the
Sailor's
Sketchbook

the Sailor's Sketchbook

by Bruce Bingham, N.A.

SEVEN SEAS

Seven Seas Press

A sketch drawn for *Sabrina's* christening invitation. The author's Flicka-class sloop loved to spread her tri-colored radial-head reacher in a fresh breeze.

TO SUSAN . . . proofreader, editor, organizer, typist, counselor and confidante; helmsman, cook and bottlewasher, sheet trimmer, sail bagger; friend, lover, wife; a patient, wonderful woman who helped put it all together.

Published by Seven Seas Press

10 9 8 7 6

Published by Seven Seas Press, an imprint of TAB BOOKS. TAB BOOKS is a division of McGraw-Hill, Inc.

Library of Congress Cataloging in Publication Data

Bingham, Bruce, 1940–
    The sailor's sketchbook.

    1. Sailboats—Maintenance and repair.
I. Title.
VM351.B48   1983   623.8′223′0288   83-531
ISBN 0-915160-55-2

TAB BOOKS offers software for sale. For information and a catalog, please contact TAB Software Department, Blue Ridge Summit, PA 17294-0850.

Questions regarding the content of this book should be addressed to:

Seven Seas Press/International Marine Publishing
P.O. Box 220
Camden, ME 04843

Design by Bruce Bingham
Edited by James Gilbert

Preface

When I began drawing *Sailor's Sketchbook* pages in 1974, I really didn't think that many boat owners would actually pick up tools and execute the *Sketchbook* projects. That was not the prime intent of the *Sailor's Sketchbook*. It was designed to generate the concept that a boat owner needn't settle for the mediocrity of a plain stock yacht, that his boat can be more functional, custom-styled, easier to handle, and more accommodating than as purchased from the showroom floor.

The Sailor's Sketchbook has done its work well throughout these six years. Many boat owners, feeling inadequate with tools, have turned to professional yards for custom installations and special effects. Several major yacht manufacturers have even included *Sketchbook* ideas as standard or optional features within their product line. More importantly, thousands of yachtsmen have begun to think of their own personal ways of customizing their boats; ways to make them different from all others; details to make them distinctive.

No single *Sketchbook* page is the one-and-only ideal solution for a given situation. They are simply suggestions . . . points of departure . . . seeds of thought. In fact, every time I draw a new *Sketchbook* page, many alternative methods and applications come to my mind. Only the lack of available space restrains my pen. At the same time, I realize that each represented solution may require modification to fit the owner's particular requirements. If your thoughts follow the same pattern, you will undoubtedly develop many more *Sketchbook* ideas of your own.

A carefully customized boat can raise the brows of onlookers in every harbor. You'll experience an overwhelming sense of pride when fellow yachtsmen express their admiration for a boat that's been painstakingly graced with touches of quality and excellence. And the added comforts will make your boat more opulent and serviceable. They can even make your boat seem larger . . . and who doesn't strive towards a larger boat?

I have executed each *Sketchbook* project prior to its commitment to paper. Each idea has had a thorough proving ground. Most projects have been designed so as not to require sophisticated tools or years of experience to accomplish. In fact, many of these projects were actually undertaken while underway without the benefit of a shore-based workshop or electrical power. Only simple hand tools were used. Needless to say, however, adequate equipment will make a difference in the resulting quality.

There's absolutely nothing to lose by giving some of these ideas a try. If you've never done any handiwork, put your fears aside . . . your own capabilities might surprise you! If your first project is not a professional success, the next one probably will be. So don't be hesitant . . . you may find that tinkering is one of the most enjoyable aspects of sailing. The rewards of creativity and accomplishment simply cannot be measured.

Bruce Bingham

Introduction

The first time I met Bruce Bingham, I was two hours late for our appointment. We were meeting in the revolving restaurant in the middle of the Los Angeles airport, a rendezvous straight out of a novel about big-time journalism.

We had struck simultaneously on an idea for something new for *Sail Magazine* . . . a page of sketches in the tradition of Hervey Garrett Smith, Jim Emmitt and "Ham" De-Fontaine. As an editor for *Sail,* I wanted someone with original ideas, a fine skill with pen or pencil, and a keen knowledge of boats.

Above all, I was looking for someone who would not merely be content grinding out how-to drawings for the nautical handiman. Of course, what I had in mind would be useful for such a sailor. However, I thought that the sketches should show something about the fine details of a well-found yacht.

When I finally found Bruce that first time, we were both a bit fuzzy, Bruce from whirling for hours past a panorama of L.A. airport and I from racing bumper-to-bumper on the freeways. But, fuzzy or not, from the outset we knew we had something.

Bruce immediately struck me as having a rare combination of a thorough knowledge of boats and an illustrator's talent. Just in case, though, I brought a list of perhaps a dozen possible *Sketchbook* topics. After all, I reasoned, a monthly page can tax anyone's ingenuity sooner or later.

The just-in-case was never needed. I can't recall Bruce ever expressing the slightest concern that he might run out of ideas for his *Sketchbooks.* He gets them from everywhere: suggestions from sailors he meets (he seems to meet everyone), adaptations of ideas he sees on other boats (he also seems to get everywhere) but most he just seems to come up with on his own.

Afloat, sailors seem to live in a world wrapped in plastic . . . a world that encourages us to buy everything for our boats from ropework to seamanship in prepackaged form off the shelf. The *Sketchbooks* have done their bit to bring charm, personality and, yes, tradition to that plastic world.

Mix the *Sketchbooks* with other pieces from Bruce's deft touch and keen eye for detail, then blend in bits of his feisty prose, and you'll find a true love for boats, for sailing and, above all, for the right way to do things.

That first meeting with Bruce was thoroughly amicable, a splendid success. We settled the details of the *Sailor's Sketchbook* series one by one, most of them agreed upon tacitly with no need to spell out particulars. In the seven years since that meeting, the *Sailor's Sketchbook* has become one of the most popular features ever to appear in a boating magazine. Better still, the concept has never been changed; the *Sketchbooks* evolved but, apart from some minor matters of style, you'd be hard pressed to know whether a particular page was among the most recent or one of the earliest.

More importantly, for me at least, is that Bruce and I have become warm friends. We've had a relationship that transcends the usual close but professional ties between artist and editor.

Through those years the friendship grew. Bruce and I, in the midst of a New England blizzard, drove to look at a boat he had heard about and considered buying. Tramping through knee-deep snow, we found her . . . just her masts sticking above the ice in the slip where she had settled. Our laughter over the absurdity of the moment was as thick and deep as the swirling snow.

Then a year later, again in the midst of winter, my wife and I drove to Hyannis on Cape Cod to visit Bruce aboard a small schooner he was refurbishing while living aboard. We found him, snug within *At Last* locked in harbor ice. It was a long convivial evening with not one mention of magazines, editing, *Sketchbooks* . . . just a protracted blend of sea tales interspersed with thunderous arguments on half-mast matters.

And more recently when, on the maiden voyage of the boat I had just built, my wife and

I rafted with Bruce's previous boat, *Sabrina.*
We come alongside ready, albeit with trepidations, to subject my amateur efforts to Bruce's
critical eye. He looked *Skratch* over, peering
into crannies and under hatches, asking questions, silently raising an eyebrow now and
then, and commenting on a *Sketchbook* idea
or two he noted I had incorporated.

Finally he settled down, took a swig of his
tepid coffee and pronounced *Skratch* a yacht,
not merely a boat. He must have meant it: I've
never known Bruce to give a phony answer for
convenience.

Jeff Spranger
Editor, *The Practical Sailor*
Former editor, *Sail Magazine*
Newport
May 1983

Contents

CHAPTER

Deck Hands

Compass Mounting Without Pedestals

BOATS WITHOUT STEERING PEDESTALS POSE SPECIAL COMPASS-MOUNTING PROBLEMS THAT MUST BE SOLVED TO ASSURE COMFORTABLE AND CONVENIENT COMPASS STEERING. JUST CUTTING A HOLE THROUGH ONE SIDE OF THE CABIN END AND INSTALLING A SINGLE, BULKHEAD-MOUNT COMPASS IS RARELY AN ADEQUATE ARRANGEMENT (BUT MOST BOAT MANUFACTURERS SEEM TO THINK IT IS).

CONSIDER THAT YOU MAY BE STUCK AT THE HELM FOR MANY HOURS A DAY, PERHAPS FOR DAYS AND NIGHTS AT A TIME. YOUR EYES (OR GLASSES) MAY BE PELTED WITH SPRAY AND YOUR VISION BLURRED BY LACK OF SLEEP. YOU'RE HYPNOTIZED BY THE MOTION OF THE LUBBER'S LINE AND ALL THE NUMBERS BEGIN TO LOOK ALIKE. IT'S AT TIMES LIKE THIS WHEN THE COMPASS POSITION BECOMES MOST IMPORTANT, SO TRY TO FULFILL THE FOLLOWING CRITERIA BEFORE CHOOSING YOUR COMPASS(ES) OR CUTTING INTO YOUR PRECIOUS BOAT:

● YOU SHOULD BE ABLE TO SEE YOUR MIDSHIP LUBBER'S LINE EVEN WHEN SITTING A NORMAL DISTANCE OFF OF CENTER ON EITHER SIDE OF THE BOAT.

● YOU SHOULD BE ABLE TO SEE AT LEAST A 45° LUBBER'S LINE WHILE SEATED MOST COMFORTABLY ON EITHER SIDE OF THE BOAT WHETHER UPRIGHT UNDER POWER OR HEELED HEAVILY UNDER SAIL.

● YOU SHOULD NEVER HAVE TO CROUCH DOWN TO SEE THE COMPASS CLEARLY.

● YOU SHOULD BE ABLE TO SEE THE MIDSHIP LUBBER'S LINE WHILE STANDING.

● IT IS ALSO BENEFICIAL TO BE ABLE TO SEE THE MIDSHIP LUBBER'S LINE WHILE STANDING ON THE COCKPIT SEAT (AS WHEN PILOTING IN VERY TIGHT QUARTERS).

● THE COMPASS IS BEST LOCATED AS NEARLY AS POSSIBLE TO YOUR NORMAL, FORWARD LINE OF SIGHT (COURSE/SAILS).

● THE COMPASS MUST NOT BE VULNERABLE TO DAMAGE.

● BEING ABLE TO TAKE A FULL ROUND OF VISUAL BEARINGS FROM THE STEERING COMPASS IS VERY HANDY.

● BUY A GOOD COMPASS; ONE THAT IS FULLY PIVOTAL AND INTERNALLY GIMBALED. IT SHOULD ALSO BE OF A COMPENSATING TYPE WITH LIGHTING. BE SURE THAT THE BULB CAN BE EASILY CHANGED (WITHOUT SOLDERING) AND THAT THE COMPASS HAS A LIQUID-EXPANSION DEVICE.

● BE SURE THAT THE COMPASS NUMBERS ARE VERY LEGIBLE BY THE POOREST-SIGHTED MEMBER OF THE CREW, ESPECIALLY AT NIGHT.

THE FOLLOWING SKETCHES ARE ONLY INTRODUCTIONS TO INNUMERABLE POSSIBLE COMPASS ARRANGEMENTS. EACH HAS ITS OWN MERITS AND DRAWBACKS THAT MUST BE JUDGED IN THE CONTEXT OF YOUR OWN BOAT.

IN MY OPINION, THIS IS THE BEST OF ALL COMPASS ARRANGEMENTS. OF COURSE, IF CABIN-TOP WINCHES AND CLEATS ARE USED, THERE MIGHT NOT BE ROOM FOR A COMPASS. A FLUSH-MOUNT IN A BRIDGE DECK MIGHT DO.

THIS IS AN IDEAL SOLUTION FOR FLUSH-CABIN BOATS SUCH AS THE *CAL-20* AND THE *STONEHORSE*. BUT AS THE COMPASSES SHARE WALKING SPACES, THEY SHOULD BE FITTED WITH STOCK OR HOMEMADE PROTECTIVE CAGES.

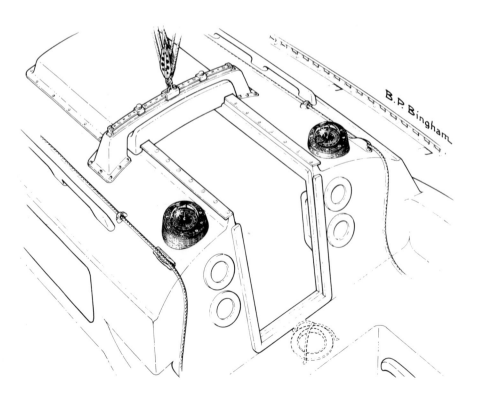

B.P. Bingham

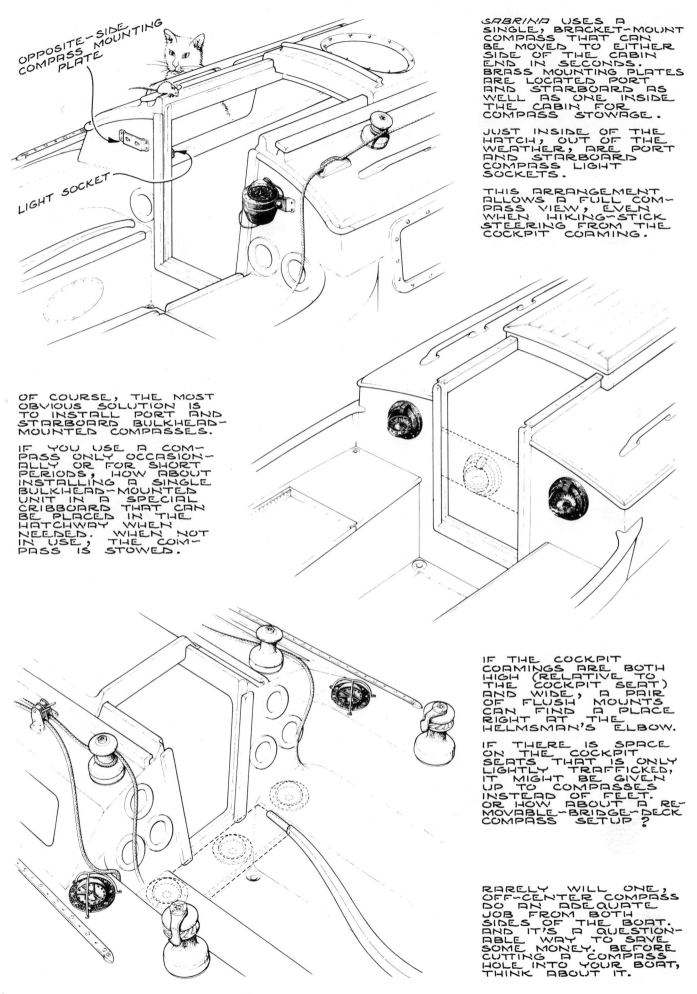

OPPOSITE-SIDE
COMPASS MOUNTING
PLATE

LIGHT SOCKET

SABRINA USES A
SINGLE, BRACKET-MOUNT
COMPASS THAT CAN
BE MOVED TO EITHER
SIDE OF THE CABIN
END IN SECONDS.
BRASS MOUNTING PLATES
ARE LOCATED PORT
AND STARBOARD AS
WELL AS ONE INSIDE
THE CABIN FOR
COMPASS STOWAGE.

JUST INSIDE OF THE
HATCH, OUT OF THE
WEATHER, ARE PORT
AND STARBOARD
COMPASS LIGHT
SOCKETS.

THIS ARRANGEMENT
ALLOWS A FULL COM-
PASS VIEW, EVEN
WHEN HIKING-STICK
STEERING FROM THE
COCKPIT COAMING.

OF COURSE, THE MOST
OBVIOUS SOLUTION IS
TO INSTALL PORT AND
STARBOARD BULKHEAD-
MOUNTED COMPASSES.

IF YOU USE A COM-
PASS ONLY OCCASION-
ALLY OR FOR SHORT
PERIODS, HOW ABOUT
INSTALLING A SINGLE
BULKHEAD-MOUNTED
UNIT IN A SPECIAL
CRIBBOARD THAT CAN
BE PLACED IN THE
HATCHWAY WHEN
NEEDED. WHEN NOT
IN USE, THE COM-
PASS IS STOWED.

IF THE COCKPIT
COAMINGS ARE BOTH
HIGH (RELATIVE TO
THE COCKPIT SEAT)
AND WIDE, A PAIR
OF FLUSH MOUNTS
CAN FIND A PLACE
RIGHT AT THE
HELMSMAN'S ELBOW.

IF THERE IS SPACE
ON THE COCKPIT
SEATS THAT IS ONLY
LIGHTLY TRAFFICKED,
IT MIGHT BE GIVEN
UP TO COMPASSES
INSTEAD OF FEET.
OR HOW ABOUT A RE-
MOVABLE-BRIDGE-DECK
COMPASS SETUP?

RARELY WILL ONE,
OFF-CENTER COMPASS
DO AN ADEQUATE
JOB FROM BOTH
SIDES OF THE BOAT.
AND IT'S A QUESTION-
ABLE WAY TO SAVE
SOME MONEY. BEFORE
CUTTING A COMPASS
HOLE INTO YOUR BOAT,
THINK ABOUT IT.

3

Compass Pedestals Without Wheels

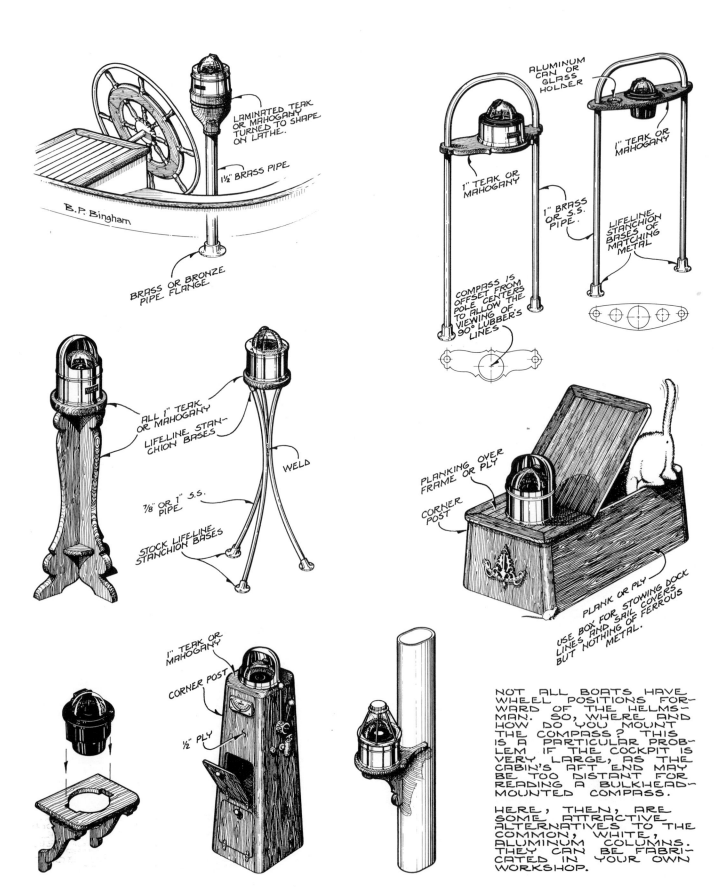

LAMINATED TEAK OR MAHOGANY TURNED TO SHAPE ON LATHE.

1½" BRASS PIPE

B.P. Bingham

BRASS OR BRONZE PIPE FLANGE

ALUMINUM CAN OR GLASS HOLDER

1" TEAK OR MAHOGANY

1" BRASS OR S.S. PIPE.

1" TEAK OR MAHOGANY

LIFELINE STANCHION BASES OF MATCHING METAL

COMPASS IS OFFSET FROM POLE CENTERS TO ALLOW THE VIEWING OF 90° LUBBER'S LINES

ALL 1" TEAK OR MAHOGANY

LIFELINE STAN-CHION BASES

WELD

7/8" OR 1" S.S. PIPE

STOCK LIFELINE STANCHION BASES

PLANKING OVER FRAME OR PLY

CORNER POST

PLANK OR PLY

USE BOX FOR STOWING DOCK LINES AND SAIL COVERS BUT NOTHING OF FERROUS METAL.

1" TEAK OR MAHOGANY

CORNER POST

½" PLY

NOT ALL BOATS HAVE WHEEL POSITIONS FOR-WARD OF THE HELMS-MAN. SO, WHERE AND HOW DO YOU MOUNT THE COMPASS? THIS IS A PARTICULAR PROB-LEM IF THE COCKPIT IS VERY LARGE, AS THE CABIN'S AFT END MAY BE TOO DISTANT FOR READING A BULKHEAD-MOUNTED COMPASS.

HERE, THEN, ARE SOME ATTRACTIVE ALTERNATIVES TO THE COMMON, WHITE, ALUMINUM COLUMNS. THEY CAN BE FABRI-CATED IN YOUR OWN WORKSHOP.

Three Cockpit Navigation Centers

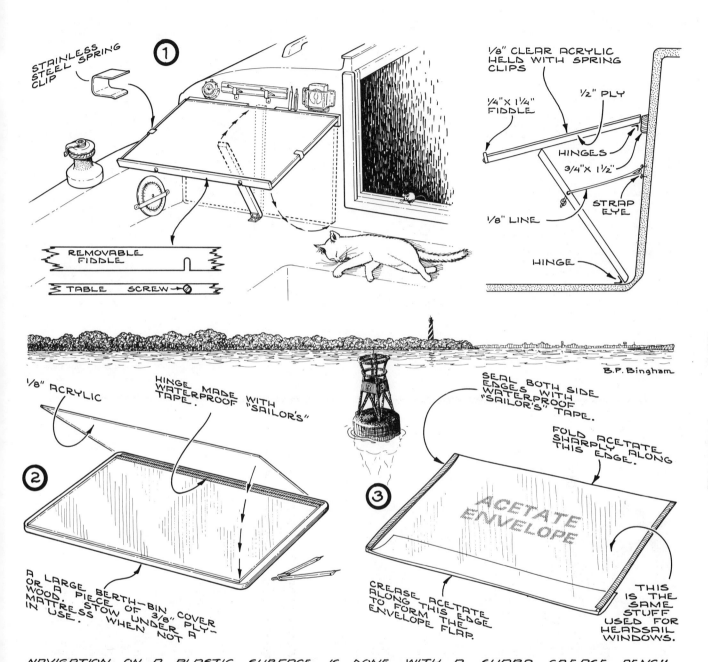

① STAINLESS STEEL SPRING CLIP

REMOVABLE FIDDLE

TABLE SCREW →

⅛" CLEAR ACRYLIC HELD WITH SPRING CLIPS

¼" X 1¼" FIDDLE

½" PLY

HINGES

¾" X 1½"

STRAP EYE

⅛" LINE

HINGE

② ⅛" ACRYLIC

HINGE MADE WITH WATERPROOF "SAILOR'S" TAPE.

A LARGE BERTH-BIN COVER OR A PIECE OF ⅜" PLY-WOOD. STOW UNDER A MATTRESS WHEN NOT IN USE.

B.P. Bingham

③ SEAL BOTH SIDE EDGES WITH WATERPROOF "SAILOR'S" TAPE.

FOLD ACETATE SHARPLY ALONG THIS EDGE.

ACETATE ENVELOPE

CREASE ACETATE ALONG THIS EDGE TO FORM THE ENVELOPE FLAP.

THIS IS THE SAME STUFF USED FOR HEADSAIL WINDOWS.

NAVIGATION ON A PLASTIC SURFACE IS DONE WITH A SHARP GREASE PENCIL.

WHETHER IT BE SAILING A WEEKEND RACE, CRUISING THE WATERWAY, PILOTING A TIGHT COASTLINE OR ENTERING A STRANGE HARBOR, THERE ARE TIMES WHEN NAVIGATING JUST CAN'T BE DONE FROM BELOW. INSTANTANEOUS CHECKS AND DOUBLE CHECKS, BEARINGS AND MORE BEARINGS, ESTIMATING CURRENTS ON RANGES AND BUOY WAKES, KEEPING TRACK OF TRAFFIC (OR COMPETITION), NOTING THE PASSAGE OR CONSTANT PROGRESS OF LIGHTS

AND MARKS DEMAND THE NAVIGATOR'S VIGILANT PRESENCE ON DECK ... NOT PLAYING "BOWDITCH" AT A CHART TABLE INSIDE. THAT MAY NOT ONLY BE DANGEROUS, BUT THE PHYSICAL ACT OF CLIMBING UP AND DOWN THE COMPANIONWAY CAN GET A LITTLE TIRING.

COCKPIT NAVIGATION POSES ITS OWN PROBLEMS HOWEVER: BLOWING CHARTS, SPRAY OR RAIN, FINDING A SURFACE UPON WHICH TO USE DIVIDERS AND

PARALLEL RULERS, A SURFACE THAT CAN BE CONVENIENTLY SET ASIDE (OR STOWED) TO CLEAR THE COCKPIT FOR ACTION.

THE FOREGOING SKETCHES OFFER A FEW SIMPLE AND PRACTICAL SOLUTIONS. THERE CAN BE MANY VARIATIONS ON THESE THEMES, OF COURSE, SO VIEW THESE IDEAS AS POINTS OF DEPARTURE. ONLY YOU KNOW BEST WHAT WILL FIT YOUR OWN PREREQUISITES, SO TAKE IT FROM HERE.

Cockpit Tables

THE PLEASURE OF DINING IN THE COCKPIT IS RARELY ENJOYED NOWADAYS, BUT IT'S A WONDERFUL WAY TO UNWIND AFTER A HOT AFTERNOON'S JAUNT DOWN THE BAY. IT'S A RELAXING WAY OF TAKING ADVANTAGE OF A COOLING BREEZE WHILE COCKTAILING WITH A FEW GUESTS. A COCKPIT TABLE CAN ALSO SERVE AS A 'FIXIT' BENCH OR AS A NAVIGATION STATION UNDER MILD CONDITIONS.

UNFORTUNATELY, VERY FEW MANUFACTURERS OFFER A COCKPIT-TABLE OPTION, SO YOU'D PROBABLY HAVE TO FABRICATE YOUR OWN. HERE ARE SEVERAL THAT HAVE CAUGHT MY FANCY; MAYBE ONE WOULD WORK ON YOUR BOAT.

THE "HINCKLEY TABLE" IS ONE OF THE EASIEST TO FABRICATE AND THE QUICKEST TO SET UP AND STOW. THE SAME ARRANGEMENT CAN EVEN BE APPLIED TO THE MIZZEN MAST OF A KETCH.

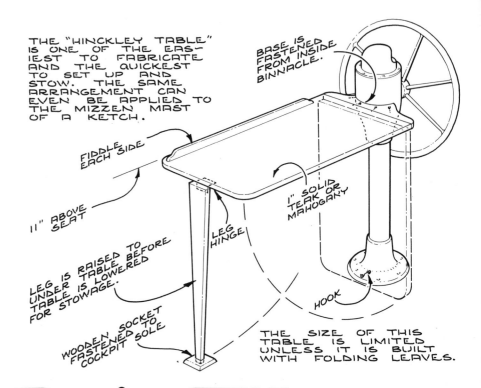

BASE IS FASTENED FROM INSIDE BINNACLE.

FIDDLE EACH SIDE

11" ABOVE SEAT

1" SOLID TEAK OR MAHOGANY

LEG HINGE

LEG IS RAISED TO UNDER TABLE BEFORE TABLE IS LOWERED FOR STOWAGE.

HOOK

WOODEN SOCKET FASTENED TO COCKPIT SOLE

THE SIZE OF THIS TABLE IS LIMITED UNLESS IT IS BUILT WITH FOLDING LEAVES.

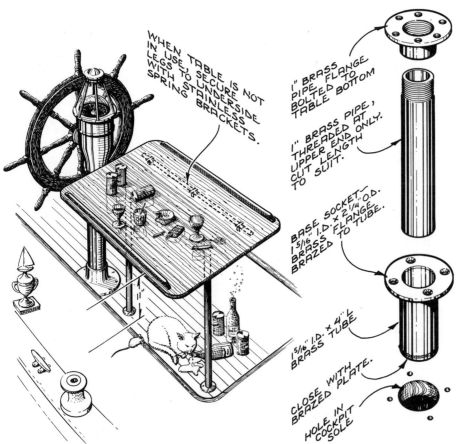

WHEN TABLE IS NOT IN USE, SECURE LEGS TO UNDERSIDE WITH STAINLESS SPRING BRACKETS.

1" BRASS PIPE FLANGE BOLTED TO TABLE BOTTOM

1" BRASS PIPE, THREADED AT UPPER END ONLY. CUT LENGTH TO SUIT.

BASE SOCKET.— 1 5/16" I.D. × 2 1/4" O.D. BRASS FLANGE BRAZED TO TUBE.

1 5/16" I.D. × 4" L BRASS TUBE

CLOSE WITH BRAZED PLATE.

HOLE IN COCKPIT SOLE

THIS TABLE TAKES A FEW MINUTES TO SET UP BUT PROVIDES A CONTINUOUS SURFACE TO ANY DESIRED LENGTH OR WIDTH. FINDING A CONVENIENT STORAGE SPACE MAY BE A PROBLEM TO BE SOLVED.

THE TABLE TOP MAY BE STRIP-PLANKED, VARNISHED PINE; EDGE-PLANKED MAHOGANY OR TEAK; OR A GOOD GRADE OF PLYWOOD. IN ANY EVENT, IT SHOULD NOT EXCEED 5/8" THICKNESS.

EVEN THOUGH THE FABRICATION OF THE PAIR OF BASE SOCKETS WILL REQUIRE THE SERVICES OF A GOOD WELDER AND THE BRASS PIECES WILL BE QUITE EXPENSIVE, THIS IS ONE OF THE STURDIEST TABLES YOU CAN INSTALL.

AT LAST'S DINETTE TABLE WAS DESIGNED TO ALSO SERVE AS THE COCKPIT TABLE. HENCE, IT IS A PORTABLE AFFAIR THAT IS QUICKLY DETACHED FROM THE BULKHEAD AND SOLE BELOW, FOLDED COMPACTLY, PASSED TOPSIDE AND RE-ATTACHED IN THE COCKPIT. THE ENTIRE OPERATION TAKES ONLY THREE MINUTES.

THE KEY TO THIS TABLE IS THAT THE BULKHEAD AND SOLE BRACKETS THAT SECURE THE TABLE BELOW HAVE BEEN PERFECTLY MATCHED IN THE COCKPIT. THE TABLE IS JUST AS AT HOME IN EITHER PLACE.

THE ONLY PROBLEM WITH THIS TABLE IS THAT IT PARTIALLY RESTRICTS THE HATCH OPENING. FORTUNATELY, AT LAST HAS TWO COMPANIONWAYS. BUT, IF YOU WERE TO ROTATE THE TABLE 180°, THE "BULKHEAD" BRACKETS MIGHT BE FASTENED TO THE STEERING PEDESTAL.

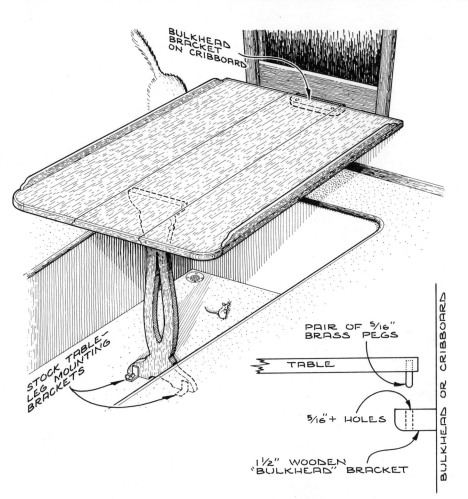

BULKHEAD BRACKET ON CRIBBOARD

STOCK TABLE-LEG MOUNTING BRACKETS

PAIR OF 5/16" BRASS PEGS

TABLE

5/16"+ HOLES

1 1/2" WOODEN "BULKHEAD" BRACKET

BULKHEAD OR CRIBBOARD

BECAUSE SABRINA IS ONLY TWENTY FEET ON DECK BUT MUST DO ALL THE TRICKS THE BIG BOATS DO, MANY THINGS ON BOARD HAVE DUAL FUNCTIONS. WHEN NOT IN USE AS SUCH, HER COCKPIT TABLE LIVES UNDER A CUSHION AS A BERTH-STOWAGE-BIN COVER. IT MEASURES 21" X 36" SO IS LARGE ENOUGH TO ACCOMMODATE FOUR FOR DINNER.

TO SET UP THE TABLE, IT IS ONLY A MATTER OF PLACING THE AFFIXED BRACKETS OF THE BIN COVER ONTO THE TILLER THEN DROPPING IN THE TWO RETAINING BOLTS. EVEN HERE, THE BOLT HOLES SERVE DUAL ROLES: THE FORWARD HOLE NORMALLY SECURES A REMOVABLE HIKING STICK WHILE THE AFTER HOLE RECEIVES THE TILLER-MASTER PIN.

THIS TABLE WILL WORK ON ALMOST ANY TILLER-STEERED BOAT, BUT THE TABLE/TILLER BRACKETS MUST BE DESIGNED IN LENGTH SO THE TABLE SITS LEVEL.

OH, YOU MUST TIE OFF THE TILLER TO PREVENT THE TABLE FROM SAILING BACK AND FORTH.

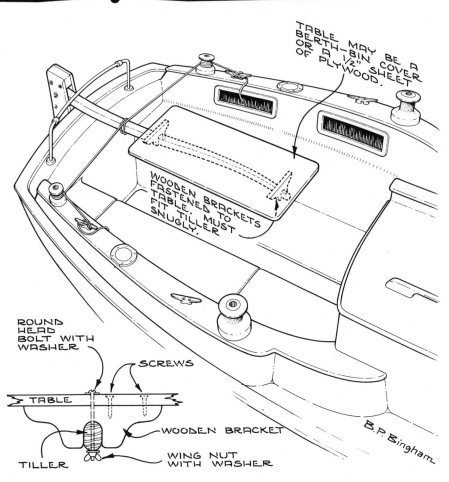

TABLE MAY BE A BERTH-BIN COVER OR A 1/2" SHEET OF PLYWOOD.

WOODEN BRACKETS FASTENED TO TABLE. MUST FIT TILLER SNUGLY.

ROUND HEAD BOLT WITH WASHER

SCREWS

TABLE

WOODEN BRACKET

WING NUT WITH WASHER

TILLER

B.P. Bingham

Getting On The Stick

ALL SMALL RACING DINGHIES HAVE 'EM. MOST, TILLER-STEERED OCEAN RACERS HAVE 'EM. EVEN THE 12 METER *SVERIGE* HAD ONE. BUT, FOR SOME REASON, YOU HARDLY EVER SEE THEM ON A CRUISING BOAT.

CONSIDER THE ADVANTAGES OF A HIKING STICK OR TILLER EXTENSION.

● IT ALLOWS THE HELMSMAN TO MOVE HIS WEIGHT SEVERAL FEET TO WEATHER FOR ADDITIONAL STABILITY.
● IT INCREASES THE HELMSMAN'S RANGE OF SEATING OPTIONS FOR MORE COMFORT.
● IT ALLOWS THE HELMSMAN TO STAND ON THE COCKPIT SEAT FOR INCREASED VISIBILITY WHEN PILOTING IN "TIGHT" WATERS OR WHILE UNDER POWER (ESPECIALLY IF THE BOAT HAS A DODGER).
● IT ALLOWS BETTER VISIBILITY OF SAILS.
● IT ALLOWS THE HELMSMAN TO REACH THINGS (SHEETS, WINCH HANDLES, ETC.) THAT MIGHT OTHERWISE BE JUST TOO FAR AWAY.

SO, YOU SEE, A HIKING STICK NEED NOT BE STRICTLY A RACING GIMMICK FOR LITTLE BOATS. I THINK EVERY TILLER-STEERED YACHT COULD USE ONE, COMPETITOR AND CRUISER ALIKE.

BUT SOME PEOPLE JUST DON'T LIKE THE "FEEL" OF A HIKING STICK. MOSTLY, THEY DON'T LIKE THE UNNATURAL POSITION OF HOLDING ONTO A ROUND KNOB AND THE TWIST OF THE WRIST REQUIRED. BESIDES, THERE'S JUST SOMETHING "TINNY" ABOUT STEERING WITH AN ALUMINUM TUBE. I AGREE FULLY.

SO, I CONCEIVED AND BUILT A DIFFERENT TYPE OF HIKING STICK FOR MY SCHOONER *AT LAST* OUT OF MAHOGANY, THEN ONE OUT OF TEAK FOR MY LITTLE *SABRINA*. THEY NOT ONLY LOOK APPROPRIATE, THEY'RE VERY STRONG. MORE IMPORTANT, THEY REALLY FEEL LIKE TILLERS BECAUSE THE SAME "FIST GRIP" IS USED.

SO MANY BOAT OWNERS HAVE ADMIRED THESE HIKING STICKS (FROM ONE TONNERS TO WESTSAILS, I OFFER THEIR DESIGN HERE.

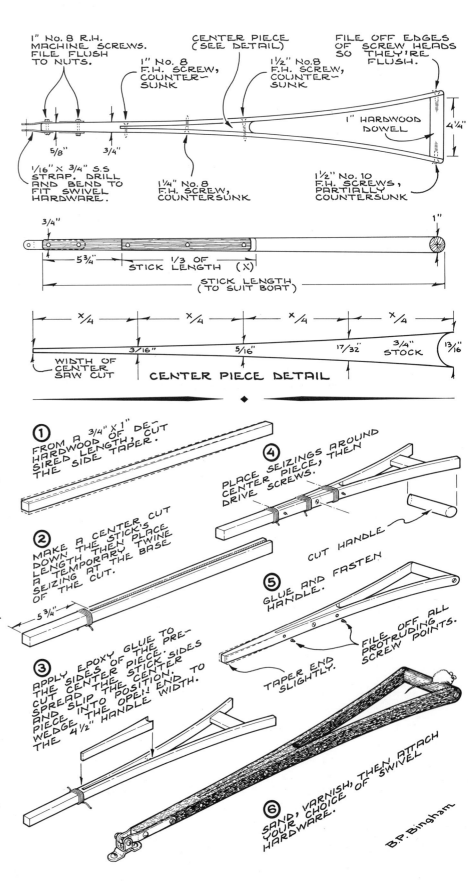

1" No. 8 R.H. MACHINE SCREWS. FILE FLUSH TO NUTS.

1" No. 8 F.H. SCREW, COUNTERSUNK

CENTER PIECE (SEE DETAIL)

1½" No.8 F.H. SCREW, COUNTERSUNK

FILE OFF EDGES OF SCREW HEADS SO THEY'RE FLUSH.

1" HARDWOOD DOWEL

4¼"

5/8"   3/4"

1/16" X 3/4" S.S STRAP. DRILL AND BEND TO FIT SWIVEL HARDWARE.

1¼" No. 8 F.H. SCREW, COUNTERSUNK

1½" No. 10 F.H. SCREWS, PARTIALLY COUNTERSUNK

3/4"

5¾"   1/3 OF STICK LENGTH (X)

STICK LENGTH (TO SUIT BOAT)

1"

X/4   X/4   X/4   X/4

WIDTH OF CENTER SAW CUT

3/16"   5/16"   17/32"   3/4" STOCK   13/16"

CENTER PIECE DETAIL

① FROM A 3/4" X 1" HARDWOOD OF DESIRED LENGTH, CUT THE SIDE TAPER.

② MAKE A CENTER CUT DOWN THE STICK'S LENGTH, THEN PLACE A TEMPORARY TWINE SEIZING AT THE BASE OF THE CUT.

5¾"

③ APPLY EPOXY GLUE TO THE SIDES OF THE PRE-CUT CENTER PIECE. SPREAD THE STICK'S SIDES AND SLIP THE CENTER PIECE INTO POSITION, TO WEDGE THE OPEN END TO THE 4½" HANDLE WIDTH.

④ PLACE SEIZINGS AROUND CENTER PIECE, THEN DRIVE SCREWS.

CUT HANDLE

⑤ GLUE AND FASTEN HANDLE.

TAPER END SLIGHTLY.

FILE OFF ALL PROTRUDING SCREW POINTS.

⑥ SAND, VARNISH, THEN ATTACH YOUR CHOICE OF SWIVEL HARDWARE.

B.P. Bingham

A Unique Non-Skid System

GRANTED, MOST NEW BOATS COME OUT OF THE MOLD WITH A NON-SKID PATTERN ON DECKS, CABIN TOPS AND COCKPIT. BUT WHAT ABOUT THE SOLE INSIDE YOUR DINGHY OR THE FLOORBOARDS OF YOUR LITTLE *PENGUIN* OR *BLUE JAY*? HOW ABOUT A NON-SKID FINISH ON THE COMPANIONWAY TREADS? MAYBE YOU'RE BUILDING A NEW BOAT FOR YOURSELF OR FIXING UP AN OLD ONE. WHAT DO YOU DO FOR NON-SKID?

SURE, YOU CAN BUY A LITTLE BOTTLE OF NON-SKID COMPOUND FROM YOUR MARINE STORE AND MIX IT INTO YOUR PAINT, BUT THIS STUFF INVARIABLY RESULTS IN AN IRREGULAR, BLOTCHY FINISH WITH BARE SPOTS AND BRUSH STREAKS.

THE ANSWER? **MODEL-RAILROAD BALLAST!** IT IS A PERFECTLY REGULAR, FINE, CRYSTALLINE SAND SOLD IN ONE POUND BAGS AT YOUR LOCAL HOBBY SHOP.

WHEN APPLIED IN THE MANNER ILLUSTRATED BELOW, IT WILL RESULT IN A SURFACE SO PERFECT IT WILL LOOK AS IF IT CAME FROM A ROLL. THE FINISH MAY BE RE-PAINTED OR VARNISHED FOR YEARS AND WILL NOT WEAR OFF UNDER CONSTANT FOOT WORK.

YES, I DID SAY VARNISHED NON-SKID? MODEL RAILROAD BALLAST BECOMES TRANSPARENT WHEN VARNISHED AND HOLDS UP REMARKABLY.

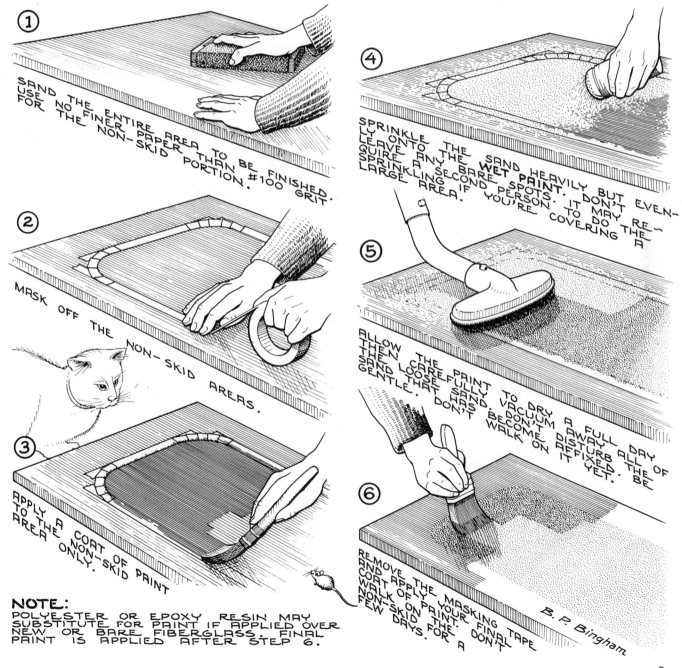

1. SAND THE ENTIRE AREA TO BE FINISHED. USE NO FINER PAPER THAN #100 GRIT FOR THE NON-SKID PORTION.

2. MASK OFF THE NON-SKID AREAS.

3. APPLY A COAT OF PAINT TO THE NON-SKID AREA ONLY.

4. SPRINKLE THE SAND HEAVILY BUT EVENLY ONTO THE **WET PAINT**. DON'T LEAVE ANY BARE SPOTS. IT MAY REQUIRE A SECOND PERSON TO DO THE SPRINKLING IF YOU'RE COVERING A LARGE AREA.

5. ALLOW THE PAINT TO DRY A FULL DAY THEN CAREFULLY VACUUM ALL OF THEN LOOSE SAND. DON'T DISTURB THE SAND THAT HAS BECOME AFFIXED. BE GENTLE. DON'T WALK ON IT YET.

6. REMOVE THE MASKING TAPE AND APPLY YOUR FINAL COAT OF PAINT. WALK ON THE NON-SKID. DON'T FEW DAYS FOR A

B. P. Bingham

NOTE:
POLYESTER OR EPOXY RESIN MAY SUBSTITUTE FOR PAINT IF APPLIED OVER NEW OR BARE FIBERGLASS. FINAL PAINT IS APPLIED AFTER STEP 6.

Wooden Planking On Fiberglass Hatches

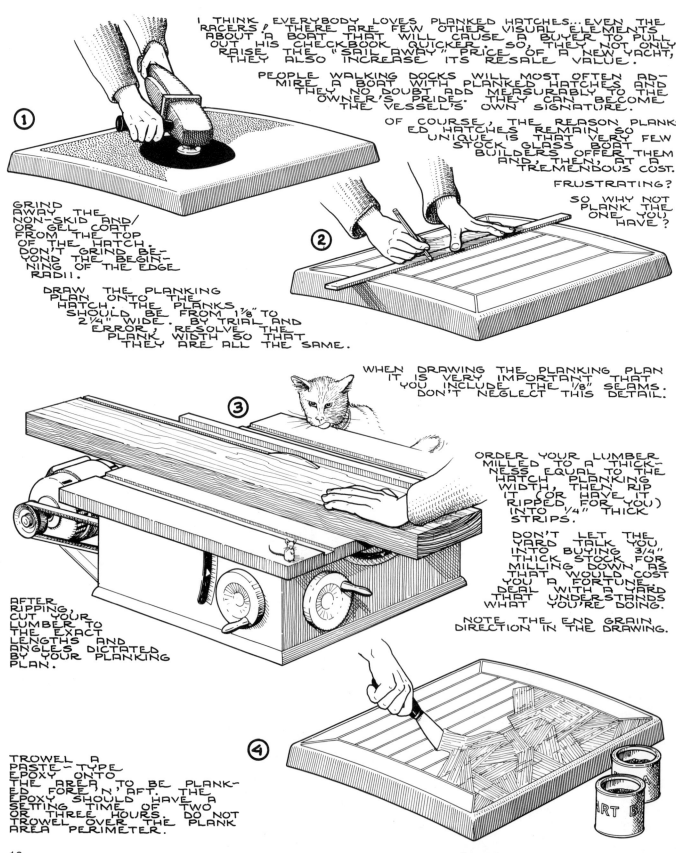

I THINK EVERYBODY LOVES PLANKED HATCHES...EVEN THE RACERS! THERE ARE FEW OTHER VISUAL ELEMENTS ABOUT A BOAT THAT WILL CAUSE A BUYER TO PULL OUT HIS CHECKBOOK QUICKER. SO, THEY NOT ONLY RAISE THE "SAIL AWAY" PRICE OF A NEW YACHT, THEY ALSO INCREASE ITS RESALE VALUE.

PEOPLE WALKING DOCKS WILL MOST OFTEN ADMIRE A BOAT WITH PLANKED HATCHES AND THEY NO DOUBT ADD MEASURABLY TO THE OWNER'S PRIDE. THEY CAN BECOME THE VESSEL'S OWN SIGNATURE.

OF COURSE, THE REASON PLANKED HATCHES REMAIN SO UNIQUE IS THAT VERY FEW STOCK GLASS BOAT BUILDERS OFFER THEM AND, THEN, AT A TREMENDOUS COST.

FRUSTRATING?

SO WHY NOT PLANK THE ONE YOU HAVE?

GRIND AWAY THE NON-SKID AND/OR GEL COAT FROM THE TOP OF THE HATCH. DON'T GRIND BEYOND THE BEGINNING OF THE EDGE RADII.

DRAW THE PLANKING PLAN ONTO THE HATCH. THE PLANKS SHOULD BE FROM 1⅛" TO 2¼" WIDE. BY TRIAL AND ERROR, RESOLVE THE PLANK WIDTH SO THAT THEY ARE ALL THE SAME.

WHEN DRAWING THE PLANKING PLAN IT IS VERY IMPORTANT THAT YOU INCLUDE THE ⅛" SEAMS. DON'T NEGLECT THIS DETAIL.

ORDER YOUR LUMBER MILLED TO A THICKNESS EQUAL TO THE HATCH PLANKING WIDTH, THEN RIP IT (OR HAVE IT RIPPED FOR YOU) INTO ¼" THICK STRIPS.

DON'T LET THE YARD TALK YOU INTO BUYING ¾" THICK STOCK FOR MILLING DOWN AS THAT WOULD COST YOU A FORTUNE. DEAL WITH A YARD THAT UNDERSTANDS WHAT YOU'RE DOING.

NOTE THE END GRAIN DIRECTION IN THE DRAWING.

AFTER RIPPING, CUT YOUR LUMBER TO THE EXACT LENGTHS AND ANGLES DICTATED BY YOUR PLANKING PLAN.

TROWEL A PASTE-TYPE EPOXY ONTO THE AREA TO BE PLANKED FORE 'N AFT. THE EPOXY SHOULD HAVE A SETTING TIME OF TWO OR THREE HOURS. DO NOT TROWEL OVER THE PLANK AREA PERIMETER.

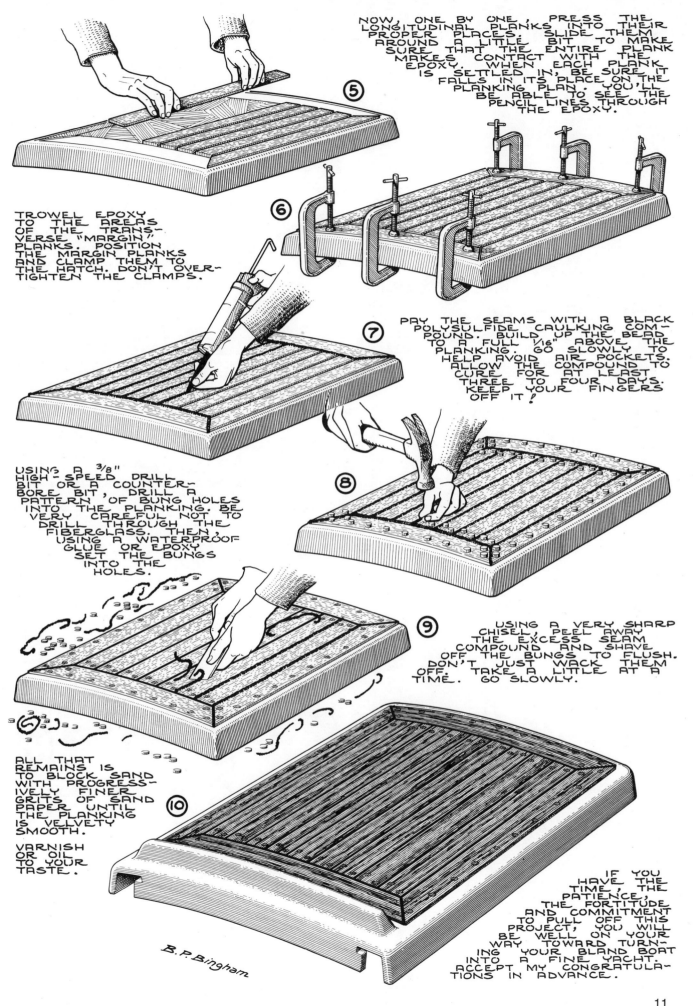

NOW, ONE BY ONE, PRESS THE LONGITUDINAL PLANKS INTO THEIR PROPER PLACES. SLIDE THEM AROUND A LITTLE BIT TO MAKE SURE THAT THE ENTIRE PLANK MAKES CONTACT WITH THE EPOXY. WHEN EACH PLANK IS SETTLED IN, BE SURE IT FALLS IN ITS PLACE ON THE PLANKING PLAN. YOU'LL BE ABLE TO SEE THE PENCIL LINES THROUGH THE EPOXY.

⑤

TROWEL EPOXY TO THE AREAS OF THE TRANS-VERSE "MARGIN" PLANKS. POSITION THE MARGIN PLANKS AND CLAMP THEM TO THE HATCH. DON'T OVER-TIGHTEN THE CLAMPS.

⑥

PAY THE SEAMS WITH A BLACK POLYSULFIDE CAULKING COM-POUND. BUILD UP THE BEAD TO A FULL 1/16" ABOVE THE PLANKING. GO SLOWLY TO HELP AVOID AIR POCKETS. ALLOW THE COMPOUND TO CURE FOR AT LEAST THREE TO FOUR DAYS. KEEP YOUR FINGERS OFF IT!

⑦

USING A 3/8" HIGH-SPEED DRILL BIT OR A COUNTER-BORE BIT, DRILL A PATTERN OF BUNG HOLES INTO THE PLANKING. BE VERY CAREFUL NOT TO DRILL THROUGH THE FIBERGLASS. THEN, USING A WATERPROOF GLUE OR EPOXY SET THE BUNGS INTO THE HOLES.

⑧

⑨ USING A VERY SHARP CHISEL, PEEL AWAY THE EXCESS SEAM COMPOUND AND SHAVE OFF THE BUNGS TO FLUSH. DON'T JUST WACK THEM OFF. TAKE A LITTLE AT A TIME. GO SLOWLY.

ALL THAT REMAINS IS TO BLOCK SAND WITH PROGRESS-IVELY FINER GRITS OF SAND PAPER UNTIL THE PLANKING IS VELVETY SMOOTH.

VARNISH OR OIL TO YOUR TASTE.

⑩

IF YOU HAVE THE TIME, THE PATIENCE, THE FORTITUDE AND COMMITMENT TO PULL OFF THIS PROJECT, YOU WILL BE WELL ON YOUR WAY TOWARD TURN-ING YOUR BLAND BOAT INTO A FINE YACHT. ACCEPT MY CONGRATULA-TIONS IN ADVANCE.

B.P.Bingham

Self-Contained Deck Vents

SOMETIMES STOCK COWL VENTILATORS JUST DON'T FIT THE BOAT. MORE OFTEN, THEY MAY NOT FIT THE POCKETBOOK!

FOR ANYONE HANDY WITH TOOLS AND WOOD, THESE SELF-CONTAIN-ED, LOW-PROFILE, FUNCTIONAL AND AT-TRACTIVE AIR SCOOPS

MAY BE A PRACTICAL ALTERNATIVE. THE TOTAL COST WILL BE LESS THAN $8.00 AND A FEW HOURS TIME. WHY NOT TRY ONE?

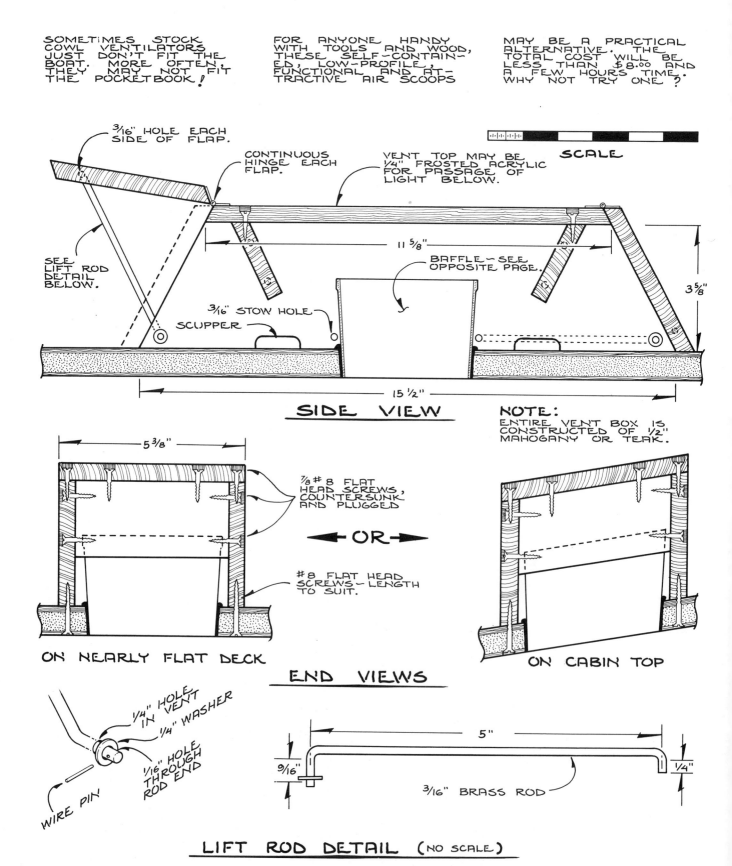

3/16" HOLE EACH SIDE OF FLAP.

CONTINUOUS HINGE EACH FLAP.

VENT TOP MAY BE 1/4" FROSTED ACRYLIC FOR PASSAGE OF LIGHT BELOW.

SCALE

SEE LIFT ROD DETAIL BELOW.

11 5/8"

BAFFLE—SEE OPPOSITE PAGE.

3 5/8"

3/16" STOW HOLE

SCUPPER

15 1/2"

SIDE VIEW

NOTE:
ENTIRE VENT BOX IS CONSTRUCTED OF 1/2" MAHOGANY OR TEAK.

5 3/8"

7/8 #8 FLAT HEAD SCREWS, COUNTERSUNK AND PLUGGED

←OR→

#8 FLAT HEAD SCREWS — LENGTH TO SUIT.

ON NEARLY FLAT DECK

ON CABIN TOP

END VIEWS

1/4" HOLE IN VENT

1/4" WASHER

1/16" HOLE THROUGH ROD END

WIRE PIN

5"

9/16"

1/4"

3/16" BRASS ROD

LIFT ROD DETAIL (NO SCALE)

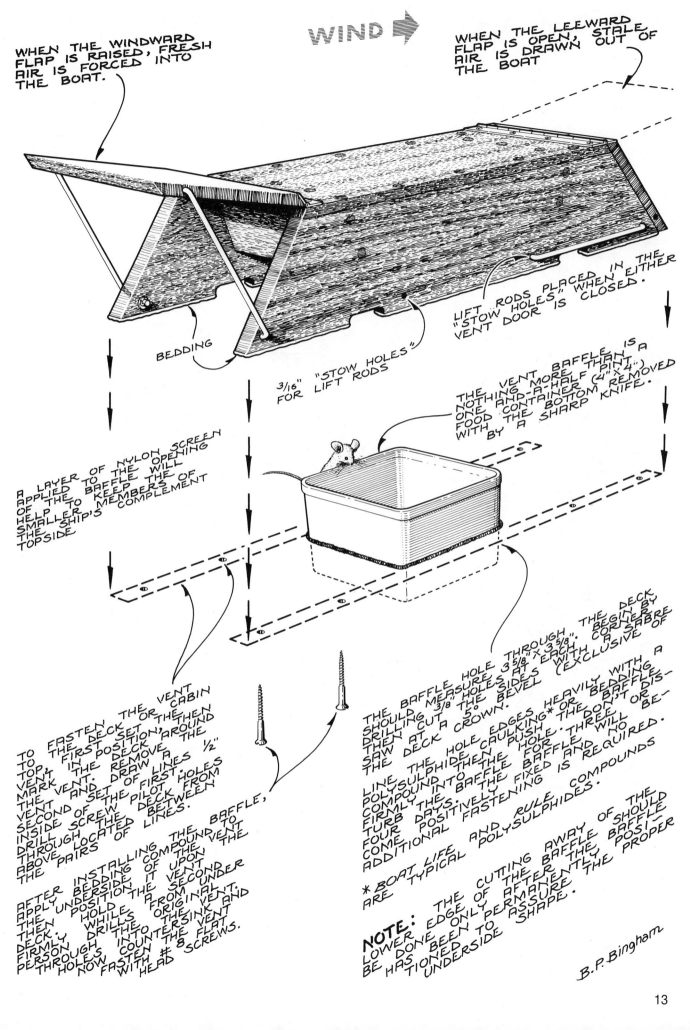

WHEN THE WINDWARD FLAP IS RAISED, FRESH AIR IS FORCED INTO THE BOAT.

WHEN THE LEEWARD FLAP IS OPEN, STALE AIR IS DRAWN OUT OF THE BOAT

BEDDING

LIFT RODS PLACED IN "STOW HOLES" WHEN IN THE EITHER VENT DOOR IS CLOSED.

3/16" "STOW HOLES" FOR LIFT RODS

THE VENT BAFFLE IS NOTHING MORE THAN A ONE AND-A-HALF (PINT) FOOD CONTAINER (4"X4") WITH THE BOTTOM REMOVED BY A SHARP KNIFE.

A LAYER OF NYLON SCREEN APPLIED TO THE OPENING OF THE BAFFLE WILL HELP TO KEEP THE SMALLER MEMBERS OF THE SHIP'S COMPLEMENT TOPSIDE

THE BAFFLE HOLE THROUGH THE DECK SHOULD MEASURE 3 5/8"X 3 5/8". BEGIN BY DRILLING 3/8" HOLES AT EACH CORNER BY THEN CUT THE SIDES WITH A SABRE SAW AT A 5° BEVEL (EXCLUSIVE OF THE DECK CROWN.

TO FASTEN THE VENT TO THE DECK OR THE CABIN TOP, FIRST SET IN POSITION, THEN MARK THE DECK AROUND THE VENT. REMOVE THE VENT AND DRAW A 1/2" INSIDE SECOND SET OF LINES DRILL THE FIRST SCREW PILOT HOLES ABOVE THROUGH THE DECK FROM THE PAIRS LOCATED BETWEEN OF LINES.

LINE THE HOLE EDGES HEAVILY WITH POLYSULPHIDE CAULKING* OR BEDDING COMPOUND THEN PUSH THE BAFFLE FIRMLY INTO THE HOLE. DON'T DIS-TURB FOR THREE OR FOUR DAYS. THE BAFFLE WILL BE-COME POSITIVELY FIXED AND NO ADDITIONAL FASTENING IS REQUIRED.

AFTER INSTALLING THE BAFFLE, APPLY BEDDING COMPOUND TO THE UNDERSIDE OF THE VENT THEN POSITION IT UPON THE DECK. WHILE A SECOND PERSON HOLD THE VENT FIRMLY DRILLS FROM UNDER THROUGH INTO THE ORIGINAL HOLES COUNTERSINK AND NOW FASTEN THE VENT WITH #8 FLAT HEAD SCREWS.

* BOAT LIFE AND RULE COMPOUNDS ARE TYPICAL POLYSULPHIDES.

NOTE: THE CUTTING AWAY OF THE LOWER EDGE OF THE BAFFLE SHOULD BE DONE ONLY AFTER THE BAFFLE HAS BEEN PERMANENTLY POSI-TIONED TO ASSURE THE PROPER UNDERSIDE SHAPE.

B.P.Bingham

Deck Drainage

HAVE YOU EVER GONE
ON DECK TO TAKE
YOUR STINT AT THE
HELM AND ENDED
UP SITTING IN A
PUDDLE OF WATER?
HAVE YOU EVER
SPENT FIVE MINUTES
WASHING YOUR BOAT
THEN TEN MINUTES
DRYING UP THE
PUDDLES AT THE
CORNERS OF THE
COCKPIT SEATS?
HAVE YOU EVER RID-
DEN THE RAIL
WHILE SLAMMING TO
WEATHER ONLY TO
FIND THAT HALF OF
THE OCEAN FOUND
ITS WAY INTO YOUR
OIL-SKIN BRITCHES
BECAUSE THE WATER
WOULDN'T RUN OFF
THE DECK?

IT'S TIME THAT YOU
WERE INTRODUCED TO
THE "BARB", MORE
COMMONLY KNOWN AS
A "PIPE-TO-HOSE CON-
NECTOR". THE BARB
IS THE KEY TO IN-
STALLING DRAIN HOSES
INTO FIBERGLASS OR
WOOD. ONLY BRASS
BARBS SHOULD BE
USED. THEY ARE
AVAILABLE IN AN IN-
FINITE VARIETY OF
SIZES AT BETTER
HARDWARE STORES
AND AUTO SUPPLY
SHOPS. THE 3/8" PIPE-
TO-3/8" HOSE BARB
SEEMS TO BE THE
MOST PRACTICAL.

THE BARB HAS THE
ADVANTAGE OF PRO-
VIDING A FLUSH
HOLE WHILE A
THROUGH-HULL FITTING
WILL NOT (WITHOUT
A GREAT DEAL OF
WORK). THE BARBS
ALSO COST A FRAC-
TION OF A PLASTIC
THROUGH-HULL.

TO INSTALL A BARB:
DRILL A HOLE THE
SAME SIZE AS THE
PIPE-THREADED END,
APPLY GASKET CE-
MENT TO THE BARB
THREADS, SCREW
THE BARB INTO THE
HOLE (IT WILL CUT
ITS OWN THREADING)
THEN TIGHTEN IT
WITH A WRENCH.

THE FOLLOWING ILLUS-
TRATIONS SHOW
SEVERAL HOSE AND
BARB DRAIN
ARRANGEMENTS.

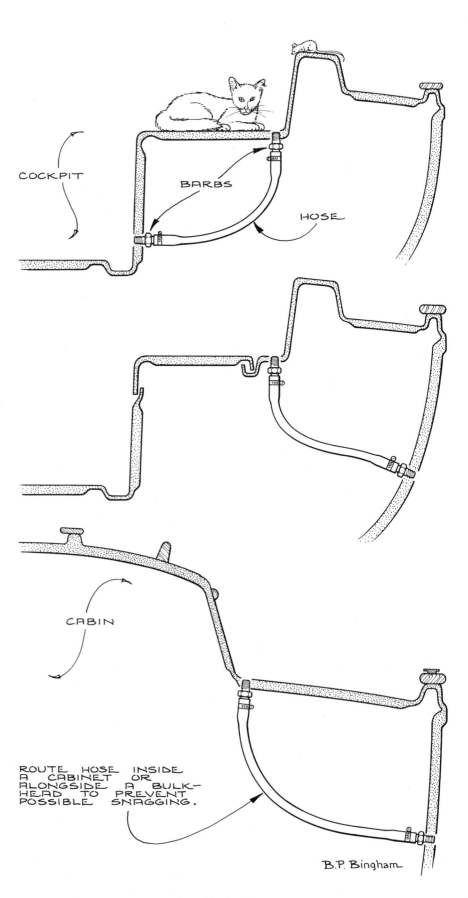

COCKPIT

BARBS

HOSE

CABIN

ROUTE HOSE INSIDE
A CABINET OR
ALONGSIDE A BULK-
HEAD TO PREVENT
POSSIBLE SNAGGING.

B.P. Bingham

On-Deck Line Stowage

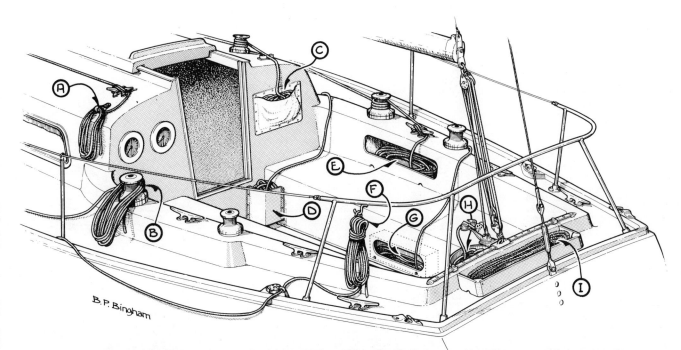

B. P. Bingham

(A) COIL SECURED TO CABIN TOP, CABIN SIDES, CABIN END, LIFELINES OR ON BULKHEADS OF SAIL LOCKER USING VELCRO STRAPS OR SNAP STRAPS.

(B) A LOOSE COIL WITHOUT SEIZING OR "ROUND TURNS" PLACED OVER CORRESPONDING WINCH OR BIT. BEST USED FOR HEADS'L SHEETS THAT ARE CONSTANTLY BEING ADJUSTED.

(C) A HEAVY, FLAT CANVAS BAG FASTENED TO THE CABIN END, SIDES OF COCKPIT SEATS OR INSIDE OF SAIL LOCKER IS AN IDEAL WAY OF STOWING SMALL OR SHORT LINES SUCH AS THE VANG TAIL.

(D) A PLASTIC WASTE BASKET CUT TO FIT THE COCKPIT CORNER WITH FASTENING FLANGES BENT TO PROVIDE ATTACHMENT. PERFECT FOR STOWING LONG LINES.

(E) A LARGE BIN WITH DRAINAGE SCUPPERS INSTALLED WITHIN THE COCKPIT COAMING IS THE LEAST CLUTTERING OF ALL LINE STOWAGE SYSTEMS, BUT THE BIN WILL NOT FIT INTO ALL BOATS. IT MUST BE AMPLE.

(F) STAINLESS STEEL HOOKS SCREWED INTO (OR WIRE SEIZED TO) BOW OR STERN PULPITS KEEP OCCASIONALLY USED LINES READY BUT OFF OF THE DECK. LOCATE TO AVOID SNAGS.

(G) BINS INSTALLED AT THE BASE OF COCKPIT SEATS MUST BE "WATER TIGHT" FROM INSIDE AND DRILLED FOR SCUPPERS. GREAT FOR ANY SHEET OR LINE STOWAGE.

(H) HALF OF A PLASTIC BUCKET FASTENED TO A COCKPIT BULKHEAD OR SEAT FRONT IS AN IDEAL PLACE TO KEEP THE MAINSHEET OUT FROM UNDER FOOT.

(I) SHALLOW, LIGHTLY CONSTRUCTED WOODEN BOXES FASTENED TO CABIN OR COAMING SIDES MAKE PERFECT NICHES TO STOW DOCK LINES WHEN OUT FOR A SHORT SAIL.

(J) A SNAP HOOK SEIZED TO THE LIFELINE IS A PERFECT SETUP FOR HANGING SMALL COILS IN THE AREAS WHERE THEY'LL BE MOST USED.

(K) A "FIDDLE BOX" FASTENED TO THE CABIN TOP IS MOST CONVENIENT FOR STOWING THE HALYARDS WHILE LOWERING WEIGHT AND REDUCING WINDAGE.

(L) NET BAGS SEIZED TO THE BASES OF SHROUDS OR THE PULPITS KEEPS DOCK LINES HANDY BUT OUT OF THE WAY.

(M) SNAP HOOKS MAY BE SEIZED TO HAND RAILS FOR HANGING SMALL COILS.

(N) SMALL STRAP EYES FASTENED TO THE CABIN TOP OR DECK ARE VERY SUITABLE FOR TYING DOWN LARGE COILS SUCH AS AN EXTRA ANCHOR RODE OR TOWING WARP.

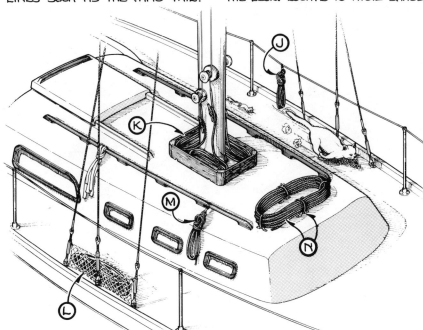

YOU SEE, EVERY LINE ON THE BOAT SHOULD HAVE A SPECIFIC STOWAGE PLACE WHEN UNDER WAY SO THAT IT CAN BE EASILY IDENTIFIED AND READY FOR RUNNING AT A MOMENT'S NOTICE. EVERY COIL SHOULD BE SECURED TO PREVENT TUMBLING, BEING TRAMPLED OR MIXED TOGETHER WITH OTHER COILS. KEEP YOUR LINES LOW, OUT OF WALKWAYS AND WORKWAYS. IT'S SEAMANLY AND PRUDENT.

Custom Wooden Coaming Caps

ADDING A WOODEN CAP TO A FIBERGLASS COCKPIT COAMING IS RIDICULOUSLY EASY TO DO. CHARLIE TINKER DID IT TO *POOH BEAR*, I DID IT TO *SABRINA*, AND YOU CAN DO IT TO YOUR BOAT IN ABOUT A DAY AND A HALF.

① REMOVE ALL HARDWARE FROM THE COAMINGS.

② MAKE A PAPER PATTERN OF EACH COAMING. DON'T ASSUME THAT THE BOAT IS SYMMETRICAL.

③ TO PREVENT THE ADDITION OF UNNECESSARY WEIGHT, YOU MAY CUT AWAY PORTIONS OF THE COAMING NOT REQUIRED TO WITHSTAND A STRAIN.

④ TRANSFER THE SHAPE TO A GOOD GRADE OF 3/4" TEAK OR MAHOGANY. ADD 1/2" TO ALL SIDE EDGES.

④a IF YOU CAN'T PURCHASE LUMBER WIDE ENOUGH TO COMPLETELY COVER THE COAMING, IT WILL HAVE TO BE EDGE-JOINED WITH EPOXY GLUE AND 1/4" BRASS DOWELS.

⑤ CUT AND SMOOTH THE EDGES OF THE FINISHED PIECES. TEST FOR FIT.

⑥ ROUND ALL OF THE EXPOSED EDGES WITH A SHAPER, PLANE OR RASP. SAND.

⑦ SAND THE TOP OF THE FIBERGLASS COAMING AND TROWEL ON A PASTE-TYPE EPOXY.

⑧ FASTEN THE CAP WITH 1½" No. 8 S.S. SHEET METAL SCREWS, COUNTERSUNK AND PLUGGED.

⑨ DRILL THE COAMING THROUGH THE ORIGINAL HOLES FROM INSIDE THE BOAT THEN RE-ATTACH THE HARDWARE WITH LONGER BOLTS.

NOW, STAND BACK AND ADMIRE YOUR WORK.

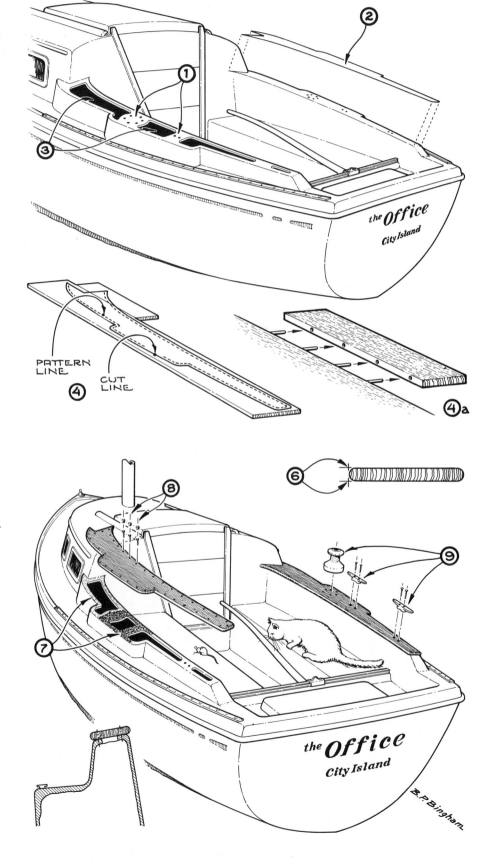

PATTERN LINE

CUT LINE

16

Wooden Transoms For Glass Yachts

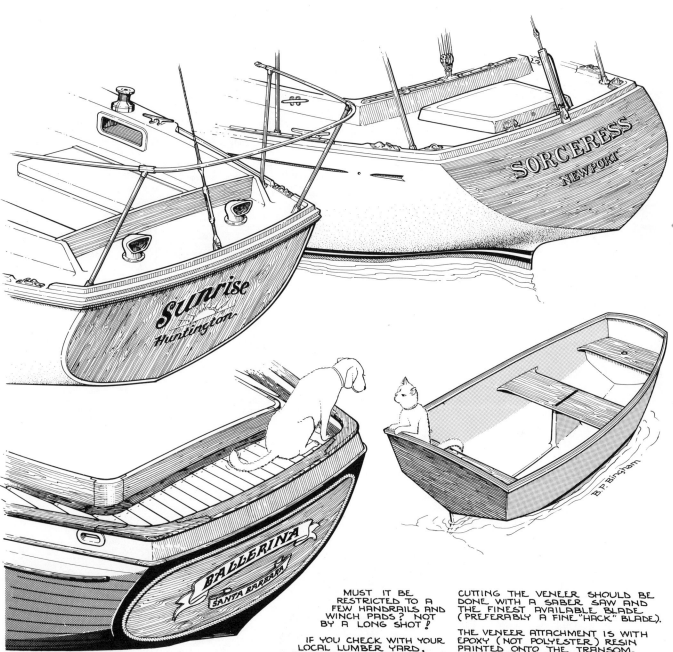

B.P. Bingham

THERE'S LITTLE THAT DISCOURAGES ME MORE THAN LOOKING DOWN ON THE MARINA FROM MY OFFICE WINDOW OR AT THE TAIL END OF A RACING FLEET (MY USUAL VANTAGE POINT) AND SEEING NOTHING BUT WHITE GEL-COAT. ONCE IN A WHILE, ONE MIGHT SEE A SPOT OF RED OR YELLOW BUT RARELY ARE WE WARMED BY THE HUE OF MAHOGANY.

I CAN THINK OF NOTHING ELSE THAT BESPEAKS A BOAT'S OR OWNER'S PERSONALITY AND PHILOSOPHY MORE THAN THE VESSEL'S TRANSOM. MUST OUR IDENTITIES BE SO PLASTICIZED? WHAT HAPPENED TO OUR LOVE FOR WOOD?

MUST IT BE RESTRICTED TO A FEW HANDRAILS AND WINCH PADS? NOT BY A LONG SHOT!

IF YOU CHECK WITH YOUR LOCAL LUMBER YARD, YOU ARE SURE TO FIND ⅛" MAHOGANY "DOOR SKINS" MANUFACTURED WITH PHENOLIC GLUE. IT MAKES A FABULOUS TRANSOM COVERING MATERIAL. YOU MAY ALSO ORDER SHEETS OF TEAK VENEER UPON SPECIAL REQUEST.

TO COVER THE TRANSOM OF A WOODEN OR ALUMINUM BOAT, IT IS NECESSARY TO STRIP THE PAINT. A GLASS TRANSOM REQUIRES A VERY THOROUGH SANDING WITH NOTHING FINER THAN #60 GRIT PAPER.

ONCE DONE, THE PLY OR VENEER IS HELD AGAINST THE TRANSOM WHILE A SECOND HAND SCRIBES ITS SHAPE ONTO THE WOOD. FOR A TRULY PLANKED EFFECT, THE VENEER MAY FIRST BE RIPPED INTO 6" STRIPS, EVERY OTHER PLANK TURNED END FOR END BEFORE SCRIBING.

CUTTING THE VENEER SHOULD BE DONE WITH A SABER SAW AND THE FINEST AVAILABLE BLADE (PREFERABLY A FINE "HACK" BLADE).

THE VENEER ATTACHMENT IS WITH EPOXY (NOT POLYESTER) RESIN PAINTED ONTO THE TRANSOM. TEMPORARY WOODEN BATTENS ARE THEN SPRUNG TIGHTLY AGAINST THE NEW TRANSOM, BEING HELD TO THE HULL WITH PLENTY OF TAPE UNTIL THE EPOXY HAS FULLY CURED.

THE TRANSOM VENEER MAY BE EXTENDED FULLY TO THE EDGE OF THE HULL IF THE TRANSOM CORNER IS VERY SHARP. SMALL GAPS MAY BE FILLED WITH POLYESTER GLAZING, THEN TOUCHED UP WITH PAINT TO MATCH THE HULL. IT MAY BE WISE TO CONSIDER LEAVING A NARROW MARGIN OF THE ORIGINAL HULL EXPOSED AROUND THE TRANSOM AS THIS WILL PREVENT POSSIBLE FITTING PROBLEMS AS WELL AS LENDING A DISTINCTIVE APPEARANCE.

USE YOUR IMAGINATION. BALLERINA'S TRANSOM HAS BEEN BORDERED WITH EPOXY SATURATED LINE. THERE'S NO END TO THE POSSIBILITIES.

The Boom Gallows

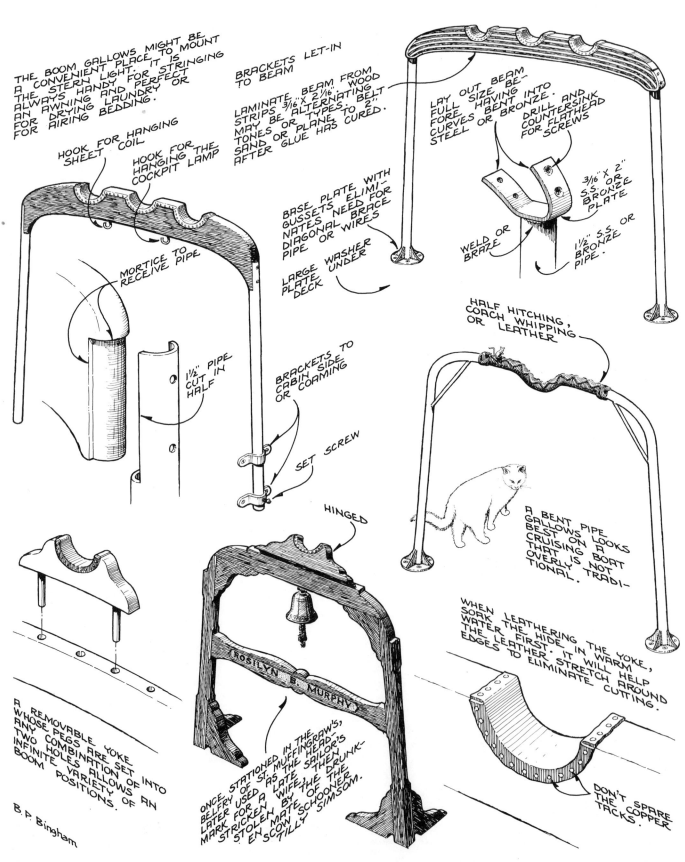

THE BOOM GALLOWS MIGHT BE A CONVENIENT PLACE TO MOUNT THE STERN LIGHT. IT IS ALWAYS HANDY FOR STRINGING AN AWNING AND PERFECT FOR DRYING LAUNDRY OR FOR AIRING BEDDING.

BRACKETS LET-IN TO BEAM

LAMINATE BEAM FROM STRIPS 3/16" X 2 1/16" WOOD MAY BE ALTERNATING TONES OR TYPES. BELT SAND OR PLANE TO 2" AFTER GLUE HAS CURED.

LAY OUT BEAM FULL SIZE BEFORE HAVING CURVES BENT INTO STEEL OR BRONZE.

DRILL AND COUNTERSINK FOR FLATHEAD SCREWS

3/16" X 2" S.S. OR BRONZE PLATE

HOOK FOR HANGING SHEET COIL

HOOK FOR HANGING THE COCKPIT LAMP

BASE PLATE WITH GUSSETS ELIMINATES NEED FOR DIAGONAL BRACE PIPE OR WIRES

WELD OR BRAZE

1½" S.S. OR BRONZE PIPE.

MORTICE TO RECEIVE PIPE

LARGE WASHER PLATE UNDER DECK

1½" PIPE CUT IN HALF

HALF HITCHING, COACH WHIPPING OR LEATHER

BRACKETS TO CABIN SIDE OR COAMING

SET SCREW

HINGED

A BENT PIPE GALLOWS LOOKS BEST ON A CRUISING BOAT THAT IS NOT OVERLY TRADITIONAL.

WHEN LEATHERING THE YOKE, SOAK THE HIDE IN WARM WATER FIRST. IT WILL HELP THE LEATHER STRETCH AROUND EDGES TO ELIMINATE CUTTING.

"ROSILYN B. MURPHY"

A REMOVABLE YOKE WHOSE PEGS ARE SET INTO ANY COMBINATION OF TWO HOLES ALLOWS AN INFINITE VARIETY OF BOOM POSITIONS.

B.P. Bingham

ONCE STATIONED IN THE BELFRY OF ST. MUFFINGRAW'S, LATER USED AS THE SAILOR'S MARK FOR A LATE HEAD-STRICKEN WIFE, THEN STOLEN BY THE DRUNKEN MATE OF THE SCOW SCHOONER TILLY SIMSOM.

DON'T SPARE THE COPPER TACKS.

CHAPTER **2** # Of Sails and Rigging

The Roller-Furling Storm Sleeve

EVERY FALL GALE, SUMMER SQUALL AND UNEXPECTED SPRING STORM PROVIDES A "WINDFALL" FOR THE SAILMAKER. BESIDES THE USUAL BLOWN MAINS'L SEAMS, TORN BATTEN POCKETS AND PARTED LEACH TABLINGS, THERE INEVITABLY RESULTS AT LEAST A WEEK'S WORK OF REPAIRING ROLLER-FURLING GENNIES AND MAINS'LS (SET ON OUT-MAST LUFF WIRES).

HIGH WINDS, FINDING A LOOSE OPENING ALONG THE SPIRALED FURLED LEACH, FORCE THE SAIL TO BALLOON UNDER THE PRESSURE. OFTEN, THIS WILL ACTUALLY UNLAY THE LUFF WIRE OR PART THE FURLING LINE. THE SAIL THEN UNROLLS (FULLY OR PARTIALLY) AND PROCEEDS TO FLOG ITSELF TO DEATH.

ONE SOLUTION, OF COURSE, IS TO RE-MOVE THE SAIL BE-FORE TROUBLE ARISES. MORE CONVENIENT, HOWEVER, IS THE PLACING OF A STORM SLEEVE.

PUTTING ON THE SLEEVE ONLY TAKES A MINUTE, IT STOWS AS A COMPACT BUNDLE, AND ITS COST IS A VERY SMALL FRACTION OF THE INVESTMENT IN YOUR SAIL.

LUFF-FOIL FURLING SAILS ARE FAR LESS SUSCEPTIBLE TO STORM DAMAGE THAN WIRE-LUFF SAILS.

WHY NOT TALK TO YOUR SAILMAKER ABOUT IT?

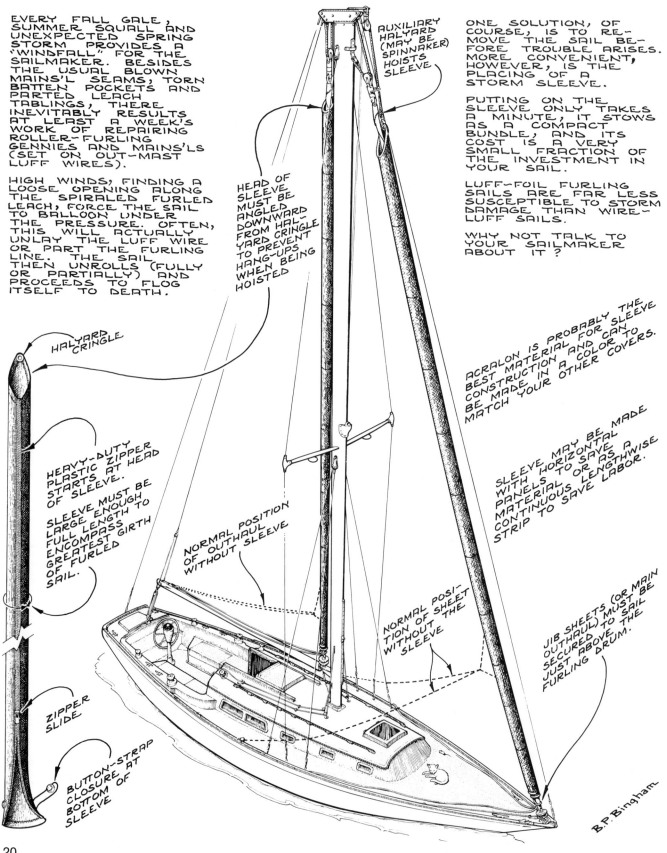

AUXILIARY HALYARD (MAY BE SPINNAKER) HOISTS SLEEVE

HEAD OF SLEEVE MUST BE ANGLED DOWNWARD FROM HAL-YARD CRINGLE TO PREVENT HANG-UPS WHEN BEING HOISTED

HALYARD CRINGLE

HEAVY-DUTY PLASTIC ZIPPER STARTS AT HEAD OF SLEEVE.

SLEEVE MUST BE LARGE ENOUGH FULL LENGTH TO ENCOMPASS GREATEST GIRTH OF FURLED SAIL.

ACRALON IS PROBABLY THE BEST MATERIAL FOR SLEEVE CONSTRUCTION AND CAN BE MADE IN A COLOR TO MATCH YOUR OTHER COVERS.

SLEEVE MAY BE MADE WITH HORIZONTAL PANELS TO SAVE MATERIAL OR AS A CONTINUOUS LENGTHWISE STRIP TO SAVE LABOR.

NORMAL POSITION OF OUTHAUL WITHOUT SLEEVE

NORMAL POSI-TION OF SHEET WITHOUT THE SLEEVE

JIB SHEETS (OR MAIN OUTHAUL) MUST BE SECURED TO SAIL JUST ABOVE THE FURLING DRUM.

ZIPPER SLIDE

BUTTON-STRAP CLOSURE AT BOTTOM OF SLEEVE

B.P.Bingham

20

Furling With Shock Cord

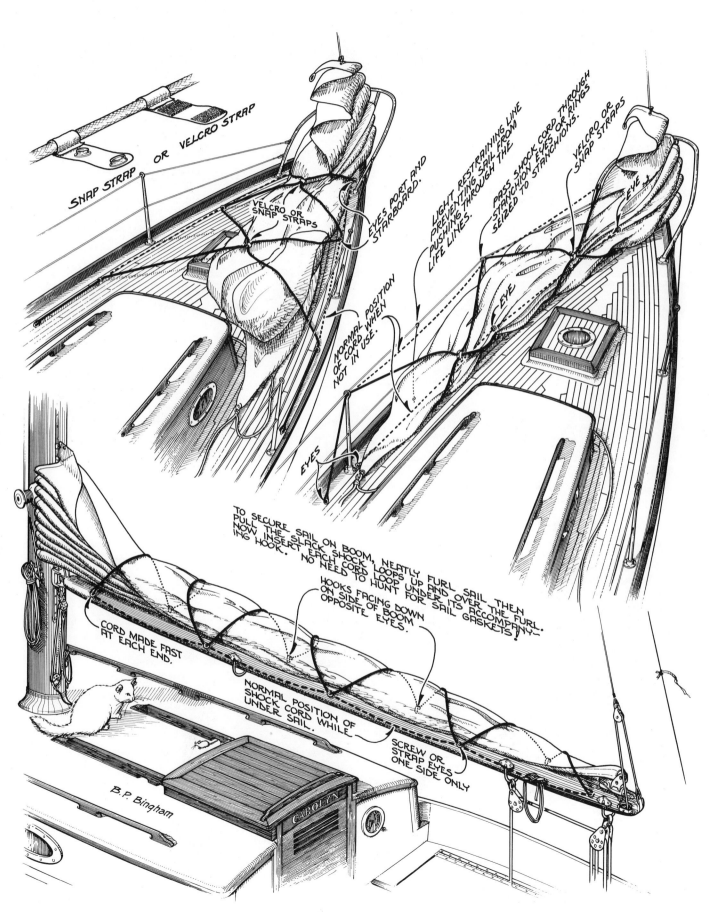

SNAP STRAP OR VELCRO STRAP

VELCRO OR SNAP STRAPS

EYES PORT AND STARBOARD.

NORMAL POSITION OF CORD WHEN NOT IN USE.

EYES

LIGHT RESTRAINING LINE PREVENTING SAIL FROM PUSHING THROUGH THE LIFE LINES.

PASS SHOCK CORD THROUGH STANCHION EYES OR RINGS SEIZED TO STANCHIONS.

VELCRO OR SNAP STRAPS

EYE

EYE

TO SECURE SAIL ON BOOM, NEATLY FURL SAIL THEN PULL THE SLACK SHOCK CORD LOOPS UP AND OVER THE FURL. NOW INSERT EACH CORD LOOP UNDER ITS ACCOMPANY-ING HOOK. NO NEED TO HUNT FOR SAIL GASKETS!

HOOKS FACING DOWN ON SIDE OF BOOM OPPOSITE EYES.

CORD MADE FAST AT EACH END.

NORMAL POSITION OF SHOCK CORD WHILE UNDER SAIL.

SCREW OR STRAP EYES ONE SIDE ONLY

B.P. Bingham

CAROLYN

Genoa Reefing

CRUISING SAILORS HAVE ALWAYS PURSUED, AND BEEN ELUDED BY, THE ABILITY TO REDUCE SAIL QUICKLY. THE MOST PUZZLING PROBLEM HAS BEEN THE REEFING OF A LARGE, OVERLAPPING HEADS'L.

UNFORTUNATELY (AND CONTRARY TO POPULAR BELIEF), FEW ROLLER-FURLING SYSTEMS ARE DESIGNED TO BE ROLLER REEFING (AS ANY SAILMAKER WILL TELL YOU).

BUT A JIFFY-REEFING HEADS'L IS A VIABLE ALTERNATIVE.

IT IS BEST LIMITED TO 135-140% L.P. SUCH A SAIL SHOULD BE BUILT OF SLIGHTLY HEAVIER CLOTH THAN NORMAL AND MUST BE DESIGNED WITH SECOND TACK AND CLEW CRINGLES, FOOT REINFORCING PATCHES AND TYING POINTS.

THE SAME ARRANGEMENT MAY BE APPLIED TO A WORKING JIB TO REDUCE IT TO STORM SIZE.

THE REEFING IS DONE JUST LIKE A MAINS'L.

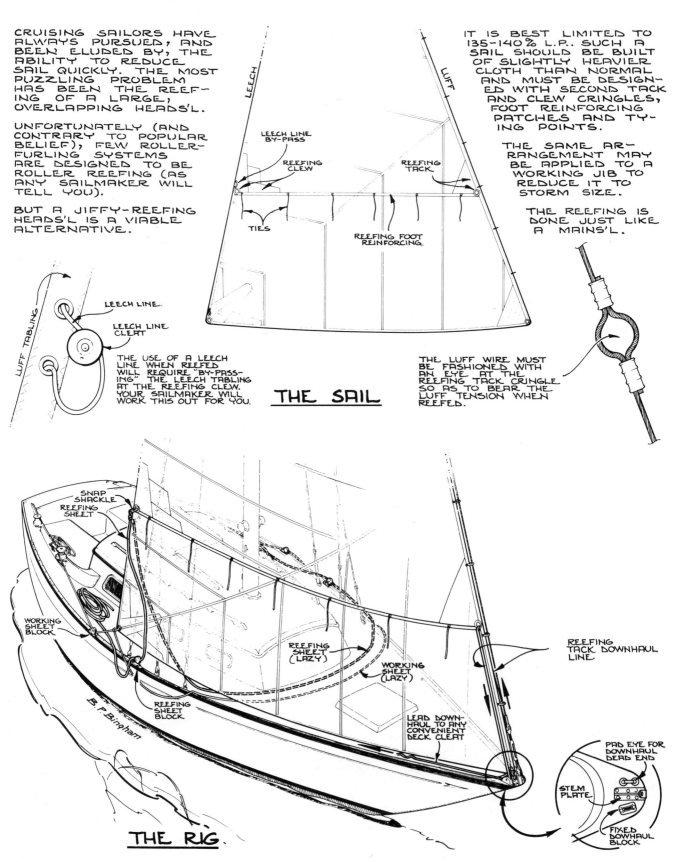

LEECH

LUFF

LEECH LINE BY-PASS

REEFING CLEW

REEFING TACK

TIES

REEFING FOOT REINFORCING

LEECH LINE

LEECH LINE CLEAT

LUFF TABLING

THE USE OF A LEECH LINE WHEN REEFED WILL REQUIRE "BY-PASSING" THE LEECH TABLING AT THE REEFING CLEW. YOUR SAILMAKER WILL WORK THIS OUT FOR YOU.

THE SAIL

THE LUFF WIRE MUST BE FASHIONED WITH AN EYE AT THE REEFING TACK CRINGLE SO AS TO BEAR THE LUFF TENSION WHEN REEFED.

SNAP SHACKLE

REEFING SHEET

WORKING SHEET BLOCK

REEFING SHEET BLOCK

B. P. Bingham

REEFING SHEET (LAZY)

WORKING SHEET (LAZY)

LEAD DOWNHAUL TO ANY CONVENIENT DECK CLEAT

REEFING TACK DOWNHAUL LINE

PAD EYE FOR DOWNHAUL DEAD END

STEM PLATE

FIXED DOWNHAUL BLOCK

THE RIG.

① AS THE WIND INCREASES TO THE POINT OF OVER-POWERING THE BOAT, THE MOST LOGICAL SHORT MAIN REEF IS TAKEN. THIS WILL NOT ONLY HELP TO PUT THE BOAT BACK ON ITS FEET BUT WILL EASE THE WEATHER HELM. RARELY WILL SHORTENING THE HEADS'L ACCOMPLISH AS MUCH.

② IF THE WIND CONTINUES TO INCREASE... OR IF THE BOAT IS STILL OVERPOWERED FOL-LOWING THE MAIN REEF, IT IS TIME TO REAVE THE REEFING DOWNHAUL AND TO ATTACH THE HEADS'L REEFING SHEETS.

③ HEADS'L REEFING TIME HAS COME. EASE THE GENNY SHEETS.

④ EASE THE HEADS'L HALYARD. TAKE UP ON THE REEFING DOWNHAUL AND MAKE IT FAST.

⑤ BUCK UP THE HEADS'L HAL-YARD AND MAKE IT FAST.

NOW, TAKE IN THE HEADS'L SHEET, TRIMMING FOR THE CORRECT BOAT HEADING.

⑥ WHEN TIME PERMITS, FURL UP THE LOOSE PORTION OF THE HEADS'L ALONG THE FOOT. SECURE THE FURL WITH THE TIES.

IF YOU PLAN ON TACKING, YOU MAY REMOVE THE WORKING SHEETS.

B. P. Bingham

Wood-Shelled Blocks

SOME HINTS

TO AVOID ERRORS WHEN RE-PRODUCING THE PATTERN DRAWING ON THE OPPOSITE PAGE, HAVE IT "PHOTOSTATED" TO THE PECENTAGE SHOWN ON THE TABLE.

THE SHEAVES ARE AVAILABLE FOR ALL LINE SIZES FROM SCORES OF HARDWARE MANU-FACTURERS. THEY VARY IN TYPE FROM BRONZE WITH "OILITE" BUSHINGS (HEAVY) TO NYLON AND "DELRIN" WITHOUT BUSHINGS. THE CHOICE IS YOURS.... BUT, DO NOT MILL YOUR SPACER LUMBER OR ORDER THE AXLE ROD UNTIL YOU HAVE THE SHEAVES IN HAND. THE SHEAVE THICKNESS AND AXLE DIAMETERS LISTED BY SUPPLIERS MAY NOT EXACTLY MATCH WHAT THEY SEND YOU. SO, TO AVOID UNDUE SLOP WITHIN THE BLOCK, MODIFY THE TABLED DIMENSIONS TO COMPLEMENT YOUR OWN SHEAVES BEFORE STARTING.

THE MOST ATTRACTIVE BLOCKS ARE THOSE WITH CONTRAST-ING CHEEK AND SPACER WOODS & MAHOGANY CHEEKS WITH BIRCH SPACERS: OAK CHEEKS WITH TEAK SPACERS: TEAK CHEEKS WITH MAPLE SPACERS.

THE GRAIN OF THE CHEEKS MUST RUN THE LENGTH OF THE BLOCK BUT THE GRAIN OF THE SPACERS RUNS ACROSS.

ROUT THE STRAP MORTICES INTO THE CHEEK LUMBER WITH THE "FLAT FOOT" **BEFORE** TRANSFERRING THE CHEEK (OR DOUBLE BLOCK CENTER) SHAPES. IT WILL HELP AVOID ALIGNMENT DIFFICULTIES.

THE MORTICES SHOULD BE A "HAIR" DEEPER THAN THE STRAP THICKNESS.

USE TISSUE AND CARBON PAPER FOR TRANSFERRING WOOD PARTS SHAPES AS WELL AS GLUEING AND DRILL-ING POSITIONS. DON'T DRILL CHEEKS UNTIL ASSEMBLED.

GIVE THE INNER SIDES OF THE CHEEKS AT LEAST TWO COATS OF VARNISH BEFORE GLUE-ING BLOCK PARTS TOGETHER. DO NOT APPLY VARNISH TO FAYING SURFACE, HOWEVER.

DON'T SAND BLOCK PERIMET-ER TO FINAL SHAPE UNTIL GLUEING ALL WOOD PARTS.

TO AVOID THE NECESSITY OF HAVING TO CLAMP THE BLOCK PARTS DURING GLUEING (BOTH COSTLY AND DIFFICULT TO ACHIEVE PROPER ALIGNMENT), USE A 3-HOUR EPOXY. YOU WILL NOT HAVE TO BE TOO CONCERNED WITH TEMPERATURE AND YOUR BLOCKS WILL BE VERY STRONG. YOU MAY ALSO ELIMINATE THE CHEEK THRU-PINS.

WHEN GLUEING UP, DON'T TRY TO ASSEMBLE THE ENTIRE BLOCK AT ONCE. FIRST, GLUE THE SPACERS TO ONE CHEEK ONLY. WHEN THIS GLUE HAS SET, APPLY THE OPPOSITE CHEEK.

"ROUND EDGE" THE CHEEK PERIM-ETERS ONLY AFTER SANDING TO FINAL SHAPE.

TO CUT THE BRASS COVER PLATE, BEGIN WITH A SMALL SQUARE THEN PROGRESSIVELY SNIP OFF THE CORNERS UNTIL ONLY A SMOOTH, ROUND DISC REMAINS.

WHEN I DECIDED TO REPLACE ALL OF THE DECK AND RIG-GING HARDWARE ABOARD MY LITTLE SCHOONER, *AT LAST*, I WAS NOT FULLY PREPARED FOR THE OVERWHELMING COST. AFTER ALL, SHE IS GAFF HEADED, CARRIES A TOPS'L AND FISHERMAN AS WELL AS DOUBLE HEADS'LS. SHE ALSO SPORTS LAZYJACKS, VANGS, RUNNING BACKS AND JIB BOOM GUYS.

THE GREATEST EXPENSE, IT TURNED OUT, WOULD BE THE PURCHASING OF BLOCKS; ALL FIVE DOZEN OF THEM (OF VARIOUS SIZES AND TYPES) HAD TO BE WOOD SHELLED TO BE IN KEEPING WITH THE CHARACTER OF THE BOAT. UPON REVIEWING THE QUOTES FROM A HALF-DOZEN SUPPLIERS, IT LOOKED LIKE A CASH LAYOUT OF $1,500 TO $2,200 WAS UN-AVOIDABLE....MONEY I DIDN'T HAVE!

ENTER THE DESIGNER/CRAFTS-MAN WITH LIMITED TOOLS.

WITHIN 120 HOURS, EVERY BLOCK WAS FINISHED WITH STAINLESS STEEL STRAP, NYLON SHEAVES, ALL NECESSARY SHACKLES AND CRINGLES, STAINLESS AXLES, BRASS COVER PLATES AND FOUR COATS OF VARNISH. THE TOTAL COST WAS UNDER $160 (INCLUDING A SILICON/CAR-BIDE SANDING DISC FOR SHAP-ING THE SHELLS, SPECIAL SAW BLADES AND BITS FOR WORKING STAINLESS, AND EPOXY GLUE FOR ASSEMBLING THE WOOD SHELL PARTS).

SO, THE AVERAGE COST OF EACH BLOCK RAN $2.50 AND LESS THAN TWO HOURS OF MY TIME. IN MY OPINION, THIS ISN'T A BAD WAY TO INCREASE THE VALUE AND APPEARANCE OF AN OLDER BOAT WHILE INDULGING IN SOME VERY RELAXING AND ENJOYABLE THERAPY.

BE AWARE AT THE OUTSET THAT THE FEWER BLOCKS YOU MAKE, THE MORE EX-PENSIVE EACH WILL BE. SUCH COSTS AS A "SHEARING SET-UP" CHARGE FOR CUTTING THE STAINLESS STRAP, THE MINIMUM MILLING FEE FOR LUMBER, THE PRICES FOR SPECIAL TOOLS WILL RE-MAIN ALMOST FIXED.

TOOLS YOU'LL NEED

A SABER SAW, A HACK SAW WITH A SILICON/CAR-BIDE BLADE, A ROUTER FITTED WITH A CARBIDE "FLAT FOOT" BIT (THE SIZE OF BIT TO EQUAL THE BLOCK'S STRAP WIDTH), A CARBIDE 5/16" "ROUND-EDGE" ROUTER BIT, TUNGSTEN DRILL BITS FOR THE AXLE AND CRINGLE CLEVIS PIN HOLES. A VISE FOR HOLDING WORK AND BENDING STRAP, A MEDIUM-COARSE 1/4" RAT-TAIL FILE, A PAIR OF STRAIGHT-CUTTING TIN SNIPS, EITHER A TABLE SAW FIT-TED WITH A SILICON/CARBIDE SANDING DISC OR A BELT SANDER WITH No. 60 CAR-BORUNDUM BELTS, A DRILL PRESS (PREF.) OR HAND DRILL.

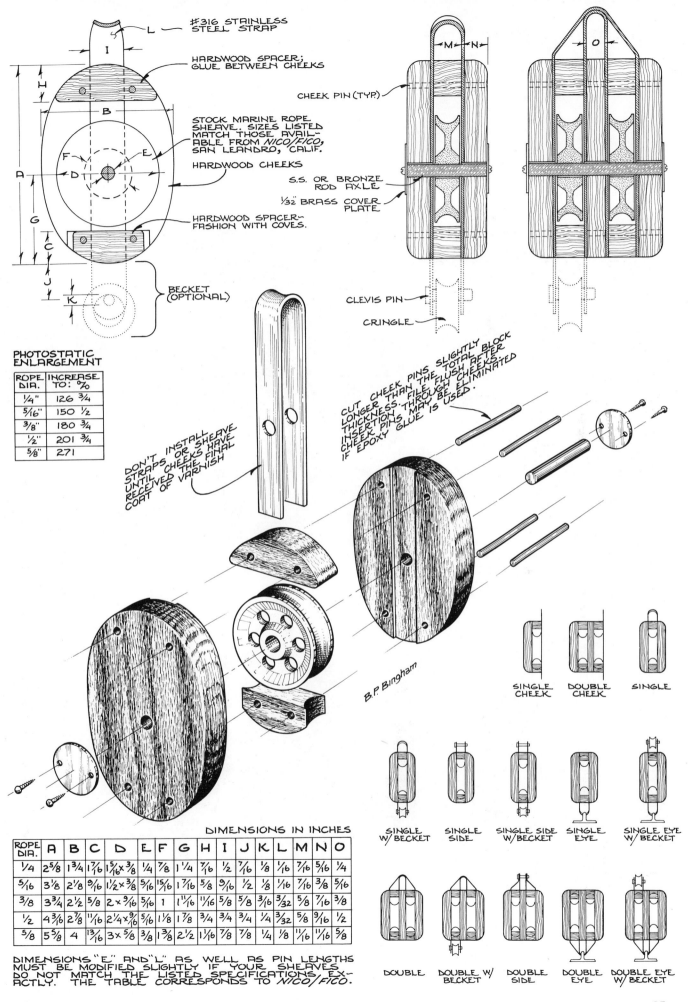

#316 STAINLESS STEEL STRAP

HARDWOOD SPACER; GLUE BETWEEN CHEEKS

CHEEK PIN (TYP.)

STOCK MARINE ROPE SHEAVE. SIZES LISTED MATCH THOSE AVAILABLE FROM *NICO/FICO*, SAN LEANDRO, CALIF.

HARDWOOD CHEEKS

S.S. OR BRONZE ROD AXLE

1/32" BRASS COVER PLATE

HARDWOOD SPACER- FASHION WITH COVES.

BECKET (OPTIONAL)

CLEVIS PIN

CRINGLE

PHOTOSTATIC ENLARGEMENT

ROPE DIA.	INCREASE TO: %
1/4"	126 3/4
5/16"	150 1/2
3/8"	180 3/4
1/2"	201 3/4
5/8"	271

DON'T INSTALL STRAPS OR SHEAVE UNTIL CHEEKS HAVE RECEIVED THE FINAL COAT OF VARNISH

CUT CHEEK PINS SLIGHTLY LONGER THAN THE TOTAL BLOCK THICKNESS. FILE FLUSH AFTER INSERTION THROUGH CHEEKS. CHEEK PINS MAY BE ELIMINATED IF EPOXY GLUE IS USED.

B.P. Bingham

SINGLE CHEEK

DOUBLE CHEEK

SINGLE

SINGLE W/ BECKET

SINGLE SIDE

SINGLE SIDE W/ BECKET

SINGLE EYE

SINGLE EYE W/ BECKET

DOUBLE

DOUBLE W/ BECKET

DOUBLE SIDE

DOUBLE EYE

DOUBLE EYE W/ BECKET

DIMENSIONS IN INCHES

ROPE DIA.	A	B	C	D	E	F	G	H	I	J	K	L	M	N	O
1/4	2 5/8	1 3/4	1 7/16	1 5/16 × 3/8	1/4	7/8	1 1/4	7/16	1/2	7/16	1/8	1/16	7/16	5/16	1/4
5/16	3 1/8	2 1/8	9/16	1 1/2 × 3/8	5/16	15/16	1 7/16	5/8	9/16	1/2	1/8	1/16	7/16	3/8	5/16
3/8	3 3/4	2 1/2	5/8	2 × 9/16	5/16	1	1 11/16	11/16	5/8	5/8	3/16	3/32	5/8	7/16	3/8
1/2	4 3/16	2 7/8	11/16	2 1/4 × 9/16	5/16	1 1/8	1 7/8	3/4	3/4	3/4	1/4	3/32	5/8	9/16	1/2
5/8	5 5/8	4	13/16	3 × 5/8	3/8	1 3/8	2 1/2	1 1/16	7/8	7/8	1/4	1/8	11/16	11/16	5/8

DIMENSIONS "E" AND "L" AS WELL AS PIN LENGTHS MUST BE MODIFIED SLIGHTLY IF YOUR SHEAVES DO NOT MATCH THE LISTED SPECIFICATIONS, EXACTLY. THE TABLE CORRESPONDS TO *NICO/FICO*.

Belaying Pins

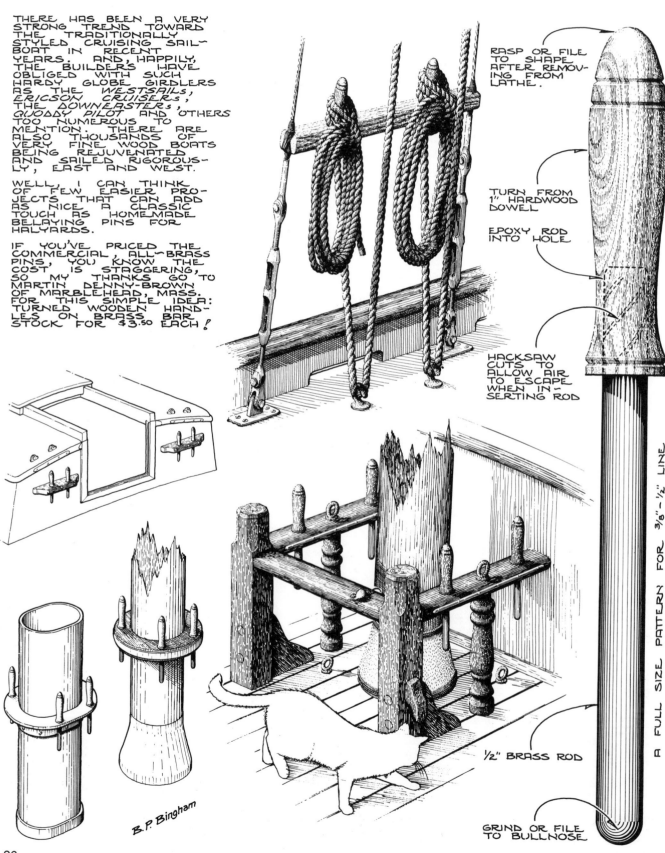

THERE HAS BEEN A VERY STRONG TREND TOWARD THE TRADITIONALLY STYLED CRUISING SAIL-BOAT IN RECENT YEARS. AND, HAPPILY, THE BUILDERS HAVE OBLIGED WITH SUCH HARDY GLOBE GIRDLERS AS THE WESTSAILS, ERICSON CRUISERS, THE DOWNEASTERS, QUODDY PILOT AND OTHERS TOO NUMEROUS TO MENTION. THERE ARE ALSO THOUSANDS OF VERY FINE WOOD BOATS BEING REJUVENATED AND SAILED RIGOROUS-LY, EAST AND WEST.

WELL, I CAN THINK OF FEW EASIER PRO-JECTS THAT CAN ADD AS NICE A CLASSIC TOUCH AS HOMEMADE BELAYING PINS FOR HALYARDS.

IF YOU'VE PRICED THE COMMERCIAL, ALL-BRASS PINS, YOU KNOW THE COST IS STAGGERING, SO MY THANKS GO TO MARTIN DENNY-BROWN OF MARBLEHEAD, MASS. FOR THIS SIMPLE IDEA: TURNED WOODEN HAND-LES ON BRASS BAR STOCK FOR $3.50 EACH!

RASP OR FILE TO SHAPE AFTER REMOV-ING FROM LATHE.

TURN FROM 1" HARDWOOD DOWEL

EPOXY ROD INTO HOLE

HACKSAW CUTS TO ALLOW AIR TO ESCAPE WHEN IN-SERTING ROD

½" BRASS ROD

A FULL SIZE PATTERN FOR ⅜"–½" LINE

GRIND OR FILE TO BULLNOSE

B. P. Bingham

26

Modern Baggywrinkles

BAGGYWRINKLES: THEY RAIN DOWN SHREDS OF MANILA BITS ONTO THE DECK; THEY ADD WINDAGE; THEY MESS UP THE APPEARANCE OF AN OTHERWISE TIDY RIG AND THEY WEIGH A TON WHEN THEY'RE WET. BUT, BAGGY-WRINKLES SERVE THE VITAL FUNCTION OF MINIMIZING SAIL CHAFE ABOARD THE VOYAGING YACHT, MOST PARTICULARLY WHERE THE SAILS ARE WORN BY SHROUDS, SPREADER TIPS, RUNNING BACKSTAYS, TOP'N'LIFT, EVEN LIFELINES AND THE BOW PULPIT.

BAGGYWRINKLES ARE MOST USUALLY SEEN IN THE RIGGING OF VERY TRADITIONAL BOATS ONLY. THE MODERN SAILOR RESISTS THEM BECAUSE THEY'RE UNSIGHTLY TO HIM AND TEDIOUS TO MAKE.

HOWEVER, THE BEST OF BOTH WORLDS CAN BE ACHIEVED BY FABRICATING YOUR BAGGYWRINKLES IN THE MANNER SHOWN HERE. THEY ARE LIGHT AND UNOBTRUSIVE, LONG-LASTING, EASY TO INSTALL AND VERY FUNCTIONAL. JUST THE THING TO REDUCE THE SAIL REPAIR BILL AT THE END OF A LONG OFFSHORE PASSAGE.

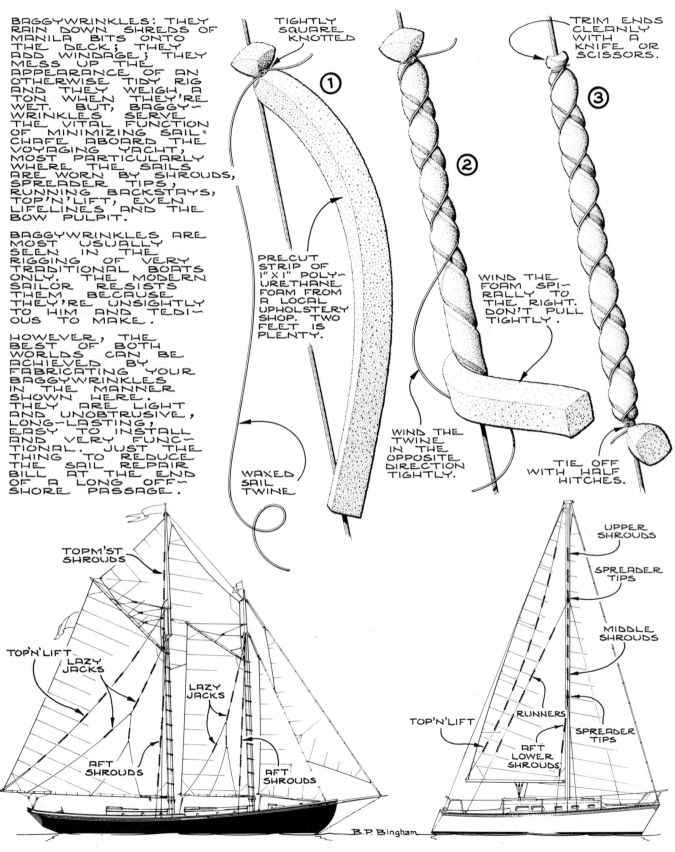

TIGHTLY SQUARE KNOTTED

①

PRECUT STRIP OF 1" X 1" POLYURETHANE FOAM FROM A LOCAL UPHOLSTERY SHOP. TWO FEET IS PLENTY.

WAXED SAIL TWINE

②

WIND THE TWINE IN THE OPPOSITE DIRECTION TIGHTLY.

WIND THE FOAM SPIRALLY TO THE RIGHT. DON'T PULL TIGHTLY.

③

TRIM ENDS CLEANLY WITH A KNIFE OR SCISSORS.

TIE OFF WITH HALF HITCHES.

TOPM'ST SHROUDS

TOP'N'LIFT

LAZY JACKS

LAZY JACKS

AFT SHROUDS

AFT SHROUDS

UPPER SHROUDS

SPREADER TIPS

MIDDLE SHROUDS

TOP'N'LIFT

RUNNERS

AFT LOWER SHROUDS

SPREADER TIPS

B.P. Bingham

Whence The Wind?

ONE OF THE MOST DIF-FICULT AND ELUSIVE ELEMENTS OF SAILING IS DETERMINING COR-RECT SAIL TRIM AND STEERING BY THE EVER-SHIFTING WIND. PURELY SENSORY JUDGEMENT WILL SUF-FICE FOR LACKADAISICAL DAY SAILS, BUT FOR PASSAGE-MAKING AND RACING, PROPER SAIL TRIM IS **VERY** IMPOR-TANT FOR MAINTAINING BEST BOAT SPEED. EVEN THE MOST EXPER-IENCED SAILOR NEEDS HELP.

YOU CAN MAKE OR BUY A FANCY MASTHEAD FLY TO DETERMINE THE WIND'S DIRECTION. BUT YOU REALLY CAN'T SAIL VERY WELL WITH YOUR HEAD TILTED BACK ALL THE TIME, SO THEY ARE ONLY GOOD FOR AN OCCASIONAL GLANCE.

MASTHEAD FLIES RARELY TELL THE TRUTH. THEY DON'T REPRESENT THE AVERAGE WIND DIREC-TION OVER THE BOAT'S SAIL PLAN, BUT ONLY AT THE TOP OF THE MAST WHERE WIND SPEEDS ARE HIGHER AND VAST-LY INFLUENCED BY THE PITCHING AND ROLLING OF THE BOAT.

THESE SAME INFLUENC-ES CAUSE AN ELEC-TRONIC WIND INDICATOR TO LIE AS WELL. THE MOST EXPENSIVE WIND INSTRUMENT MAY NOT AID YOUR DETERMINA-TION AT ALL AND CAN BE DOWNRIGHT CONFUSING TO A BEGINNING SAILOR.

YOUR BEST BET IS TO INVEST ABOUT $2.00 IN A SPOOL OF 1/4" NYLON CLOTH RIBBON TO MAKE EXTREMELY RELIABLE, ABSOLUTELY TRUTHFUL, HEADS'L-LUFF TELL-TALES.

THEY'LL TELL YOU WHEN TO TRIM OR START THE HEADS'L SHEET AND WHEN TO STEER "HIGHER" OR "LOWER" OF THE APPAR-ENT WIND. THEY CAN EVEN TELL YOU IF YOUR HEADS'L-SHEET LEAD BLOCK IS IN THE PROPER FORE-AND-AFT POSITION.

LUFF TELL-TALES, IN FACT, ARE SO INEX-PENSIVE, SO ACCURATE AND EASY TO READ THAT ALL RACERS USE THEM AND EVERY CRUISING BOAT SHOULD HAVE THEM.

TO FIND VERTICAL POSITIONS FOR TELL-TALES, JUST MULTIPLY THE LUFF LENGTH (L) BY THE SPACING FACTORS (.15, .3 AND .25).

THE BOTTOM TELL-TALE MAY BE RAISED SLIGHTLY IF THE VIEW FROM THE COCKPIT PERMITS.

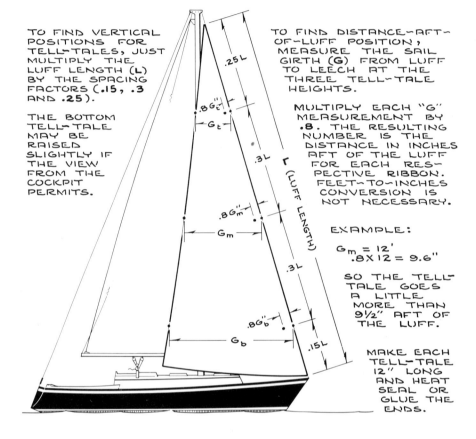

TO FIND DISTANCE-AFT-OF-LUFF POSITION, MEASURE THE SAIL GIRTH (G) FROM LUFF TO LEECH AT THE THREE TELL-TALE HEIGHTS.

MULTIPLY EACH "G" MEASUREMENT BY .8. THE RESULTING NUMBER IS THE DISTANCE IN INCHES AFT OF THE LUFF FOR EACH RES-PECTIVE RIBBON. FEET-TO-INCHES CONVERSION IS NOT NECESSARY.

EXAMPLE:

$G_m = 12'$
$.8 \times 12 = 9.6"$

SO THE TELL-TALE GOES A LITTLE MORE THAN 9 1/2" AFT OF THE LUFF.

MAKE EACH TELL-TALE 12" LONG AND HEAT SEAL OR GLUE THE ENDS.

SEVERAL METHODS FOR ATTACHING THE TELL-TALES ARE POSSIBLE:

BE SURE THE SAIL IS SALT FREE AND DRY, THEN USE A GOOD WEATHER-PROOF TAPE.

MELT A TINY HOLE IN THE SAIL WITH A HOT ICE PICK; THEN PUSH THE RIBBON THROUGH AND KNOT AT EACH SIDE.

DOUBLE OVER THE FORWARD ENDS AND SEW THEM TO THE SAIL.

THE TELL-TALES ON BOTH SIDES OF THE SAIL ARE READ TOGETHER TO ASCERTAIN CORRECT SAIL TRIM AND/OR THE BOAT'S HEADING.

ON BRIGHT DAYS WITH THE SUN ON THE OTHER SIDE OF THE SAIL, THE OBSCURED TELL-TALE WILL CAST A VISIBLE SHADOW THAT CAN BE "READ".

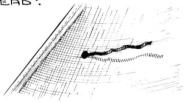

AT OTHER TIMES, HOW-EVER, IT'S IMPOSSIBLE TO SEE THEM BOTH. YOUR SAILMAKER CAN INSTALL SPECIAL TELL-TALE WINDOWS.

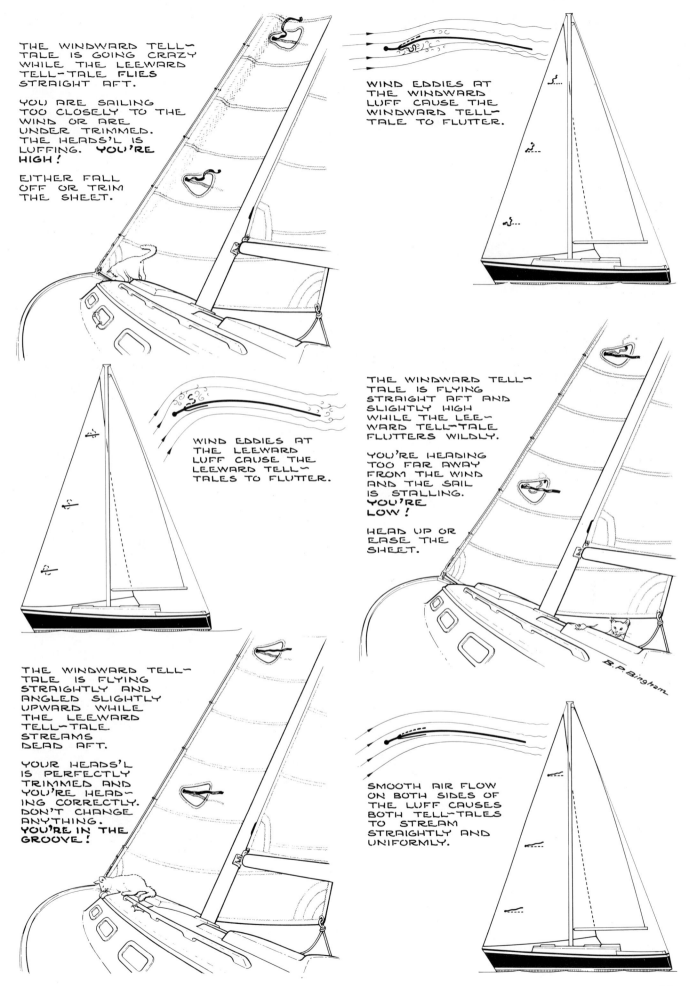

THE WINDWARD TELL-TALE IS GOING CRAZY WHILE THE LEEWARD TELL-TALE FLIES STRAIGHT AFT.

YOU ARE SAILING TOO CLOSELY TO THE WIND OR ARE UNDER TRIMMED. THE HEADS'L IS LUFFING. **YOU'RE HIGH!**

EITHER FALL OFF OR TRIM THE SHEET.

WIND EDDIES AT THE WINDWARD LUFF CAUSE THE WINDWARD TELL-TALE TO FLUTTER.

WIND EDDIES AT THE LEEWARD LUFF CAUSE THE LEEWARD TELL-TALES TO FLUTTER.

THE WINDWARD TELL-TALE IS FLYING STRAIGHT AFT AND SLIGHTLY HIGH WHILE THE LEE-WARD TELL-TALE FLUTTERS WILDLY.

YOU'RE HEADING TOO FAR AWAY FROM THE WIND AND THE SAIL IS STALLING. **YOU'RE LOW!**

HEAD UP OR EASE THE SHEET.

B. P. Bingham

THE WINDWARD TELL-TALE IS FLYING STRAIGHTLY AND ANGLED SLIGHTLY UPWARD WHILE THE LEEWARD TELL-TALE STREAMS DEAD AFT.

YOUR HEADS'L IS PERFECTLY TRIMMED AND YOU'RE HEAD-ING CORRECTLY. DON'T CHANGE ANYTHING. **YOU'RE IN THE GROOVE!**

SMOOTH AIR FLOW ON BOTH SIDES OF THE LUFF CAUSES BOTH TELL-TALES TO STREAM STRAIGHTLY AND UNIFORMLY.

Tell-Tales That Work

I BEGAN SAILING LONG BEFORE THE SOPHIS- TICATED ELECTRONIC WIND-POINT SYSTEMS WERE INVENTED. INDEED, THE MAST- HEAD FLY WAS NO MORE THAN A RO- TATING FEATHER. INSOMUCH AS LUFF "WOOLIES" HADN'T EVOLVED EITHER, THE PRIMARY WIND-DIREC- TION INDICATORS WERE SIMPLY LENGTHS OF YARN OR RIBBON TIED TO THE MAIN SHROUDS.

THINGS HAVE CHANGED A LOT SINCE THOSE DAYS. EVERY HEADS'L IS FITTED WITH WOOL- IES, I USE A WIND- POINT SYSTEM WITH DUAL INSTRUMENT HEADS AND A FANCY, GIMBALED WIND IN- DICATOR FASTENED TO THE MAIN HATCH FOR MAXIMUM VISI- BILITY. BUT... I STILL USE THE OLD SHROUD TELL-TALES AS WELL. I AM SIMPLY LOST WITHOUT THEM AND I KNOW HUNDREDS OF OTHER SAILORS WHO FEEL THE SAME WAY. IT MUST BE SOME KIND OF SECURITY- BLANKET SYNDROME.

THE PROBLEM WITH YARNS OR RIBBONS IS THEY HAVE A PROPENSITY FOR WRAP- PING THEMSELVES AROUND THE SHROUDS (IT NEVER HAPPENS WHILE YOU'RE LOOK- ING).

I'VE TRIED TO SOLVE THIS BY USING THE COMMERCIALLY MADE TELL-TALES (THE DYED GOOSE DOWN ATTACHED TO THE SPIRAL WIRE AND THE ORANGE PLASTIC STREAMER WITH THE WHITE PLASTIC ENDS). FOR SOME REASON, THEY JUST DON'T LOOK OR FEEL QUITE RIGHT.

I'VE BEEN TRYING TO COME UP WITH AN ALTERNATIVE FOR

YEARS THEN I HIT AN IDEA LAST YEAR THAT WAS WORTH A TRY. IT ONLY TOOK TEN MINUTES AND I HAVEN'T HAD TO STRAIGHTEN OUT A TELL-TALE SINCE. THAT WAS SEVEN- THOUSAND MILES AGO.

①

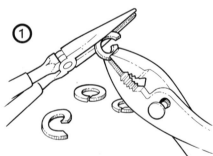

PICK ONE PAIR OF STAINLESS-STEEL LOCK WASHERS FOR EACH TELL-TALE TO BE INSTALLED. THE INSIDE DIAMETERS MUST BE ABOUT 1/8" LARGER THAN THE SHROUDS.

TWIST EACH WASHER OPEN WITH PLIERS UNTIL THEY ARE JUST ABLE TO BE SLIPPED ONTO THE SHROUDS.

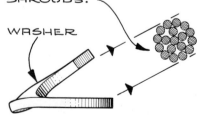

②

WRAP THE SHROUD AT THE TELL-TALE POSI- TION WITH MARINE FABRIC TAPE (SUCH AS DANFORTH "SAILOR'S TAPE") TO A THICK- NESS OF 1/8".

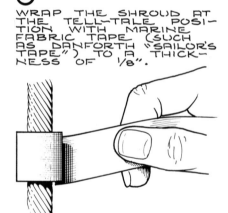

③

SLIP TWO WASHERS ONTO THE SHROUD ABOVE THE TAPE THEN CLOSE THE WASHERS SO THEIR SURFACES ARE SMOOTH.

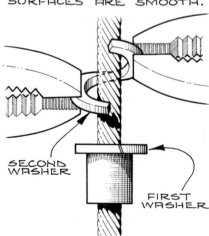

SECOND WASHER

FIRST WASHER

④

USING A GRANNY KNOT, TIE A FOURTEEN- INCH LENGTH OF WOVEN NYLON OR RAYON RIBBON TO THE UPPER WASHER.

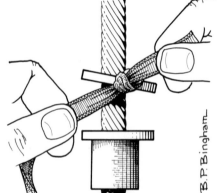

B.P.Bingham

⑤

CUT THE SHORT TAIL OF RIBBON TO WITHIN 1/4" OF THE KNOT. THEN BURN ALL OF THE RIBBON ENDS SLIGHTLY WITH A MATCH OR LIGHTER TO PREVENT UNRAVEL- ING.

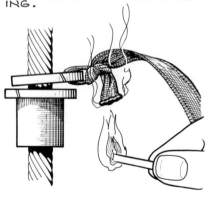

THAT'S ALL THERE IS TO IT.

The Trucker's Hitch

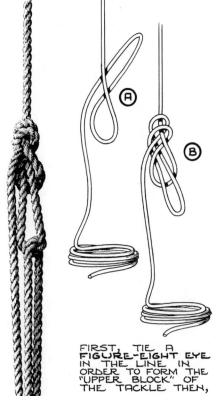

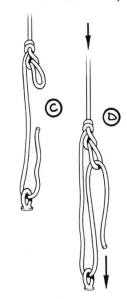

B.P. Bingham

FIRST, TIE A **FIGURE-EIGHT EYE** IN THE LINE IN ORDER TO FORM THE "UPPER BLOCK" OF THE TACKLE THEN,

PASS THE BITTER END THROUGH AN EYE, AROUND A CLEAT, THROUGH A BLOCK OR WHATEVER ELSE IS AVAILABLE TO ACT AS THE "LOWER BLOCK" OF THE TACKLE. YOU HAVE NOW INCREASED YOUR PULLING POWER BY THREE.

AT ANY MOMENT ABOARD *AT LAST,* YOU MIGHT HEAR ORDERS SUCH AS "TRUCK-UP THE FORE PEAK," OR "TRUCK THE JIB SHEET," OR "TRUCK-DOWN THE FISHERMAN TACK." BEFORE GETTING UNDERWAY, SOMEONE MAY HAVE TRUCKED-DOWN THE DINGHY OR TRUCKED-IN THE LIFELINE.

IF THESE SEEM LIKE VERY FOREIGN PHRASES, MAYBE IT'S BECAUSE THEY WERE INVENTED ON MY OWN BOAT. "TRUCKING" SIMPLY REFERS TO THE TYING OF A **TRUCKER'S HITCH** INTO A LINE TO FACILITATE ITS BEING DRAWN UP VERY TIGHTLY.

INSOMUCH AS THERE WERE NO WINCHES ABOARD MY LITTLE SCHOONER, THE TRUCKER'S HITCH WAS USED IN SHEETS AND HALYARDS TO ACHIEVE THAT "EXTRA UMPH" WHEN THE WIND WAS BRISK. THE TRUCKER'S HITCH WILL INCREASE THE ORIGINAL PULLING POWER ON A LINE BY THREE TIMES. IT IS SIMPLY A MATTER OF ADDING MECHANICAL ADVANTAGE WITHOUT THE USE OF BLOCKS.

THE UPPER "BLOCK" IS JUST A **FIGURE-EIGHT EYE** TIED INTO THE HAULING PART OF THE LINE. IT IS EASILY TIED AND EQUALLY EASY TO UNTIE, EVEN IF THE KNOT IS WET OR HAS BEEN UNDER A HEAVY STRAIN. THE REMAINDER OF THE HITCH (REAVING THE TACKLE) IS SIMPLY A MATTER OF PASSING THE BITTER END OF THE LINE THROUGH (OR AROUND) SOME TURNING POINT, THENCE THROUGH THE EYE OF THE "EIGHT".

THE BITTER END MAY BE HAULED FROM ITS ORIGINAL DIRECTION (AS SHOWN IN ⒟) OR THE HAULING DIRECTION CAN BE REVERSED BY PASSING THE BITTER END AROUND THE TURNING POINT A SECOND TIME.

THE END OF THE LINE MAY BE MADE FAST TO A CLEAT, BELAYING PIN, HANDRAIL OR UPON ITSELF THROUGH THE USE OF A STOPPER KNOT (AS I HAVE SHOWN AT THE EXTREME LEFT).

THE "EIGHT" MUST USUALLY BE UNTIED FROM HALYARDS AND SHEETS BEFORE DROPPING SAIL AS THE KNOT MAY FETCH UP AGAINST A BLOCK AS LINE IS RUN OUT.

SO, GIVE THIS ONE A LITTLE THOUGHT AND PRACTICE AS I'M SURE IT WILL FIND ITS WAY ABOARD YOUR OWN BOAT, WHETHER RACER OR CRUISER.

FOR SECURING THE DINK

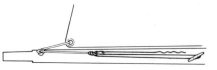

AS AN OUTHAUL

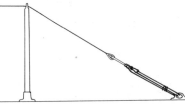

TO TIGHTEN LIFELINES, ETC.

TO TAKE UP A SHEET

AS AN EMERGENCY TURNBUCKLE

TO TIGHTEN BACKSTAYS

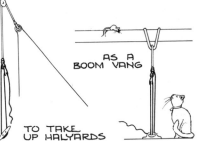

AS A BOOM VANG

TO TAKE UP HALYARDS

Single-Handed Masting

AS I APPROACHED THE ST. AUGUSTINE BRIDGE WHILE HEADING NORTH FROM MIAMI IN THE INTRACOASTAL WATERWAY, I CLEARLY SAW DOZENS OF SAILBOATS LYING AT ANCHOR ON BOTH SIDES OF THE SPAN. WITHIN SEVENTY YARDS OF THE BASCULE, I SPOTTED THE SIGN..."OUT OF ORDER". A PASSING SKIPPER THEN IN-FORMED ME THAT THE BRIDGE WOULD NOT BE OPERATING FOR FIVE DAYS. SO, I SIMPLY LOW-ERED MY MAST AND CHUGGED UNDER THE ROADWAY.

ON ANOTHER OCCA-SION, I DECIDED TO CRUISE UP THE POTOMAC RIVER INTO THE WOODED COUNTRY-SIDE JUST NORTH OF WASHINGTON, D.C. SEVERAL BRIDGES OF FOURTEEN FOOT CLEAR-ANCE STOOD IN FRONT OF MY OBJECTIVE. I JUST DROPPED *SABRINA'S* STICK AND PROCEEDED WITHOUT HINDRANCE.

THE ABILITY TO RAISE AND LOWER YOUR OWN MAST WITHOUT ON-SHORE MECHANICAL AIDS CAN OPEN MANY NEW CRUISING GROUNDS, SHORTEN DISTANCES BETWEEN PORTS AND VASTLY ENHANCE MAST AND RIGGING REPAIRS. IT MAY EVEN MAKE WEEKEND "DRY SAILING" OF YOUR TRAILERABLE BOAT A PRACTICAL ALTERNATIVE TO EX-PENSIVE DOCKAGE.

NOW, MOST YACHT MANUFACTURERS DO OFFER MAST-RAISING HARDWARE AND SYS-TEMS FOR THEIR BOATS FITTED WITH DECK-STEPPED RIGS. BUT THEIR PRICES FOR SUCH OPTIONS ARE OUTRAGEOUS. I'VE SEEN SUCH SYSTEMS RANGING FROM $150 TO $600! WELL, I'LL TELL YOU, IT JUST DOESN'T REQUIRE THAT KIND OF MONEY TO SET UP YOUR OWN SYSTEM BY YOURSELF. IN FACT, IF YOUR BOAT IS ALREADY EQUIPPED WITH A TABERNACLE MAST STEP, YOU CAN RAISE AND LOWER YOUR MAST WITH A TEN-DOLLAR INVESTMENT! BOATS WITHOUT A TABER-NACLE WILL COST SOMEWHAT MORE.

THE SYSTEMS, SHOWN HERE, ARE INTEND-ED FOR LIGHT DIS-PLACEMENT BOATS TO 34' AND HEAVY DISPLACEMENT BOATS TO 28'. IT IS AS-SUMED THAT YOUR MAST ISN'T OVERWEIGHT.

THE TABERNACLE MAST STEP

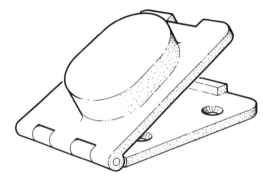
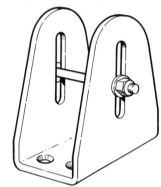

THE TABERNACLE-TYPE MAST STEPS, SHOWN HERE, ARE THE ONLY ONES I CAN RECOMMEND FOR MAST RAISING AND LOWERING OPERATIONS WITHOUT THE NEED FOR OUTSIDE EQUIP-MENT OR MANPOWER. THESE STEPS PROVIDE TOTAL CONTROL OF THE MAST FOOT AT ALL TIMES, THUS PREVENTING IT FROM TWISTING OR BECOM-ING DISLODGED.

IF YOUR MAST STEP IS NOT OF THESE TYPES, YOUR BOAT OR MAST BUILDER CAN PROVIDE YOU WITH ONE. IF NOT, YOU CAN HAVE ONE FABRICATED FROM PLANS DRAWN BY A REPUTABLE DESIGNER.

THE PIVOT-BRIDLE ATTACHMENTS

THE KEY TO RAISING OR LOWERING YOUR MAST IS PARTLY THAT OF MAINTAIN-ING SOME TENSION ON THE UPPER SHROUDS TO PREVENT THE MAST FROM SWAYING SIDE TO SIDE DURING THE OPERATIONS. THE SHROUDS DON'T HAVE TO BE DRUM TIGHT.

THE SHROUD TENSION IS MAINTAINED BY USING PIVOT BRIDLES. BEFORE PROCEEDING WITH THE BRIDLES, HOWEVER, YOU MUST PROVIDE MEANS OF ATTACHMENT TO THE SHROUDS. STAINLESS RINGS AND SHACKLES ARE USED FOR THIS PURPOSE AS SHOWN BELOW.

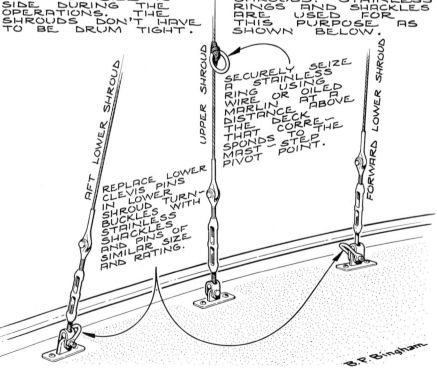

SECURELY SEIZE A STAINLESS RING USING OILED WIRE OR MARLIN AT A DISTANCE ABOVE THE DECK THAT CORRE-SPONDS TO THE MAST-STEP PIVOT POINT.

REPLACE LOWER CLEVIS PINS IN LOWER SHROUD TURN-BUCKLES WITH STAINLESS SHACKLES AND PINS OF SIMILAR SIZE AND RATING.

AFT LOWER SHROUD

UPPER SHROUD

FORWARD LOWER SHROUD

B.P. Bingham

THE SHROUD PIVOT BRIDLES

A PAIR OF SHROUD PIVOT BRIDLES MUST NOW BE MADE. THEY MAY BE FANCY WIRE AFFAIRS WITH NICO-PRESSED EYES BUT THEY CAN JUST AS WELL BE MADE OF ANY 3/8" FIBER LINE. THE SNAP HOOKS MAY BE OF BRONZE, STAINLESS OR GAL-VANIZED. THERE IS LITTLE NEED FOR THESE BRIDLES TO BE TERRIBLY STRONG BUT THEIR LENGTHS MUST BE CAREFULLY ADJUSTED SO THEY WILL JUST ALLOW THEIR SNAPPING ONTO THE LOWER-SHROUD TURNBUCKLE SHACKLES AND THE UPPER-SHROUD PIVOT RINGS.

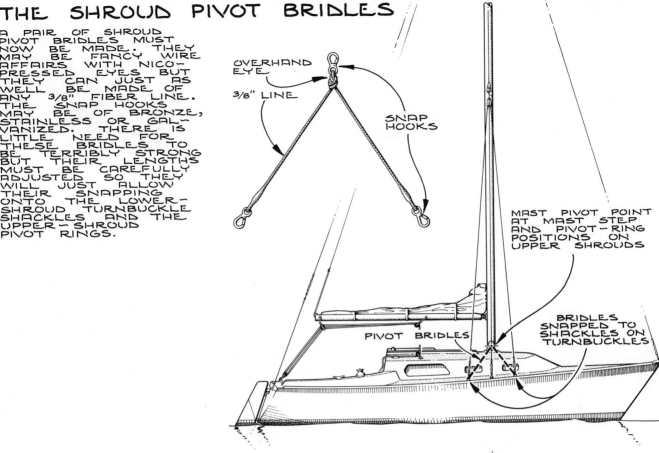

THE BOOM GUYS

THE BOOM IS USED AS A STRUT DURING MAST RAIS-ING AND LOWERING OPERATIONS. IN ORDER TO BE EFFECTIVE, HOWEVER, THE BOOM MUST NOT BE ALLOWED TO WOBBLE FROM SIDE TO SIDE. THIS IS THE FUNCTION OF THE BOOM GUYS.

THE BOOM GUYS ARE MADE UP AS A TWO-LEGGED BRIDLE, MUCH IN THE SAME MANNER AS THE PIVOT BRIDLES. USE 3/8" LINE AND SNAP HOOKS. THE LENGTH OF THE GUYS MUST BE SUCH THAT THE CENTER SNAP HOOK WILL FIT ONTO THE AFTERMOST SHEET BOOM BALE (OR THE SHEET-BLOCK SHACKLE), WHILE THE FORWARD SNAP HOOKS ATTACH TO THE SHROUD-PIVOT RINGS. THE GUYS SHOULD BE AS TIGHT AS POSSIBLE WHILE STILL ALLOW-ING ATTACHMENT.

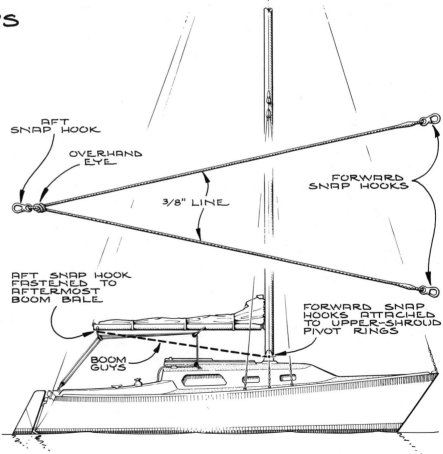

ONCE YOU'VE MADE UP THE SHROUD-PIVOT BRIDLE AND THE BOOM GUYS, YOU'VE COMPLETED THE INVENTORY OF MAST-RAISING/LOWERING GEAR. STORE THEM IN A SMALL CANVAS BAG WHEN NOT IN USE.

MAST LOWERING PROCEDURE

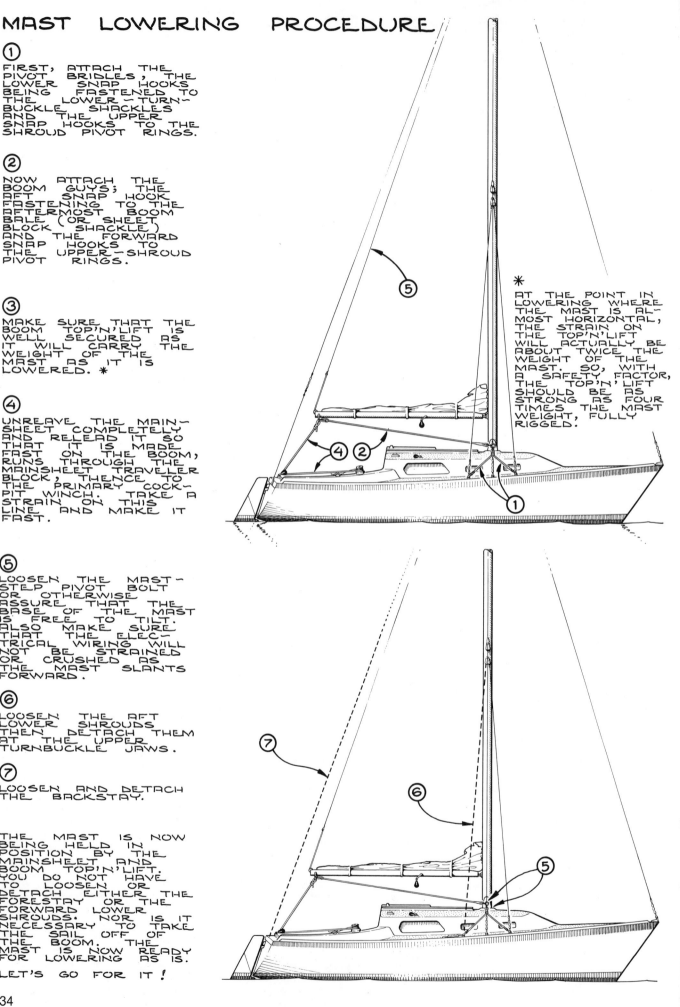

① FIRST, ATTACH THE PIVOT BRIDLES, THE LOWER SNAP HOOKS BEING FASTENED TO THE LOWER-TURN-BUCKLE SHACKLES AND THE UPPER SNAP HOOKS TO THE SHROUD PIVOT RINGS.

② NOW ATTACH THE BOOM GUYS; THE AFT SNAP HOOK FASTENING TO THE AFTERMOST BOOM BALE (OR SHEET BLOCK SHACKLE) AND THE FORWARD SNAP HOOKS TO THE UPPER-SHROUD PIVOT RINGS.

③ MAKE SURE THAT THE BOOM TOP'N'LIFT IS WELL SECURED AS IT WILL CARRY THE WEIGHT OF THE MAST AS IT IS LOWERED. ✱

④ UNREAVE THE MAINSHEET COMPLETELY AND RELEAD IT SO THAT IT IS MADE FAST ON THE BOOM, RUNS THROUGH THE MAINSHEET TRAVELER BLOCK, THENCE TO THE PRIMARY COCKPIT WINCH. TAKE A STRAIN ON THIS LINE AND MAKE IT FAST.

⑤ LOOSEN THE MAST-STEP PIVOT BOLT OR OTHERWISE ASSURE THAT THE BASE OF THE MAST IS FREE TO TILT. ALSO MAKE SURE THAT THE ELECTRICAL WIRING WILL NOT BE STRAINED OR CRUSHED AS THE MAST SLANTS FORWARD.

⑥ LOOSEN THE AFT LOWER SHROUDS THEN DETACH THEM AT THE UPPER TURNBUCKLE JAWS.

⑦ LOOSEN AND DETACH THE BACKSTAY.

THE MAST IS NOW BEING HELD IN POSITION BY THE MAINSHEET AND BOOM TOP'N'LIFT. YOU DO NOT HAVE TO LOOSEN OR DETACH EITHER THE FORESTAY OR THE FORWARD LOWER SHROUDS. NOR IS IT NECESSARY TO TAKE THE SAIL OFF OF THE BOOM. THE MAST IS NOW READY FOR LOWERING AS IS.

LET'S GO FOR IT!

✱ AT THE POINT IN LOWERING WHERE THE MAST IS ALMOST HORIZONTAL, THE STRAIN ON THE TOP'N'LIFT WILL ACTUALLY BE ABOUT TWICE THE WEIGHT OF THE MAST. SO, WITH A SAFETY FACTOR, THE TOP'N'LIFT SHOULD BE AS STRONG AS FOUR TIMES THE MAST WEIGHT, FULLY RIGGED.

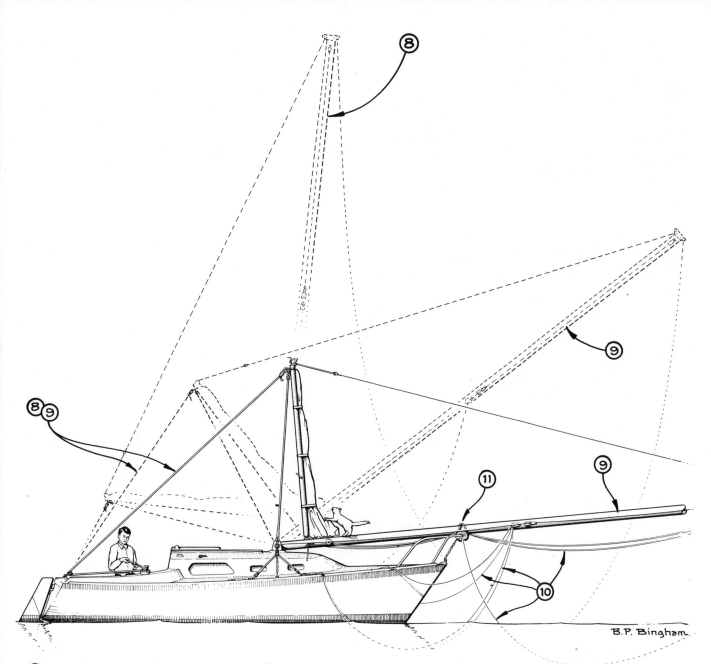

B.P. Bingham

8 VERY CAREFULLY EASE OFF ABOUT TWO FEET OF MAIN-SHEET. THERE'S A GOOD CHANCE THAT THE MAST WILL SEEM STUCK IN THE VERTICAL POSI-TION. IF THIS HAPPENS, SECURE THE MAINSHEET, WALK FORWARD AND GIVE THE FORESTAY A HEFTY PERPEN-DICULAR TUG. THE MAST WILL THEN ROCK FORWARD ABOUT FIVE DEGREES. YOU NEED NOT WORRY ABOUT IT CRASHING DOWN ONTO YOU AS THERE IS VERY LITTLE STRAIN ON ANYTHING AT THIS POINT.

9 NOW, CONTINUE EAS-ING THE MAINSHEET UNTIL THE MAST IS JUST TOUCHING THE BOW PULPIT (OR IN A POSITION THAT WILL PROVIDE SOME OTHER METHOD OF SUPPORT).

10 BUNDLE UP ALL LOOSE HALYARDS AND SHROUDS, TYING THEM TO THE MAST TO PREVENT THEIR THRASHING ABOUT.

11 THE FORWARD MAST SUPPORT MUST NOW BE PADDED AND THE MAST SECURED TO PREVENT MOVE-MENT ONCE UNDER-WAY...

OR

THE MAST MAY NOW BE COMPLETELY RE-MOVED FROM THE BOAT IN THE NOR-MAL MANNER.

IT IS USUALLY FEA-SIBLE TO OPERATE YOUR BOAT WITH THE MAST EXTEND-ING FORWARD OF THE BOW FOR SHORT PERIODS OF TIME OR WHEN ONLY

GENTLE WINDS AND WAVES ARE ANTICI-PATED SUCH AS IN PROTECTED CANALS. IF SUCH CONDITIONS ARE NOT IN THE OFFING, IT IS BEST TO LIFT THE MAST OUT OF ITS STEP, MOVE IT AFT AND SECURE IT FOR THE BUMPY RIDE.

MAST RAISING

YOU GUESSED IT: MAST RAISING IS BASICALLY THE RE-VERSE OF THE LOWERING PROCE-DURE. BECAUSE THE GREATEST STRAINS OCCUR WHEN THE MAST IS MOST NEAR-LY HORIZONTAL, YOU'LL FIND IT EASIER IF A SEC-OND PERSON HELPS LIFT THE MAST FOR THE FIRST FEW FEET. THAT'S ALL THERE IS TO IT.

VARIATIONS

THE EQUIPMENT I'VE DESCRIBED FOR MAST RAISING AND LOWERING CAN HAVE AS MANY VARIATIONS AS THERE ARE TYPES AND SIZES OF BOATS. SO FAR, I HAVE ONLY TOUCHED UPON THE BASICS.

IF YOU INTEND TO RAISE OR LOWER YOUR MAST FREQUENTLY AND/OR IN CHOPPY CONDITIONS, YOU MIGHT CONSIDER THE MORE ELABORATE GEAR AND ARRANGEMENTS SHOWN HERE. THE ADDITIONAL MONEY SPENT FOR THESE ARRANGEMENTS WILL BE ESPECIALLY WORTH IT IF YOUR MAST IS EXCEPTIONALLY HEAVY.

THE SIMPLEST AND MOST OBVIOUS VARIATION IS TO REREAVE YOUR MAINSHEET SO AS TO PROVIDE A 2:1 OR A 3:1 PURCHASE. THIS MAY REQUIRE THE INSTALLATION OF A LONGER MAINSHEET THAN YOU PRESENTLY HAVE.

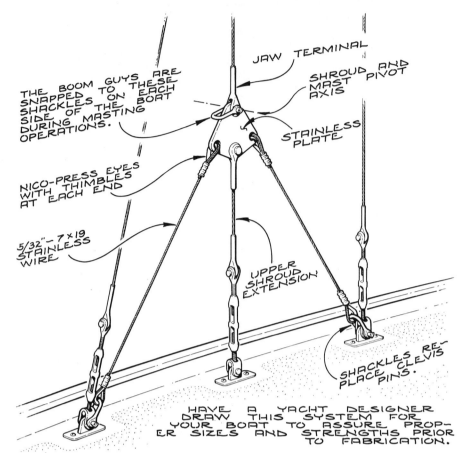

A PERMANENT UPPER-SHROUD PIVOT

HAVE A YACHT DESIGNER DRAW THIS SYSTEM FOR YOUR BOAT TO ASSURE PROPER SIZES AND STRENGTHS PRIOR TO FABRICATION.

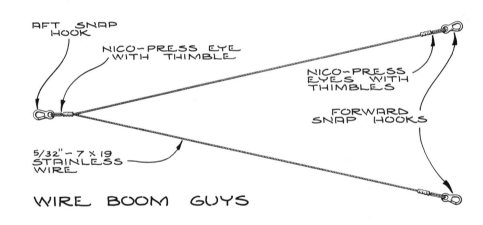

WIRE BOOM GUYS

EVEN WHILE COMPILING THIS SKETCHBOOK, I WAS FACED BY A DECOMMISSIONED BRIDGE ON THE JERSEY WATERWAY. THE COAST GUARD ADVISED ME NOT TO PROCEED NORTH, ASSURING ME THAT IT WOULD BE IMPOSSIBLE TO SLIP UNDER THE FIXED SEVEN-FOOT OBSTACLE. HOWEVER, I WAS DETERMINED NOT TO LOSE THE SEVEN-MILE INVESTMENT ALREADY ACHIEVED. SO, I SIMPLY DISCONNECTED THE BOOM GUYS, LOWERED THE BOOM AND ALLOWED IT TO REST UPON THE LIFELINE. NO SWEAT AT ALL!

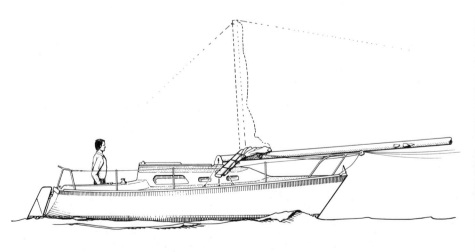

LOWERING THE BOOM

CHAPTER  **Cabin Comforts**

B. P. Bingham

A Seagoing Galley

HOW MANY FEATURES CAN YOU INCORPORATE INTO YOUR OWN BOAT?

GALLEY IS OUT OF THE CREW'S TRAFFIC PATTERN. EVERYTHING IS WITHIN ARM'S REACH. COOK MAY LEAN AGAINST SOMETHING WHILE FACING IN ANY DIRECTION. HATCH VENTILATION IS CLOSE BY. SECTIONAL ICE BOX PRESERVES THE COLD WHILE A DOUBLE SINK CAN HELP SAVE WATER. THE RANGE IS GIMBALED, FIDDLED, FITTED WITH A SWING LOCK AND A FUEL SHUT-OFF SOLENOID SWITCH WITH A "FUEL ON" WARNING LIGHT. REMOVABLE PIPE PREVENTS COOK FROM LEANING UPON OR GRABBING RANGE IF HE LOSES HIS BALANCE. RANGE OPERATING INSTRUCTIONS ARE PROMINENTLY PLACED. DRY CHEMICAL FIRE EXTINGUISHER IS READILY ACCESSIBLE. THE COUNTER TOP IS WELL FIDDLED WITH OPEN

CORNERS FOR EASY CLEANING AND COVERED WITH A STOCK NON-SKID MATTING DURING HEAVY WEATHER. ALL COUNTER CORNERS ARE WELL ROUNDED FOR SAFETY AND GALLEY IS FITTED WITH PERSONAL RETAINING BELT (WITH SNAP HOOKS AND EYES) OR RETAINING RAIL. NON-SKID STRIPS ARE PLACED ON SOLE AND CABIN CARLIN IS FITTED WITH HAND GRIP.

COUNTER HAS BEEN BUILT WITH A CORNER "DEEP BIN" TO USE OTHERWISE INCONVENIENT STORAGE SPACE. IT ALSO HAS A HINGED COUNTER EXTENSION/CUTTING BOARD. CABINET SHELVING IS WELL DIVIDED AND FIDDLED, ALSO COVERED WITH NON-SKID MATTING. BUILT-IN TRASH BIN IS REMOVABLE. GALLEY SINK AND RANGE TOP COVERS INCREASE FLAT WORKING SPACE WHEN NEEDED.

CLEANING-GEAR FIDDLES HAVE BEEN DRILLED FOR DRAINAGE. THERE ARE LARGE BINS JUST FOR POTS 'N' PANS WHILE CANNED STAPLES ARE KEPT IN DRY BILGE BINS UNDER THE SOLE.

ALSO NOTE: WELL SECTIONED DISH RACKS • CUP HANGERS • OPEN FIDDLE BIN FOR FREQUENTLY USED FOODS • A.C. ELECTRICAL OUTLET • TOWEL RACK • PAPER TOWEL HOLDER • MOUNTED BOTTLE OPENER AND CAP CATCHER • ICE PICK HOLDER • HOT PADS • SEA WATER HAND PUMP AT SINK • SEA WATER SPIGOT TAPPED FROM ANY CLEAN SEA WATER LINE • ALL DRY FOOD IS STORED IN PLASTIC CONTAINERS OR SEALED IN PLASTIC WRAP.

AND... THERE'S A BULKHEAD-MOUNTED THERMAL JUG WITH SPIGOT TO HOLD A SUPPLY OF HOT GROG FOR THE WATCH.

Quarter Berth Galley Extension

LIKE MANY OTHER BOATS, *SABRINA* HAS A QUARTER BERTH THAT SHARES A BULKHEAD AT THE AFT END OF THE GALLEY. AND, LIKE MOST OTHER BOATS, THE QUARTER BERTH IS RARELY EVER SLEPT IN. RATHER, IT MORE OFTEN SERVES AS A STORAGE SPACE FOR LIGHT SAILS, THE COCKPIT AWNING AND SACKS OF DOG FOOD. IF IT WERE NOT FOR THE QUARTER BERTH, HER 4'6" GALLEY WOULD BE OVER SIX FEET LONG WITH MORE THAN TWO ADDITIONAL FEET OF UNOBSTRUCTED COUNTER SPACE.

SO, I BUILT THIS TRIPLE-JOINTED, ACCORDION-FOLDING GALLEY EXTENSION, GIVING ME A VERY LONG COUNTER TOP OR QUARTER BERTH AT THE WILL OF MY WHIM. STOWING OR OPENING THIS HANDY COUNTER EXTENSION TAKES ONLY SECONDS AND ITS ADVANTAGES ARE IMMEASURABLE.

WITH SOME CAREFUL PLANNING, YOU MIGHT INCORPORATE THIS FEATURE INTO YOUR OWN BOAT.

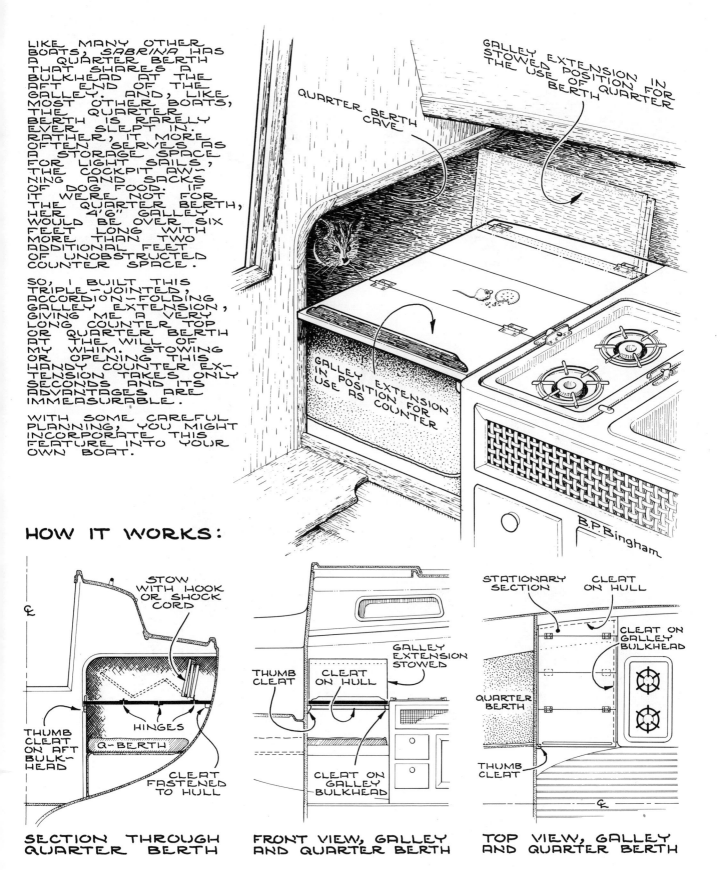

QUARTER BERTH CAVE

GALLEY EXTENSION IN STOWED POSITION FOR THE USE OF QUARTER BERTH

GALLEY EXTENSION IN POSITION FOR USE AS COUNTER

B.P.Bingham

HOW IT WORKS:

STOW WITH HOOK OR SHOCK CORD

HINGES

THUMB CLEAT ON AFT BULKHEAD

Q-BERTH

CLEAT FASTENED TO HULL

SECTION THROUGH QUARTER BERTH

THUMB CLEAT

CLEAT ON HULL

GALLEY EXTENSION STOWED

CLEAT ON GALLEY BULKHEAD

FRONT VIEW, GALLEY AND QUARTER BERTH

STATIONARY SECTION

CLEAT ON HULL

CLEAT ON GALLEY BULKHEAD

QUARTER BERTH

THUMB CLEAT

TOP VIEW, GALLEY AND QUARTER BERTH

Sabrina's Hot Water System

MAYBE "HOT WATER SYSTEM" IS A SLIGHT OVERSTATEMENT. ACTUALLY, IT'S A *THERMOS*, ALL STAINLESS STEEL, TWO-QUART VACUUM BOTTLE.

I MADE A VERY CONVENIENT STORAGE SPACE FOR IT BY VERY CAREFULLY CUTTING A PERFECTLY ROUND HOLE THROUGH THE COUNTER TOP USING A SABRE SAW WITH A NO. 24 METAL CUTTING BLADE. THE DIAMETER OF THE HOLE IS ONLY 1/32" GREATER THAN THE BODY OF THE BOTTLE, SO THE FINAL SHAPING OF THE HOLE WAS DONE WITH A RAT-TAIL FILE. A RIDGE AT THE TOP OF THE BOTTLE PREVENTS IT FROM FALLING COMPLETELY THROUGH THE HOLE.

NOW, I ONLY HAVE TO HEAT WATER ONCE A DAY TO PROVIDE FOR ENOUGH COFFEE FOR TWO PEOPLE. THE TWO QUARTS ALWAYS GETS US THROUGH TWENTY-FOUR HOURS OF SAILING. I MUST ADMIT, HOWEVER, THAT OCCASIONALLY I CUT THE HOT WATER A LITTLE WITH COLD. BUT THE POINT IS THAT I ONLY HAVE TO FIRE UP THE STOVE ONE TIME INSTEAD OF TEN. THAT'S QUITE A SAVING OF FUEL AND HASSLE.

THE KEY TO THE SYSTEM'S CONVENIENCE IS THAT THE BOTTLE IS ALWAYS AT YOUR FINGERTIPS, BUT NOT SLAMMING AROUND INSIDE THE SINK. I NEVER HAVE TO STOW THE BOTTLE OTHER THAN PLACING IT BACK INTO ITS HOLE. THE BODY OF THE BOTTLE OCCUPIES SPACE BEHIND THE SINK THAT WOULD BE UNUSED OTHERWISE.

NOW, I CAN HAVE MY COFFEE ON THE SPUR OF THE MOMENT. I DON'T HAVE TO BOIL WATER FOR A DROWSY, ONCOMING WATCH EITHER. THE WATER IS ALWAYS READY FOR THE UNEXPECTED ARRIVAL OF GUESTS.

WELL, IT'S SO SIMPLE IT VERGE'S ON THE RIDICULOUS. I THINK EVERY BOAT SHOULD HAVE AT LEAST ONE OF THESE INSTALLATIONS.

B.P. Bingham

Port-O-Showers For MiniCruisers

AH, THE GOOD OLE DAYS! REMEMBER WHEN YOU SAILED OUT TO THE ISLAND FOR A WEEKEND IN YOUR LITTLE MINI-CRUISER... AND THE TIME YOU DECIDED TO TAKE A JAUNT UP THE COAST? IT WAS TO WINDWARD ALL THE WAY AND NOT QUITE AS DRY AS YOU THOUGHT IT WOULD BE. YOUR HAIR KNOTTED UP LIKE A SIX-STRAND TURK'S HEAD, AND YOU FELT LIKE A PIECE OF WASHED-UP SEAWEED FOR THE NEXT TWO DAYS. YOUR EYES FELT LIKE PEELED GRAPES, AND YOUR PANTS STUCK TO YOU LIKE FLYPAPER.

IT DOESN'T HAVE TO BE THAT WAY. THERE'S NO REASON TO REMAIN TACKY AFTER A LONG DAY'S SAIL. WHY NOT TAKE ALONG A "PORT-O-SHOWER?"

THE DO-IT-YOURSELF UNITS SHOWN HERE ARE INEXPENSIVE, QUICKLY MADE AND CAN DOUBLE AS CAMPING GEAR. THEY REQUIRE VERY LITTLE WATER. THEY SURE BEAT THE LAST-RESORT SPONGE BATH.

DISH-SPRAYER SHOWER

THESE DISH SPRAYERS WITH TURN-OFF BUTTONS ARE AVAILABLE AT ANY HARDWARE STORE. THE HOSES ARE FITTED WITH RUBBER FAUCET CONNECTORS THAT WILL SLIP ONTO YOUR GALLEY SPIGOT. YOU'LL NEED A PRESSURE WATER SYSTEM, BUT THIS CAN BE A GRAVITY SYSTEM SUCH AS A HOISTED JERRY CAN FULL OF HOT WATER.

OF COURSE, THE DISH SPRAYER ALSO MAKES A HANDY GALLEY TOOL.

JERRY-CAN SHOWER

THIS IS NOTHING MORE THAN A RIGID OR COLLAPSIBLE POLYETHYLENE FIVE-GALLON JUG WITH A DISH SPRAYER ATTACHED TO THE OUTLET SPIGOT.

ONCE FILLED WITH HOT WATER, THE JUG IS SUSPENDED FROM THE BOOM OR A HALYARD IN THE INVERTED POSITION. A 1/4-INCH LINE SLING MUST BE MADE UP FOR THIS PURPOSE.

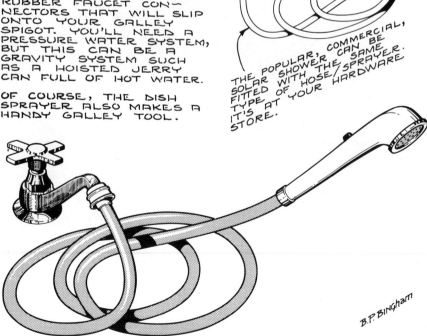

CORKED VENT. OPEN WHEN SHOWERING

THE POPULAR, COMMERCIAL, SOLAR SHOWER CAN BE FITTED WITH THE SAME TYPE OF HOSE/SPRAYER. IT'S AT YOUR HARDWARE STORE.

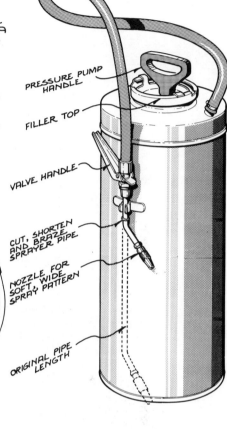

PRESSURE PUMP HANDLE

FILLER TOP

VALVE HANDLE

CUT, SHORTEN AND BRAZE SPRAYER PIPE

NOZZLE FOR SOFT, WIDE SPRAY PATTERN

ORIGINAL PIPE LENGTH

WEED-SPRAYER SHOWER

THE MOST INGENIOUS PORT-O-SHOWER I'VE USED WAS SIMPLY A PUMP-PRESSURIZED GARDEN WEED SPRAYER. IT WAS A THREE-GALLON MODEL WITH A 15-STROKE PUMP HANDLE. IT MEASURED ONLY 7" X 21".

THESE SPRAYERS ARE AVAILABLE IN MOST GARDEN-SUPPLY STORES. THE SPRAY PIPE MAY BE SHORTENED TO A CONVENIENT LENGTH BY ANY METALSMITH. I'VE SEEN THESE UNITS IN BOTH METAL AND HEAVY-DUTY PLASTIC.

EITHER TYPE CAN BE FILLED WITH HOT WATER. OR THEY CAN BE FILLED WITH COLD WATER AND LEFT IN THE SUN TO SOLAR HEAT. THIS CAN ALSO BE DONE WITH THE JERRY-CAN SHOWER. BUT FOR THE BEST SOLAR HEATING, THE CAN OR TANK SHOULD BE PAINTED BLACK. FOR PLASTICS, A VINYL OR PLASTIC PAINT IS BEST.

B.P. Bingham

Towel Tricks

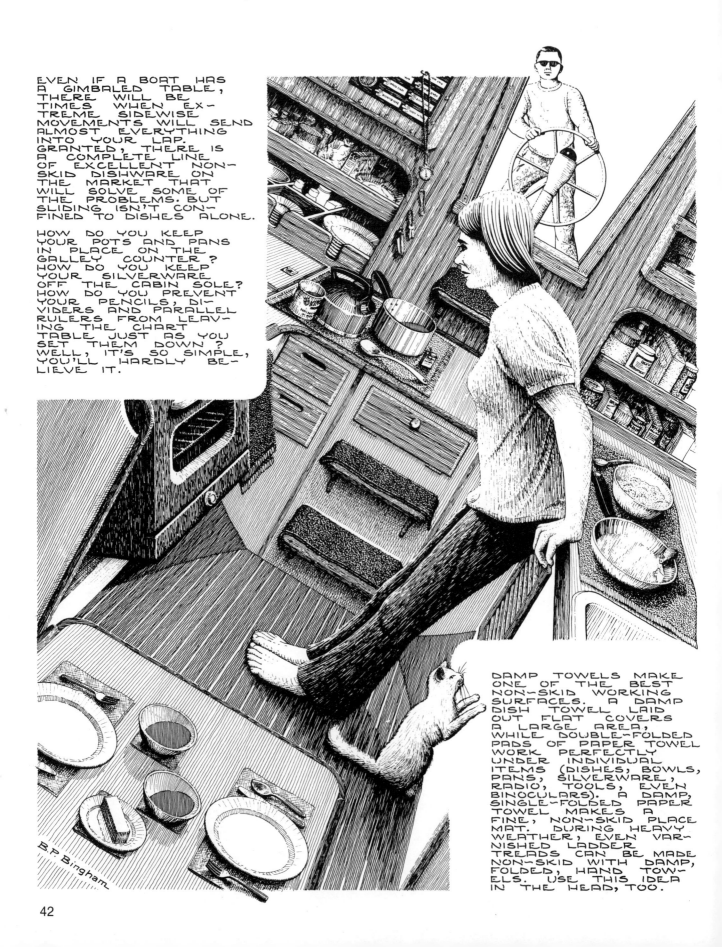

EVEN IF A BOAT HAS A GIMBALED TABLE, THERE WILL BE TIMES WHEN EXTREME SIDEWISE MOVEMENTS WILL SEND ALMOST EVERYTHING INTO YOUR LAP. GRANTED, THERE IS A COMPLETE LINE OF EXCELLENT NON-SKID DISHWARE ON THE MARKET THAT WILL SOLVE SOME OF THE PROBLEMS. BUT SLIDING ISN'T CONFINED TO DISHES ALONE.

HOW DO YOU KEEP YOUR POTS AND PANS IN PLACE ON THE GALLEY COUNTER? HOW DO YOU KEEP YOUR SILVERWARE OFF THE CABIN SOLE? HOW DO YOU PREVENT YOUR PENCILS, DIVIDERS AND PARALLEL RULERS FROM LEAVING THE CHART TABLE JUST AS YOU SET THEM DOWN? WELL, IT'S SO SIMPLE, YOU'LL HARDLY BELIEVE IT.

B.P. Bingham

DAMP TOWELS MAKE ONE OF THE BEST NON-SKID WORKING SURFACES. A DAMP DISH TOWEL LAID OUT FLAT COVERS A LARGE AREA, WHILE DOUBLE-FOLDED PADS OF PAPER TOWEL WORK PERFECTLY UNDER INDIVIDUAL ITEMS (DISHES, BOWLS, PANS, SILVERWARE, RADIO, TOOLS, EVEN BINOCULARS). A DAMP, SINGLE-FOLDED PAPER TOWEL MAKES A FINE, NON-SKID PLACE MAT. DURING HEAVY WEATHER, EVEN VARNISHED LADDER TREADS CAN BE MADE NON-SKID WITH DAMP, FOLDED, HAND TOWELS. USE THIS IDEA IN THE HEAD, TOO.

Shedding Light On A Dark Subject

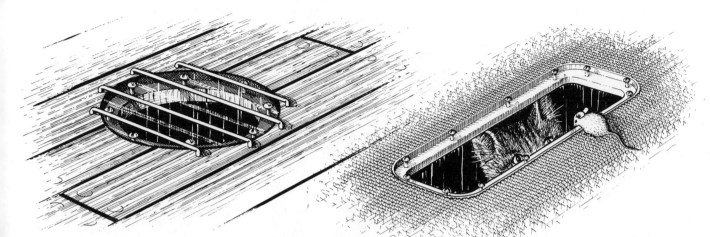

ON MY LITTLE SCHOON-ER, *AT LAST*, MY DRAWING BOARD WAS SET UP IN THE DARK AFT CABIN. I COULD BARELY SUMMON ENOUGH LIGHT BELOW TO FIND MY SOCKS IN THE MORNING, LET ALONE WORK ON MY SKETCHES.

EVEN READING DURING THE DAY BECAME AN EXPENSIVE PROSPECT, WHAT WITH THE BAT-TERY DRAIN CAUSED BY THE BUNK LIGHTS.

SO I BRIGHTENED THINGS UP BY INSTALLING

DECK LIGHTS. I LOCAT-ED THEM OVER THE BERTHS, OVER THE CHART TABLE, THE HEAD, THE SAIL LOCKER AND THE GALLEY. THE IDEA WORKED SO WELL THAT I'VE PUT THEM ON ALL MY BOATS. I'VE EVEN CONSIDERED PLACING SMALL ONES IN THE HULL TO SHED SOME LIGHT IN DARK LOCKERS, STORAGE BINS AND CUP-BOARDS.

THEIR SIZE DEPENDS ON THEIR PURPOSE AND THE AVAILABILITY OF SPACE. THEIR SHAPE IS A MATTER OF TASTE. YOU

CAN USE CLEAR OR FROSTED OR TINTED ACRYLIC RANGING FROM 5/16" (FOR SMALL LIGHTS) TO ½" (FOR LARGE LIGHTS).

DECK LIGHTS CAN ALSO BE INSTALLED IN HATCH-ES. FOR THIN FIBER-GLASS HATCHES OR DECKS, THE RABBET MAY BE ELIMINATED.

TO PREVENT SCUFFING OR POSSIBLE BREAKING FROM IMPACT OF DECK GEAR, YOU CAN INSTALL PRO-TECTIVE RODS OVER THE LIGHTS.

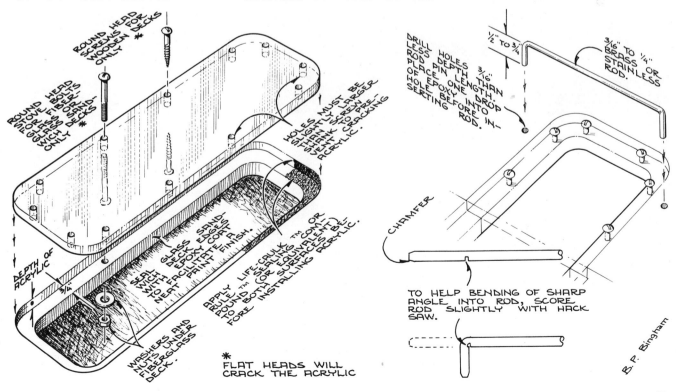

ROUND HEAD SCREWS FOR WOODEN DECKS ONLY

ROUND HEAD STOVE BOLTS FOR FIBER-GLASS OR SAND-WICH DECKS ONLY

HOLES MUST BE SLIGHTLY LARGER THAN SCREW SHANK TO PRE-VENT CRACKING ACRYLIC.

DEPTH OF ACRYLIC

GLASS SAND-ED, DECK EDGES EPOXY COAT TO FACILITATE NEAT PAINT FINISH.

SEAL WITH

APPLY LIFE-CAULK ™ OR RULE ™ SEALING COMP-ROUND ™ (OR EQUIVALENT) TO BOTH SURFACES BE-FORE INSTALLING ACRYLIC.

WASHERS AND NUTS UNDER FIBERGLASS DECK.

* FLAT HEADS WILL CRACK THE ACRYLIC

DRILL HOLES 3/16" LESS DEPTH THAN ROD PIN LENGTH. PLACE ONE DROP OF EPOXY INTO HOLE BEFORE IN-SERTING ROD.

½" TO ¾"

3/16" TO ¼" BRASS OR STAINLESS ROD.

CHAMFER

TO HELP BENDING OF SHARP ANGLE INTO ROD, SCORE ROD SLIGHTLY WITH HACK SAW.

B.P. Bingham

Fancy Lamps

B.P.Bingham

WERE VERY HOMELY, OF LOW-QUALITY MATERIAL AND HARDLY ITEMS BEFITTING A PROPER YACHT.

I RESOLVED TO GIVE THEM TO "DAVEY JONES" AT THE FIRST OPPORTUNITY. BUT MY CREW OBJECTED, CLAIMING THAT WE MIGHT NEED THEM SOMEDAY. SURE ENOUGH, SHE WAS RIGHT AGAIN.

INSOMUCH AS MY LITTLE SCHOONER HAD NOT BEEN ENDOWED WITH THE CONVENIENCE OF ELECTRICITY, I HAD TO RELY ON KEROSENE LAMPS ALONE WHILE SKETCHING INTO THE EVENING'S DARKNESS. WE ALSO USED THEM TO READ BY. BUT THE NIFTY LITTLE BRASS LAMPS DIDN'T SHED MUCH LIGHT AND, ONCE LIT, THEIR AWFUL FUMES BURNED OUR EYES AND THE ATMOSPHERE BECAME STUFFY AND UNPLEASANT.

SO... ONE NIGHT, MY CREW HAULED THE OLD, UGLY LAMPS OUT OF STORAGE, CLEANED THEIR WICKS AND LIT THEM, SETTING ONE NEXT TO MY DRAWING BOARD AND THE OTHER UPON THE GALLEY COUNTER.

MUCH TO OUR AMAZEMENT AND DELIGHT, THE LIGHT POURED FORTH, WHITE, CLEAN AND STEADY. THEIR FLAMES WERE ABSOLUTELY ODORLESS WHILE THEIR BRILLIANCE FAR EXCEEDED THEIR FANCY BRASS COUSINS. TRUE, THEY WERE SILLY-LOOKING BUT MUCH MORE EFFICIENT THAN ANY LAMPS WE HAD PREVIOUSLY USED. THEY WERE SO GOOD, IN FACT, I BOUGHT SEVERAL MORE AT A LOCAL GENERAL STORE FOR $6.00 AS WELL AS REPLACEMENT GLASS CHIMNEYS FOR $1.50 EACH. I HAVE SINCE DISCOVERED THAT NEW WICKS ARE READILY AVAILABLE AT ANY HARDWARE OR DIME STORE AS WELL AS AN ATTRACTIVE VARIETY OF LOVELY STACKS. EVEN EXTRA BURNERS ARE ONLY ABOUT $2.00.

WE HAVEN'T USED THE BRASS LAMPS SINCE!

BESIDES THE EFFICIENCY OF FUEL CARBURETION IN THESE FUNKY LAMPS, THE EXTRAORDINARY AMOUNT OF LIGHT PRODUCED CAN BE DIRECTLY ATTRIBUTED TO THE WIDTH OF THE 1" WICK (MOST NAUTICAL LAMPS USE ½" OR ¾" WICKS).

THEN... ONE RAINY EVENING, MY CREW PULLED A BALL OF WHITE COD LINE FROM HER DITTY BAG, DETERMINED TO ADD A LITTLE PERSONALITY TO THE OLD LAMPS; MAYBE A TURK'S HEAD WOULD HELP A BIT. WELL... SHE WAS STILL EXPERIMENTING WHEN I CRAWLED INTO THE BUNK.

THERE WAS A TIME WHEN I WOULD NOT HAVE ACCEPTED ANYTHING BUT THE VERY BEST BRASS, GIMBALED MARINE KEROSENE LAMPS ABOARD MY BOAT. THEIR ELEGANCE SYMBOLIZED NAUTICAL TRADITION.

OH, THEY WERE EXPENSIVE, THEY WERE DIFFICULT TO POLISH AND, ONCE BROKEN, REPLACEMENT CHIMNEYS COST MORE THAN I THOUGHT THEY SHOULD. BUT THE DRAWBACKS FADED WHENEVER THEIR WELCOME GLOW AND ENCHANTING PROFILES WARMED MY COZY LITTLE CABIN.

THEN I MOVED ABOARD *AT LAST.* THE PREVIOUS OWNER HAD ALSO FAVORED KEROSENE FOR LIGHTING AND THERE WERE, INDEED, SEVERAL LAMPS WHEN I ARRIVED TO TAKE UP QUARTERS AT HER MOORING. BUT THEY WERE NEITHER BRASS, GIMBALED NOR NAUTICAL. THEY STOOD A FULL 12" HIGH (TWICE THE SIZE OF THE PRETTY ONES I HAD PURCHASED AT "DIRTY DAN'S MARINE"). THEIR BURNERS WERE ONLY OF PLATED STEEL AND SPOTTED WITH RUST. THE FUEL RESERVOIRS CONSISTED OF CHUBBY GLASS JUGS. ALL IN ALL, THEY

WHEN I AROSE AT DAWN AND TRUDGED INTO THE GALLEY FOR MY MORNING COFFEE, THERE STOOD ONE OF THE ONCE-UGLY OLD LAMPS. IT HAD BEEN TRANSFORMED INTO A GRACEFUL WORK OF ART, IMBUED WITH ALL THE FLAVOR OF THE DEEPEST SEAGOING TRADITION. I WAS ASTOUNDED. THE LAMP WAS NOW A THING OF STRIKING, HANDCRAFTED ELEGANCE, UNIQUELY HANDSOME AND UNQUESTIONABLY PRACTICAL.

WHILE I HAD SLEPT, SHE HAD SIMPLY COVERED THE GLASS RESERVOIR WITH "FRENCH HITCHING" (SOMETIMES CALLED "RIB STITCHING"). IT NOT ONLY DECORATES BUT PREVENTS THE GLASS FROM BREAKING SHOULD IT BE KNOCKED TO THE CABIN SOLE INADVERTENTLY. SHE HAS SINCE COVERED OTHER LAMPS WITH VARIOUS OTHER FORMS OF HITCHING ("ROUND-TURN STITCHING", "NEEDLE HITCHING", "BUMPER HITCHING" AND OTHERS).

TO THIS DAY, THOSE OLD "HARDWARE STORE" LAMPS STILL SHINE ON, SAVED FROM A BRINEY DOOM. NOW DIGNIFIED AND ADMIRED BY ALL WHO BOARD MY LITTLE SHIP. I HAVE EVEN SENT A FEW OF THEM TO SAILING FRIENDS WHERE THEY GRACE DINNER TABLES AND DENS, WALLS, END BOARDS, AND MANTLE PIECES AS WELL AS BOATS, LARGE AND SMALL.

② NOW TIE THE FIRST ROW OF HITCHES "UP" THE SIDE. MAKE 14 OF THEM, EVENLY SPACED PULLED SNUGLY BUT NOT TIGHTLY.

③ SUBSEQUENT HITCHES ARE TIED, GOING ROUND 'N' ROUND, EACH TIME PRODUCING ANOTHER ROW. STUDY HOW THE HITCHES ARE TIED.

④ FROM TIME TO TIME, YOUR NEEDLE WILL RUN OUT OF TWINE. STARTING WITH A LENGTH OF ABOUT TEN FEET, THREAD THE NEEDLE, DOUBLE ALL BUT ONE FOOT OF THE TWINE THEN FEED IT INTO THE HITCHING AS SHOWN.

⑤ WITHIN ½" OF THE NECK OF THE RESERVOIR, CHANGE FROM "FRENCH HITCHING" TO "ROUND-TURN STITCHING".

TAPE HOLDS LINE IN PLACE

A DAB OF GLUE FOR A WHIPPING

#9 NEEDLE

① PASS THE LINE TWICE AROUND THE BOTTLE. PULL SNUGLY BUT NOT TIGHTLY.

B. P. Bingham

⑥ TO COMPLETE THE HITCHING OF THE RESERVOIR, TURN IT OVER, BEGIN FRENCH HITCHING (STEPS 2 and 3) THEN FINISH OFF WITH ROUND-TURN STITCHING. THERE... IT'S ALL DONE.

The Gliding Light

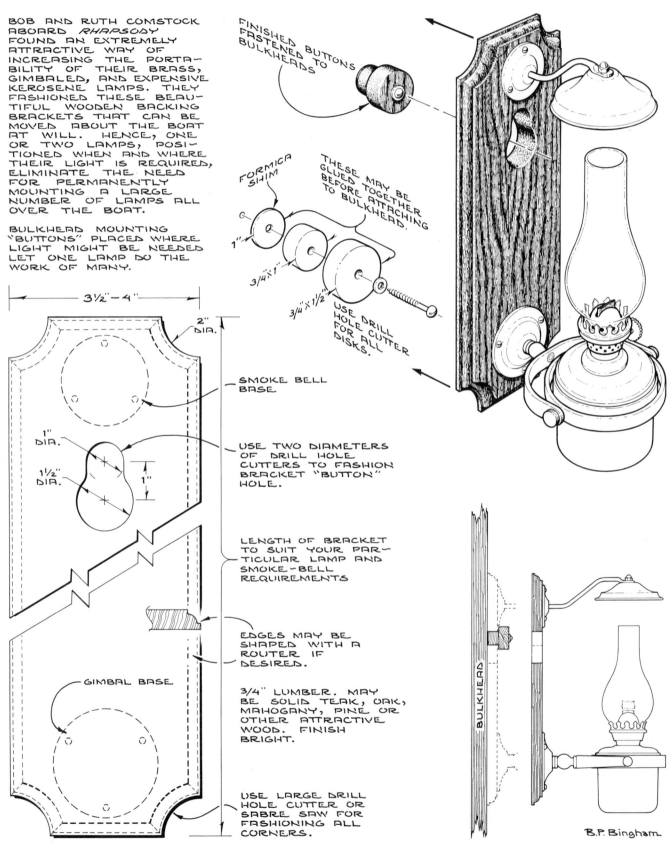

BOB AND RUTH COMSTOCK ABOARD *RHAPSODY* FOUND AN EXTREMELY ATTRACTIVE WAY OF INCREASING THE PORTABILITY OF THEIR BRASS, GIMBALED, AND EXPENSIVE KEROSENE LAMPS. THEY FASHIONED THESE BEAUTIFUL WOODEN BACKING BRACKETS THAT CAN BE MOVED ABOUT THE BOAT AT WILL. HENCE, ONE OR TWO LAMPS, POSITIONED WHEN AND WHERE THEIR LIGHT IS REQUIRED, ELIMINATE THE NEED FOR PERMANENTLY MOUNTING A LARGE NUMBER OF LAMPS ALL OVER THE BOAT.

BULKHEAD MOUNTING "BUTTONS" PLACED WHERE LIGHT MIGHT BE NEEDED LET ONE LAMP DO THE WORK OF MANY.

FINISHED BUTTONS FASTENED TO BULKHEADS

FORMICA SHIM

THESE MAY BE GLUED TOGETHER BEFORE ATTACHING TO BULKHEAD.

1"

3/4" X 1"

3/4" X 1/2

USE DRILL HOLE CUTTER FOR ALL DISKS.

3 1/2" — 4"

2" DIA.

1" DIA.

1 1/2" DIA.

1"

SMOKE BELL BASE

USE TWO DIAMETERS OF DRILL HOLE CUTTERS TO FASHION BRACKET "BUTTON" HOLE.

LENGTH OF BRACKET TO SUIT YOUR PARTICULAR LAMP AND SMOKE-BELL REQUIREMENTS

EDGES MAY BE SHAPED WITH A ROUTER IF DESIRED.

3/4" LUMBER. MAY BE SOLID TEAK, OAK, MAHOGANY, PINE OR OTHER ATTRACTIVE WOOD. FINISH BRIGHT.

GIMBAL BASE

USE LARGE DRILL HOLE CUTTER OR SABRE SAW FOR FASHIONING ALL CORNERS.

BULKHEAD

B.P. Bingham

A Folding End Table

B.P. Bingham

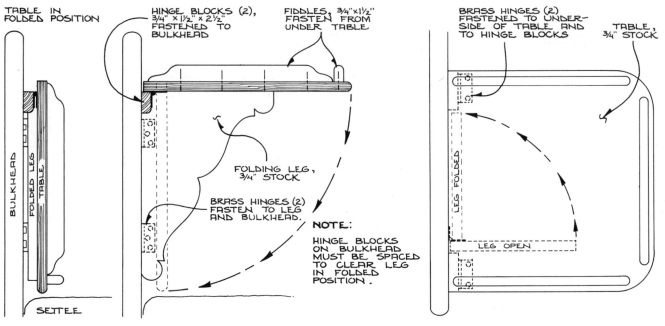

TABLE IN FOLDED POSITION

BULKHEAD

FOLDED LEG

TABLE

SETTEE

HINGE BLOCKS (2), 3/4" x 1 1/2" x 2 1/2" FASTENED TO BULKHEAD

FIDDLES, 3/4" x 1 1/2" FASTEN FROM UNDER TABLE

FOLDING LEG, 3/4" STOCK

BRASS HINGES (2) FASTEN TO LEG AND BULKHEAD.

NOTE:

HINGE BLOCKS ON BULKHEAD MUST BE SPACED TO CLEAR LEG IN FOLDED POSITION.

BRASS HINGES (2) FASTENED TO UNDER-SIDE OF TABLE AND TO HINGE BLOCKS

TABLE, 3/4" STOCK

LEG FOLDED

LEG OPEN

Gimbaled Tables

THE VALUE OF A GIM-BALED TABLE GOES WITHOUT QUESTION, ESPECIALLY IF YOU'RE CAUGHT IN HEAVY WEATHER, FORCED TO SAIL TO WINDWARD FOR A LONG PERIOD OF TIME, ANCHORED NEAR POWERBOAT WAKES OR EVEN ROLL-ING DOWNWIND JUST AT DINNER TIME. ADDITIONALLY, A GIM-BALED TABLE IS THE EPITOME OF "NAUTICA".

THEY DO HAVE A MAJOR DRAWBACK: ON ONE TACK, THE TABLE IS AT CHIN LEVEL BUT ON THE OTHER TACK IT IS AT YOUR KNEES. MOST SAILORS, THEREFORE, KNEEL OR SIT WITH THEIR FEET UNDER THEIR BUTTS WHILE EATING. IT'S NOT BAD ONCE YOU'VE GOTTEN USED TO IT. OVERALL, THOUGH, THE ADVANTAGES ARE COUNTLESS.

THE TABLE ON THIS PAGE IS A HANDSOME THING AND USES THE LEAST SOLE SPACE FOR A FIXED UNIT. BUT IN ORDER TO GIM-BAL, THE LEAVES MUST BE RAISED. THE FIXED TABLE AT THE TOP OF THE NEXT PAGE WILL GIMBAL WITH THE LEAVES DOWN BUT USES MORE SOLE SPACE.

THE LAST TABLE WAS ENGINEERED FOR DONALD STREET'S OCEAN SAILING YACHT, Vol II, AND FOLDS AWAY WHEN NOT IN USE.

A GOOD GRADE OF SOLID MAHOGANY, TEAK, OAK, MAPLE ETC. MUST BE USED FOR ALL TABLE LEGS AND PENDULUMS. SPECIALLY MILLED THICKNESSES AND WIDTHS MAY BE REQUIRED. TABLE TOPS MAY BE A GOOD GRADE OF VENEERED PLYWOOD (EDGED) BUT THE BEST LOOKING TABLE WILL ALSO HAVE A SOLID TOP. RE-COMMENDED BALLAST IS LEAD.

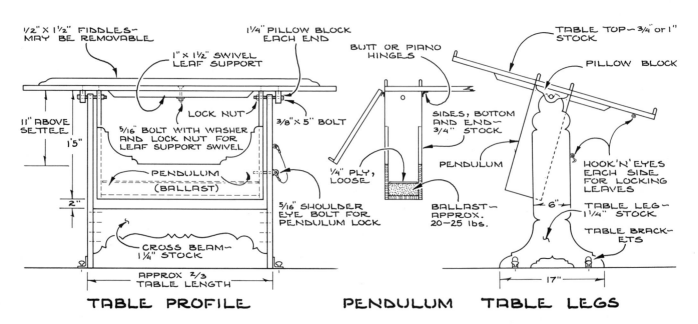

TABLE PROFILE · PENDULUM · TABLE LEGS

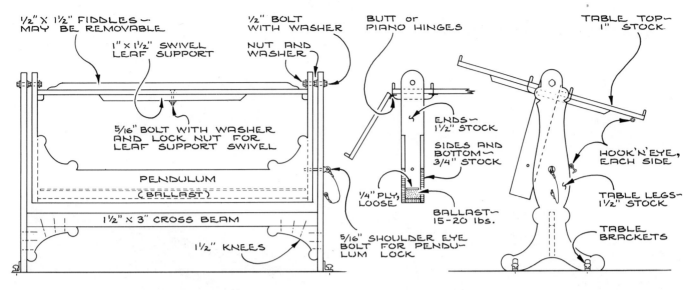

1/2" X 1 1/2" FIDDLES— MAY BE REMOVABLE

1" X 1 1/2" SWIVEL LEAF SUPPORT

1/2" BOLT WITH WASHER

NUT AND WASHER

BUTT or PIANO HINGES

TABLE TOP— 1" STOCK

5/16" BOLT WITH WASHER AND LOCK NUT FOR LEAF SUPPORT SWIVEL

ENDS— 1 1/2" STOCK

SIDES AND BOTTOM— 3/4" STOCK

PENDULUM (BALLAST)

HOOK'N'EYE, EACH SIDE

TABLE LEGS— 1 1/2" STOCK

1 1/2" X 3" CROSS BEAM

1/4" PLY, LOOSE

BALLAST— 15-20 lbs.

TABLE BRACKETS

1 1/2" KNEES

5/16" SHOULDER EYE BOLT FOR PENDU- LUM LOCK

TABLE PROFILE   PENDULUM   TABLE LEGS

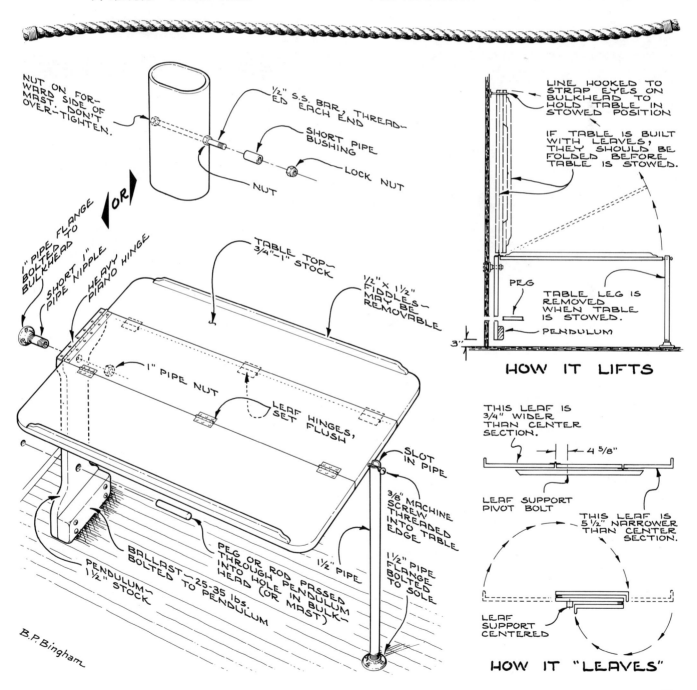

NUT ON FOR- WARD SIDE OF MAST. DON'T OVER- TIGHTEN.

1/2" S.S. BAR, THREAD- ED EACH END

SHORT PIPE BUSHING

LOCK NUT

NUT

LINE HOOKED TO STRAP EYES ON BULKHEAD TO HOLD TABLE IN STOWED POSITION

IF TABLE IS BUILT WITH LEAVES, THEY SHOULD BE FOLDED BEFORE TABLE IS STOWED.

OR

1" PIPE FLANGE BOLTED TO BULKHEAD

SHORT 1" PIPE NIPPLE

HEAVY PIANO HINGE

TABLE TOP— 3/4"-1" STOCK

1/2" X 1 1/2" FIDDLES— MAY BE REMOVABLE

1" PIPE NUT

LEAF HINGES, SET FLUSH

PEG

TABLE LEG IS REMOVED WHEN TABLE IS STOWED.

PENDULUM

3"

HOW IT LIFTS

SLOT IN PIPE

3/8" MACHINE SCREW THREADED INTO TABLE EDGE

PEG OR ROD PASSED THROUGH PENDULUM INTO HOLE IN BULK- HEAD (OR MAST)

BALLAST— 25-35 lbs. BOLTED TO PENDULUM

PENDULUM— 1 1/2" STOCK

1 1/2" PIPE

1 1/2" PIPE FLANGE BOLTED TO SOLE

B.P. Bingham

THIS LEAF IS 3/4" WIDER THAN CENTER SECTION.

4 5/8"

LEAF SUPPORT PIVOT BOLT

THIS LEAF IS 5 1/2" NARROWER THAN CENTER SECTION.

LEAF SUPPORT CENTERED

HOW IT "LEAVES"

49

Bulkhead Box Bins

THERE ARE A LOT OF LITTLE HIDDEN PLACES ON EVERY BOAT THAT ARE OUT OF ARM'S REACH AND, THUS, REMAIN WASTED SPACES: THE UPPER REGIONS OF THE CHAIN LOCKER, THE DEEPER DUNGEONS OF THE GALLEY COUNTER. SOMETIMES IT IS SIMPLY A SECTION OF BULKHEAD MORE ACCESSIBLE FROM ONE SIDE THAN ANOTHER. THE COMMON DILEMMA IS THAT A "WALL" STANDS BETWEEN YOU AND THE USABLE SPACE.

A SIMPLY BUILT, EASILY INSTALLED BULKHEAD BIN MIGHT BE ONE WAY TO USE THAT SPACE TO A VERY HANDY ADVANTAGE.

ONCE YOU'VE BUILT A FEW, YOU'LL WONDER HOW YOU GOT ALONG WITHOUT THEM.

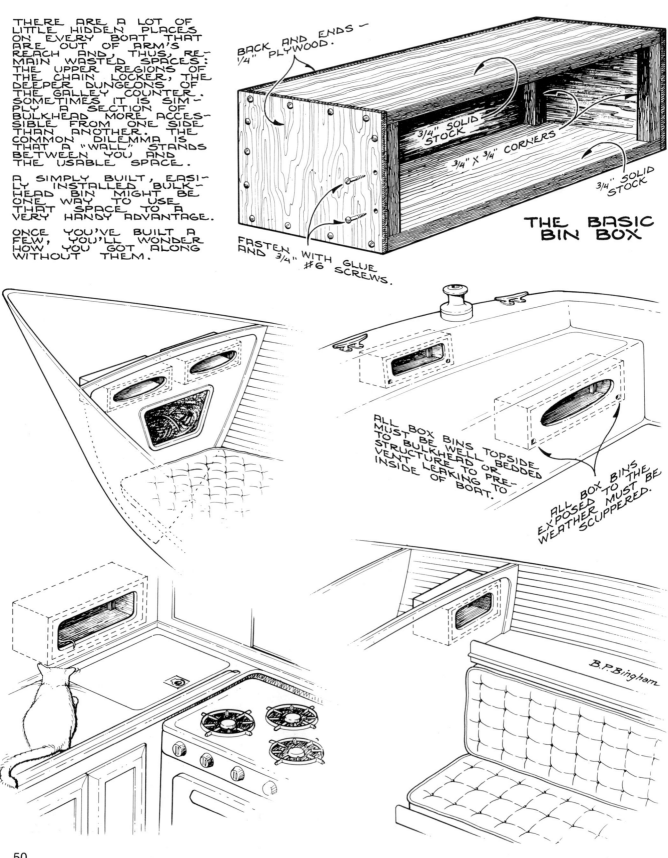

BACK AND ENDS — 1/4" PLYWOOD.

3/4" SOLID STOCK

3/4" X 3/4" CORNERS

3/4" SOLID STOCK

THE BASIC BIN BOX

FASTEN WITH GLUE AND 3/4" #6 SCREWS.

ALL BOX BINS TOPSIDE MUST BE WELL BEDDED TO BULKHEAD OR STRUCTURE TO PREVENT LEAKING TO INSIDE OF BOAT.

ALL BOX BINS EXPOSED TO THE WEATHER MUST BE SCUPPERED.

B.P. Bingham

Ladder Bins

INVARIABLY, FLASHLIGHTS, WINCH HANDLES AND SAIL GASKETS END UP STUFFED INTO THE SAME DRAWER WITH THE SILVERWARE AND POT HOLDERS. EXTRA SHACKLES AND BLOCKS GET MIXED IN WITH THE SCREWDRIVERS. THE SCREWDRIVERS, SOMEHOW, FIND THEIR WAY INTO THE SAME BIN AS THE END WRENCHES. THE WRENCHES BELONG IN THE TOOL BOX BUT IT'S STOWED UNDER THE SETTEE AND IT'S TOO MUCH TROUBLE TO GET AT!

SOUND FAMILIAR?

I HAVE YET TO SEE A BOAT THAT HAD TOO MANY SMALL, INDIVIDUAL STORAGE SPACES. SO, THE LADDER BINS SHOWN HERE MAY BE JUST THE ANSWER FOR YOUR HUNDRED LITTLE "PUT AWAY" PROBLEMS.

THEY'RE EASY TO BUILD AND INSTALL, ARE IMMEDIATELY ACCESSIBLE, WON'T INFRINGE ON STEPPING SPACE OR SAFETY AND ... THEY WON'T JAM.

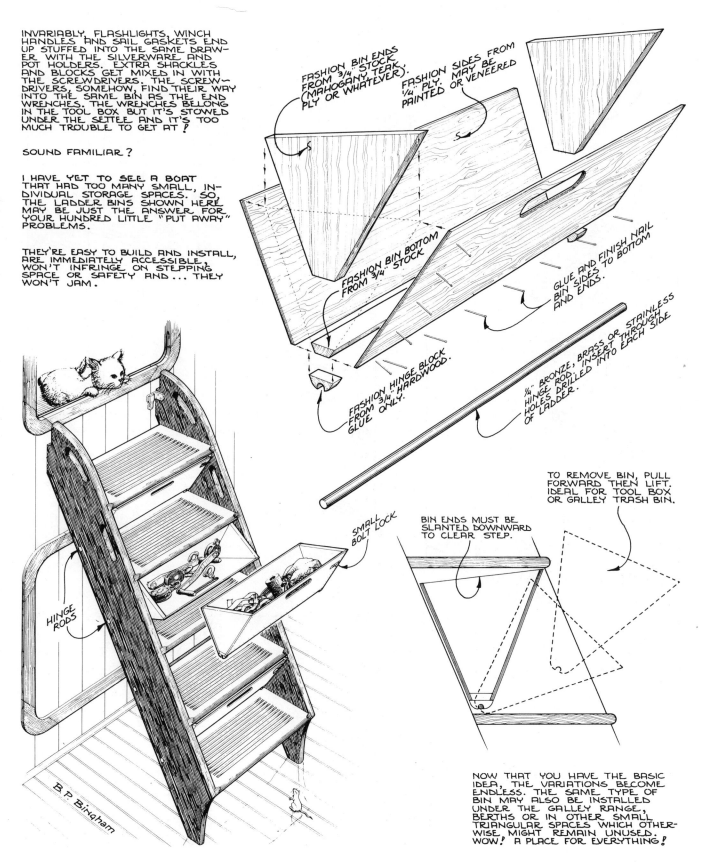

FASHION BIN ENDS FROM 3/4" STOCK (MAHOGANY TEAK, PLY OR WHATEVER).

FASHION SIDES FROM 1/4" PLY. MAY BE PAINTED OR VENEERED

FASHION BIN BOTTOM FROM 3/4" STOCK

GLUE AND FINISH NAIL BIN SIDES TO BOTTOM AND ENDS.

FASHION HINGE BLOCK FROM 3/4" HARDWOOD. GLUE ONLY.

1/4" BRONZE, BRASS OR STAINLESS HINGE ROD. INSERT THROUGH HOLES DRILLED INTO EACH SIDE OF LADDER.

TO REMOVE BIN, PULL FORWARD THEN LIFT. IDEAL FOR TOOL BOX OR GALLEY TRASH BIN.

SMALL BOLT LOCK

BIN ENDS MUST BE SLANTED DOWNWARD TO CLEAR STEP.

HINGE RODS

B. P. Bingham

NOW THAT YOU HAVE THE BASIC IDEA, THE VARIATIONS BECOME ENDLESS. THE SAME TYPE OF BIN MAY ALSO BE INSTALLED UNDER THE GALLEY RANGE, BERTHS OR IN OTHER SMALL TRIANGULAR SPACES WHICH OTHERWISE MIGHT REMAIN UNUSED. WOW! A PLACE FOR EVERYTHING!

Cassette Tape Racks

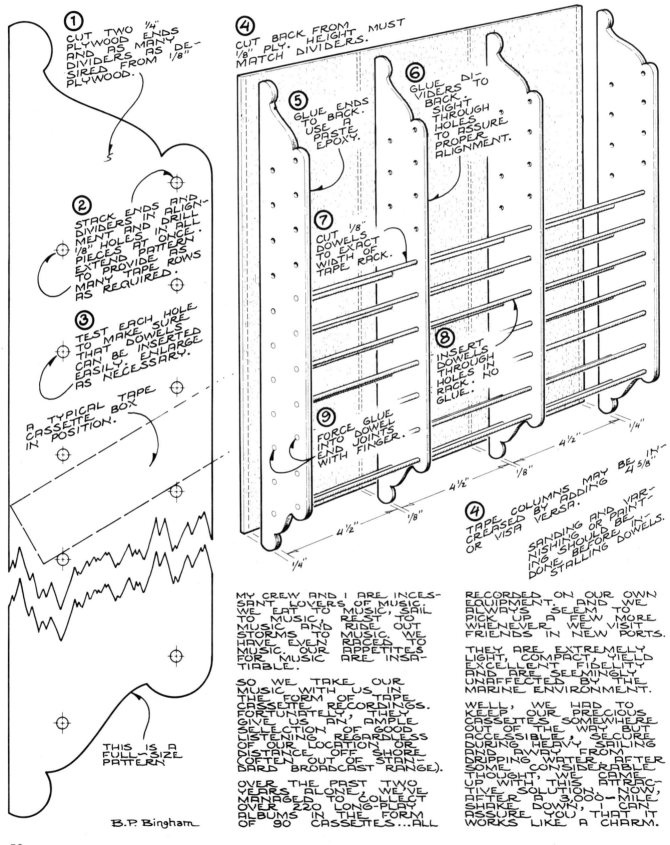

1 CUT TWO 1/4" PLYWOOD ENDS AND AS MANY DIVIDERS AS DESIRED FROM 1/8" PLYWOOD.

2 STACK ENDS AND DIVIDERS IN ALIGNMENT AND DRILL ALL 1/8" HOLES IN ALL PIECES AT ONCE. EXTEND PATTERN TO PROVIDE AS MANY TAPE ROWS AS REQUIRED.

3 TEST EACH HOLE TO MAKE SURE THAT DOWELS CAN BE INSERTED EASILY. ENLARGE AS NECESSARY.

A TYPICAL TAPE CASSETTE BOX IN POSITION.

4 CUT BACK FROM 1/8" PLY. HEIGHT MUST MATCH DIVIDERS.

5 GLUE ENDS TO BACK. USE A PASTE EPOXY.

6 GLUE DIVIDERS TO BACK. SIGHT THROUGH HOLES TO ASSURE PROPER ALIGNMENT.

7 CUT 1/8" DOWELS TO EXACT WIDTH OF TAPE RACK.

8 INSERT DOWELS THROUGH HOLES IN RACK. NO GLUE.

9 FORCE GLUE INTO DOWEL END JOINTS WITH FINGER.

4 TAPE COLUMNS MAY BE INCREASED BY ADDING OR VISA VERSA.

SANDING AND VARNISHING OR PAINTING SHOULD BE DONE BEFORE INSTALLING DOWELS.

THIS IS A FULL-SIZE PATTERN

B.P. Bingham

1/4"   4 1/2"   1/8"   4 1/2"   1/8"   4 1/2"   1/4"   4 5/8" IN.

MY CREW AND I ARE INCESSANT LOVERS OF MUSIC. WE EAT TO MUSIC, SAIL TO MUSIC, REST TO MUSIC AND RIDE OUT STORMS TO MUSIC. WE HAVE EVEN RACED TO MUSIC. OUR APPETITES FOR MUSIC ARE INSATIABLE.

SO WE TAKE OUR MUSIC WITH US IN THE FORM OF TAPE CASSETTE RECORDINGS. FORTUNATELY, THEY GIVE US AN AMPLE SELECTION OF GOOD LISTENING REGARDLESS OF OUR LOCATION OR DISTANCE OFF SHORE (OFTEN OUT OF STANDARD BROADCAST RANGE).

OVER THE PAST TWO YEARS ALONE, WE'VE MANAGED TO COLLECT OVER 220 LONG-PLAY ALBUMS IN THE FORM OF 90 CASSETTES...ALL

RECORDED ON OUR OWN EQUIPMENT. AND WE ALWAYS SEEM TO PICK UP A FEW MORE WHENEVER WE VISIT FRIENDS IN NEW PORTS.

THEY ARE EXTREMELY LIGHT, COMPACT, YIELD EXCELLENT FIDELITY AND ARE SEEMINGLY UNAFFECTED BY THE MARINE ENVIRONMENT.

WELL, WE HAD TO KEEP OUR PRECIOUS CASSETTES SOMEWHERE OUT OF THE WAY BUT ACCESSIBLE, SECURE DURING HEAVY SAILING AND AWAY FROM DRIPPING WATER. AFTER SOME CONSIDERABLE THOUGHT, WE CAME UP WITH THIS ATTRACTIVE SOLUTION. NOW, AFTER A 3,000-MILE SHAKE DOWN, I CAN ASSURE YOU THAT IT WORKS LIKE A CHARM.

Convertible Fiddles

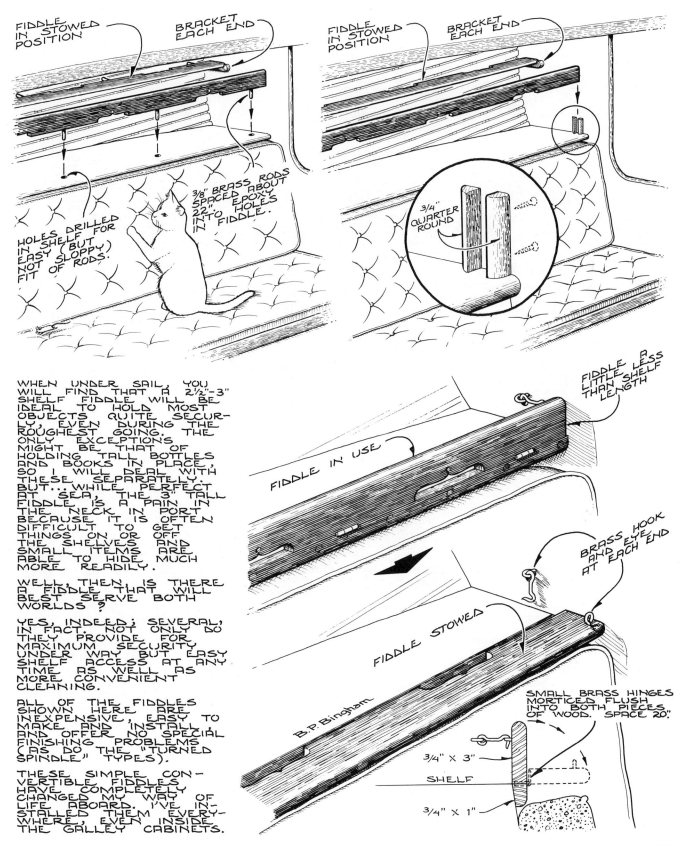

FIDDLE IN STOWED POSITION

BRACKET EACH END

HOLES DRILLED IN SHELF FOR EASY (BUT NOT SLOPPY) FIT OF RODS.

3/8" BRASS RODS SPACED ABOUT 22" EPOXY INTO HOLES IN FIDDLE.

FIDDLE IN STOWED POSITION

BRACKET EACH END

3/4" QUARTER ROUND

FIDDLE A LITTLE LESS THAN SHELF LENGTH

FIDDLE IN USE

BRASS HOOK AND EYE AT EACH END

FIDDLE STOWED

B.P. Bingham

SMALL BRASS HINGES MORTICED FLUSH INTO BOTH PIECES OF WOOD. SPACE 20".

3/4" X 3"

SHELF

3/4" X 1"

WHEN UNDER SAIL, YOU WILL FIND THAT A 2½"-3" SHELF FIDDLE WILL BE IDEAL TO HOLD MOST OBJECTS QUITE SECURELY, EVEN DURING THE ROUGHEST GOING. THE ONLY EXCEPTIONS MIGHT BE THAT OF HOLDING TALL BOTTLES AND BOOKS IN PLACE, SO I WILL DEAL WITH THESE SEPARATELY. BUT...WHILE PERFECT AT SEA, THE 3" TALL FIDDLE IS A PAIN IN THE NECK IN PORT BECAUSE IT IS OFTEN DIFFICULT TO GET THINGS ON OR OFF THE SHELVES AND SMALL ITEMS ARE ABLE TO HIDE MUCH MORE READILY.

WELL, THEN, IS THERE A FIDDLE THAT WILL BEST SERVE BOTH WORLDS?

YES, INDEED; SEVERAL, IN FACT. NOT ONLY DO THEY PROVIDE FOR MAXIMUM SECURITY UNDER WAY BUT EASY SHELF ACCESS AT ANY TIME AS WELL AS MORE CONVENIENT CLEANING.

ALL OF THE FIDDLES SHOWN HERE ARE INEXPENSIVE, EASY TO MAKE AND INSTALL AND OFFER NO SPECIAL FINISHING PROBLEMS (AS DO THE "TURNED SPINDLE" TYPES).

THESE SIMPLE CONVERTIBLE FIDDLES HAVE COMPLETELY CHANGED MY WAY OF LIFE ABOARD. I'VE INSTALLED THEM EVERYWHERE, EVEN INSIDE THE GALLEY CABINETS.

Acrylic Accessories

NOW, I LIKE TEAK AS WELL AS THE NEXT GUY BUT ENOUGH IS ENOUGH! MOST BOATS ARE ALREADY SO DARK WITH TEAK YOU CAN BARELY FIND YOUR PIPE. TACKING CLUMSY TEAK DO-DADS TO THE BULKHEADS IN THE NAME OF CUSTOMIZING ONLY MAKES YOUR SENSE OF SPACE (OR LACK OF IT) EVEN MORE NOTICEABLE.

WHY NOT TRY ACRYLIC ACCESSORIES? THE MATERIAL IS READILY AVAILABLE AT A COST WELL BELOW MOST EXOTIC WOODS, IS SOLD IN VARIOUS THICKNESSES AND COLORS AS WELL AS CLEAR, FROSTED AND SMOKED. IT LENDS ITSELF TO THE FABRICATION OF ITEMS THAT WOULD, OTHERWISE, BE VERY COMPLICATED TO CONSTRUCT, AND IS A HELL OF A LOT OF FUN ONCE YOU'VE GOTTEN THE FEEL FOR THE STUFF.

ONCE I'D STARTED MAKING THINGS IN ACRYLIC, I JUST COULDN'T STOP. IT'S SO EASY AND THE RESULTS ARE PIECES THAT ARE PRACTICAL, STRIKINGLY UNIQUE AND UNOBTRUSIVE. MOST ITEMS JUST BLEND INTO THE BOAT. YOU'LL STILL ACHIEVE THAT MATCHING, CUSTOM LOOK WITH THE ADVANTAGE OF FITTING EVERYTHING TO YOUR EXACT REQUIREMENTS.

TOOLS

ACRYLICS ARE BEST CUT WITH AN ELECTRIC SABRE SAW FITTED WITH A SPECIAL "PLASTICS" BLADE (AVAILABLE AT SEARS). YOU CAN DRILL WITH ANY STANDARD, HIGH-SPEED BIT BUT DON'T PUSH TOO HARD OR YOU COULD CRACK THE PLASTIC. AN ORDINARY "BASTARD" AND RAT-TAIL FILE WILL CLEAN UP THE

ROUGH EDGES. SANDPAPER (60 TO 120) IS USED FOR FINAL-FINISH WORK WHILE FINE WET PAPER, THEN TOOTHPASTE IS BEST FOR PUTTING THE REAL POLISH ON THE PLASTIC EDGES.

BENDING ACRYLICS REQUIRES A SPECIAL BUT LOW COST ($7.00) HEATING STRIP. THERE ARE NO TRICKS TO IT; JUST FOLLOW THE INSTRUCTIONS, HEAT, BEND AND HOLD TO SHAPE FOR ABOUT THIRTY SECONDS. BUY THE BENDER AT THE PLASTICS STORE OR A HOBBY SHOP.

PATTERNS

I WOULD SUGGEST THAT YOU DRAW A FLAT PATTERN ONTO CARDBOARD, CUT IT OUT THEN FOLD IT TO SHAPE AS A TRIAL BEFORE COMMITTING THE PLASTIC.

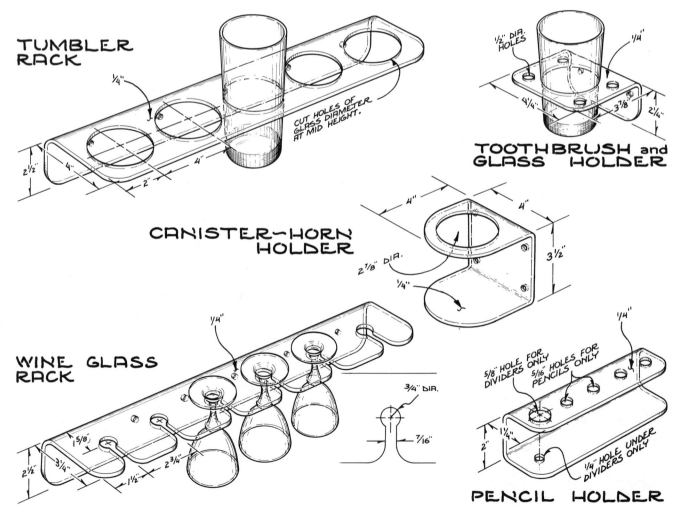

TUMBLER RACK

1/4"
CUT HOLES OF GLASS DIAMETER AT MID HEIGHT.
2 1/2"
4"
2"

TOOTHBRUSH and GLASS HOLDER

1/2" DIA. HOLES
1/4"
4 1/4"
3 7/8"
2 1/4"

CANISTER-HORN HOLDER

4"
4"
2 1/8" DIA.
1/4"
3 1/2"

WINE GLASS RACK

1/4"
3/4" DIA.
7/16"
5/8"
2 1/2"
3/4"
1/2"
2 3/4"

PENCIL HOLDER

5/8" HOLE FOR DIVIDERS ONLY
5/16" HOLES FOR PENCILS ONLY
1/4"
1 1/4"
2"
1/4" HOLE UNDER DIVIDERS ONLY

BOOK ENDS

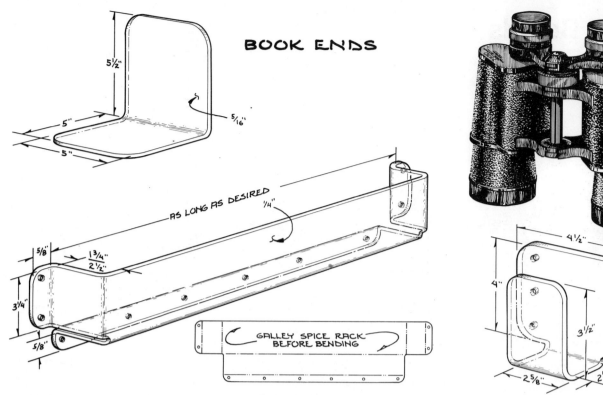

5½"

5"

5"

5/16"

AS LONG AS DESIRED

¼"

5/8"

1¾"

2½"

3¼"

5/8"

GALLEY SPICE RACK
BEFORE BENDING

GALLEY SPICE RACK or DOOR UTENSIL RACK

4½"

4"

3½"

5/16"

2 5/8"

2¼"

BINOCULAR RACK

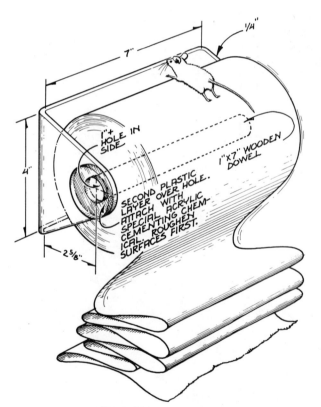

7"

¼"

1"+
HOLE IN
SIDE

1"x7" WOODEN
DOWEL

SECOND PLASTIC
LAYER OVER HOLE.
ATTACH WITH
SPECIAL ACRYLIC
CEMENTING CHEM-
ICAL. ROUGHEN
SURFACES FIRST.

4"

2 5/8"

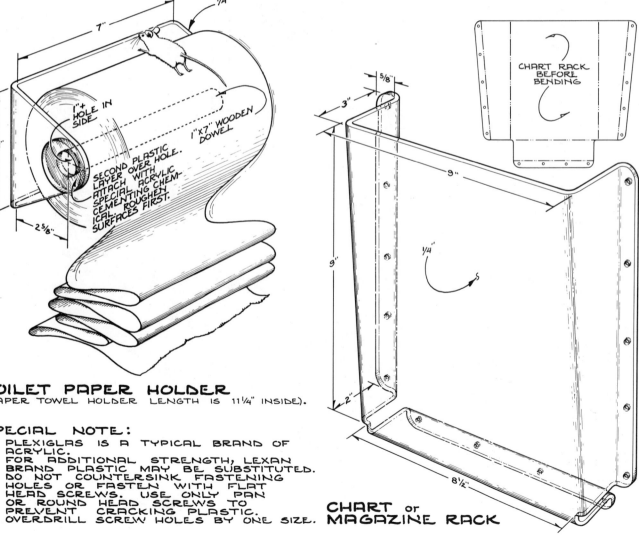

CHART RACK
BEFORE BENDING

5/8"

3"

9"

9"

¼"

2"

8½"

TOILET PAPER HOLDER
(PAPER TOWEL HOLDER LENGTH IS 11¼" INSIDE).

SPECIAL NOTE:
1. PLEXIGLAS IS A TYPICAL BRAND OF ACRYLIC.
2. FOR ADDITIONAL STRENGTH, LEXAN BRAND PLASTIC MAY BE SUBSTITUTED.
3. DO NOT COUNTERSINK FASTENING HOLES OR FASTEN WITH FLAT HEAD SCREWS. USE ONLY PAN OR ROUND HEAD SCREWS TO PREVENT CRACKING PLASTIC.
4. OVERDRILL SCREW HOLES BY ONE SIZE.

CHART or MAGAZINE RACK

Bunk Boards

IF YOU'RE SLAMMING TO WEATHER AND YOUR BOAT'S ON ITS EAR, YOU'LL PROBABLY WANT TO SLEEP ON THE HIGH SIDE TO GIVE HER A LITTLE MORE STABILITY. IF YOU'RE JUST CRUISING AROUND BUT HAVE A LARGE CREW, SOMEONE'S CHOICE OF BUNK WILL SURELY BE LIMITED TO A WINDWARD BERTH. IF YOU'RE CAUGHT OFFSHORE IN VERY LIGHT AIR AND SLOPPY SEAS, THE BOAT WILL TRY TO ROLL EVERYONE OUT OF THEIR BUNKS ONTO THE SOLE.

SOONER OR LATER, YOU'RE SURE TO FIND A NEED FOR BUNK BOARDS. I HAVE ILLUSTRATED SOME OF MY FAVORITE ONES THAT I'VE ENCOUNTERED OVER THE YEARS. THEY ARE INEXPENSIVE, EASY TO INSTALL, CONVENIENT TO USE AND DON'T POSE A STOWAGE PROBLEM.

I'VE REJECTED LEE CANVASSES BECAUSE THEY ARE TIME-CONSUMING TO RIG AND UNRIG (ALWAYS FROM INSIDE OF THE

BUNK IN A HUNCHED-OVER POSITION WHILE THE BOAT GYRATES WILDLY THROUGH THE BLACK NIGHT!). THEY MAKE IT VERY DIFFICULT TO RESPOND QUICKLY TO EMERGENCIES, TO GET UP FOR A QUICK FIX OR SIMPLY TO HIT THE HEAD. THE LAST THING I WANT TO DO AFTER (OR BEFORE) A LONG, COLD, WET, EXHAUSTING WATCH IS TO FUMBLE WITH HALF HITCHES FOR SEVEN MINUTES.

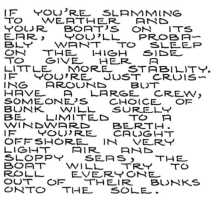

BARREL-BOLT LOCKS AT EACH END OF BUNK BOARD FIT INTO HOLES DRILLED INTO BULKHEADS.

3/8" PLYWOOD

HINGES

TO STOW BUNK BOARD: LOOSEN LOCKS, LIFT MATTRESS, LOWER BUNK BOARD AND REPLACE MATTRESS.

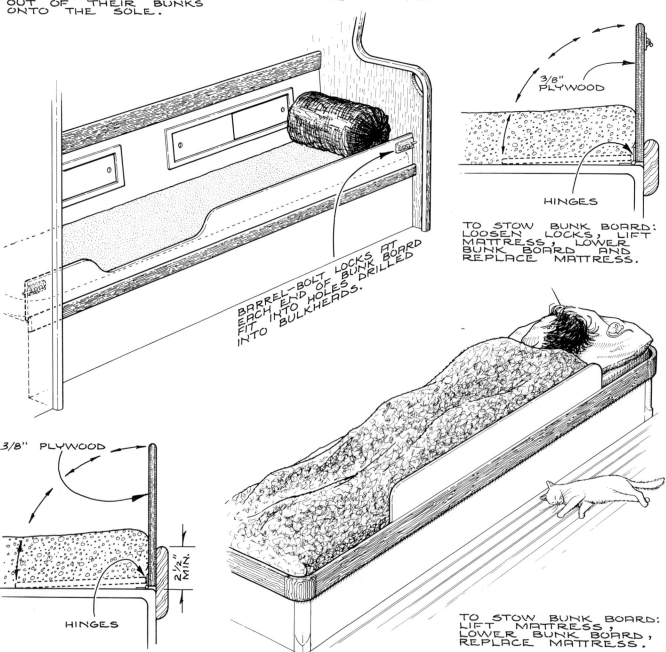

3/8" PLYWOOD

2½" MIN.

HINGES

TO STOW BUNK BOARD: LIFT MATTRESS, LOWER BUNK BOARD, REPLACE MATTRESS.

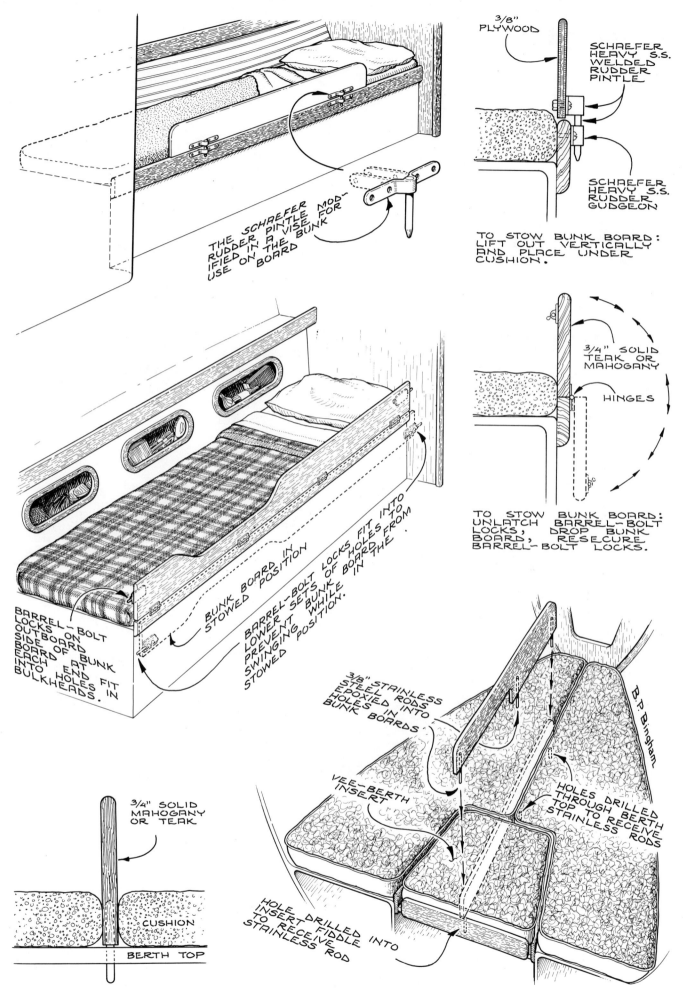

THE SCHAEFER RUDDER PINTLE MODIFIED IN A VISE FOR USE ON THE BUNK BOARD

3/8" PLYWOOD

SCHAEFER HEAVY S.S. WELDED RUDDER PINTLE

SCHAEFER HEAVY S.S. RUDDER GUDGEON

TO STOW BUNK BOARD: LIFT OUT VERTICALLY AND PLACE UNDER CUSHION.

3/4" SOLID TEAK OR MAHOGANY

HINGES

TO STOW BUNK BOARD: UNLATCH BARREL-BOLT LOCKS, DROP BUNK BOARD, RESECURE BARREL-BOLT LOCKS.

BUNK BOARD IN STOWED POSITION

BARREL-BOLT LOCKS FIT INTO LOWER SETS OF HOLES TO PREVENT BUNK BOARD FROM SWINGING WHILE IN THE STOWED POSITION.

BARREL-BOLT LOCKS ON OUTBOARD SIDE OF BUNK BOARD AT EACH END FIT INTO HOLES IN BULKHEADS.

3/8" STAINLESS STEEL RODS EPOXIED INTO HOLES IN BUNK BOARDS

VEE-BERTH INSERT

HOLES DRILLED THROUGH TOP OF BERTH TO RECEIVE STAINLESS RODS

B.P. Bingham

HOLE DRILLED INTO INSERT FIDDLE TO RECEIVE STAINLESS ROD

3/4" SOLID MAHOGANY OR TEAK

CUSHION

BERTH TOP

57

Keeping Up The Books

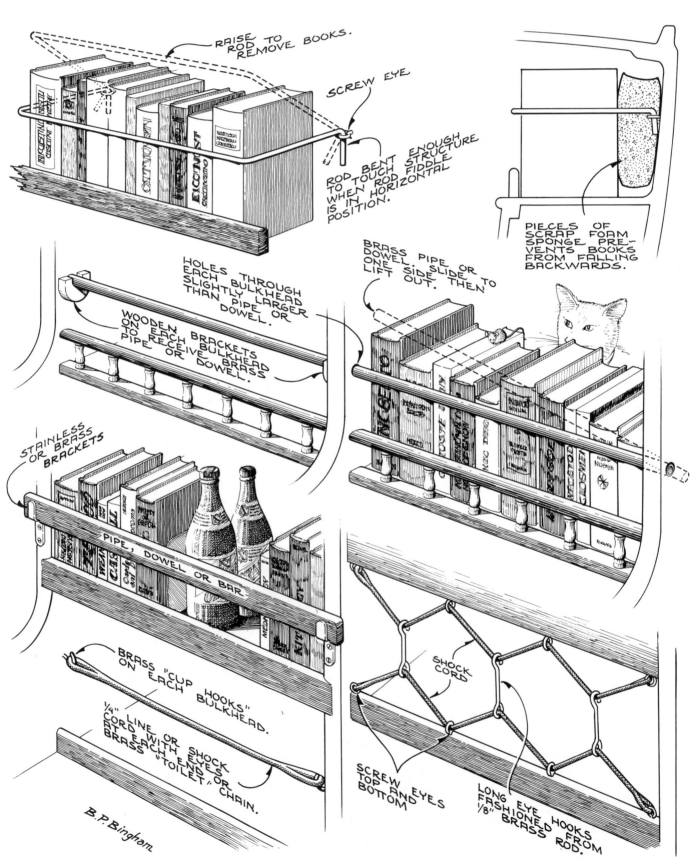

RAISE TO ROD TO REMOVE BOOKS.

SCREW EYE

ROD BENT ENOUGH TO TOUCH STRUCTURE WHEN ROD FIDDLE IS IN HORIZONTAL POSITION.

PIECES OF SCRAP FOAM SPONGE PREVENTS BOOKS FROM FALLING BACKWARDS.

HOLES THROUGH EACH BULKHEAD SLIGHTLY LARGER THAN PIPE OR DOWEL.

WOODEN BRACKETS ON EACH BULKHEAD TO RECEIVE BRASS PIPE OR DOWEL.

BRASS PIPE OR TO DOWEL. SLIDE ONE SIDE THEN LIFT OUT.

STAINLESS OR BRASS BRACKETS

PIPE, DOWEL OR BAR

BRASS "CUP" HOOKS ON EACH BULKHEAD.

1/4" LINE OR SHOCK CORD WITH EYES AT EACH END, OR BRASS "TOILET" CHAIN.

SHOCK CORD

SCREW EYES TOP AND BOTTOM

LONG EYE HOOKS FASHIONED FROM 1/8" BRASS ROD.

B.P. Bingham

Wooden Hull Ceiling For Fiberglass Boats

MANY PEOPLE (MYSELF INCLUDED) FIND THE ALL-GLOSSY WHITE INTERIOR OF MOST FIBERGLASS PRODUCTION YACHTS TO BE, AT LEAST, SOMEWHAT "PLASTIC" IN APPEARANCE. BOATS WHICH DO NOT HAVE SMOOTH HULL-LINERS, BUT ONLY PAINTED-OVER ROUGH FIBERGLASS FINISHES, MAY EVEN BE OFFENSIVE TO SOME. A PADDED VINYL HULL FINISH IS USUALLY BETTER THAN NO FINISH AT ALL.

IT DOESN'T HAVE TO BE THAT WAY. MANY FINE GLASS YACHTS ARE CONSTRUCTED WITH TRADITIONAL-LOOKING WOOD "HULL CEILING". AND....YOU CAN APPROXIMATE THE SAME RICH TREATMENT IN YOUR OWN BOAT. IF YOU'RE CONCERNED ABOUT INNER BEAUTY OR RESALE VALUE, IT MAY BE WORTH YOUR EFFORT.

HERE'S HOW:

① REMOVE ALL OBSTRUCTIONS FROM THE PORTION OF HULL TO BE COVERED.

② DRAW VERTICAL GUIDELINES ON THE HULL (OR LINER) AT INTERVALS OF 18"-24". THE GUIDELINES SHOULD DIVIDE THE COMPARTMENT INTO EQUAL SECTIONS.

③ FROM ½" ALUMINUM PIPE, CUT CEILING FRAMES TO LENGTHS MATCHING THE GUIDLINES. MARK FOR IDENTIFICATION.

④ BEND EACH FRAME SO IT FITS SNUGLY AGAINST THE HULL. USE A RENTED PIPE BENDER FOR THIS JOB. WORK SLOWLY.

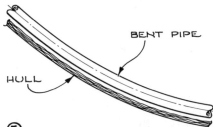

BENT PIPE

HULL

⑤ SAND THE HULL (OR LINER) ALONG THE GUIDELINES TO A WIDTH OF 4". NO GLOSS OR PAINT MUST REMAIN. USE #60 GRIT PAPER.

⑥ NOW, MIX A SMALL AMOUNT OF "FIVE MINUTE" EPOXY. APPLY IT TO THE BACK-SIDE OF A FRAME. PRESS THE FRAME AGAINST THE HULL IN ITS PREDETERMINED POSITION UNTIL THE EPOXY HAS "GONE OFF". ATTACH ALL OTHER FRAMES TO THE HULL IN THE SAME MANNER. MAKE SURE THAT EACH FRAME IS PLUMB BEFORE THE EPOXY SETS UP.

REMEMBER, THERE MUST BE A FRAME AT EACH END OF THE COMPARTMENT.

⑦ CUT LONG STRIPS OF 1oz. FIBERGLASS MAT, EACH BEING 4" WIDE, THEN CUT THE STRIPS TO MATCH THE FRAME LENGTHS.

⑧ WITH CATALIZED POLYESTER RESIN, COVER EACH FRAME WITH A MAT STRIP. ALLOW THE MAT

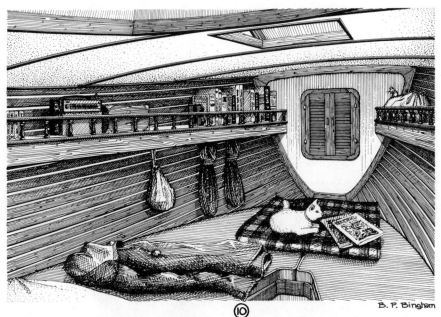

B. P. Bingham

EDGES TO LAP ABOUT 1" ONTO THE HULL. BE SURE THAT THE MAT IS THOROUGHLY SATURATED WITH RESIN AND THAT ALL BUBBLES ARE WORKED OUT BY BRUSH OR HAND.

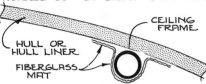

CEILING FRAME

HULL OR HULL LINER

FIBERGLASS MAT

ATTACHING THE FRAMES

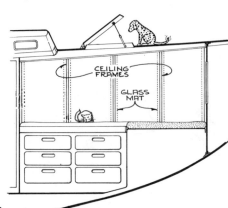

CEILING FRAMES

GLASS MAT

CEILING FRAMES IN POSITION

⑨ AFTER THE RESIN HAS CURED, THE INSIDE OF THE HULL MAY BE PAINTED WITH SEMI-GLOSS OR..... THE SPACES BETWEEN THE CEILING FRAMES MAY BE LINED WITH SEMI-RIGID FOAM USING CONTACT CEMENT ADHESIVE. THEN, COVER THE FOAM, FRAMES, AND ALL, WITH CLOTH-BACKED VINYL (AGAIN USING CONTACT CEMENT. THE VINYL COVERING IS NICE BECAUSE IT IS EASY TO KEEP CLEAN AFTER THE CEILING BATTENS ARE IN PLACE.

⑩ NOW FOR THE CEILING:

BEGIN BY MILLING LUMBER TO 5/16" X 1½". THE BATTENS MAY BE OF ANY DESIRABLE WOOD. ROUND OR CHAMFER THE OUTER EDGES SLIGHTLY.

⑪ STAIN, VARNISH OR OIL THE BATTENS. NOW...NOT LATER.

⑫ BEGINNING AT THE SHEER, CUT THE BATTENS TO LENGTH AS THEY ARE ATTACHED. FASTEN WITH S.S. PAN-HEAD, No. 6 SCREWS.

DON'T RUN THE BATTENS PARALLEL. ALLOW THEM TO BEND AS NATURALLY AS POSSIBLE AGAINST THE HULL. AVOID EDGE BENDING BY LETTING THE BATTENS TAKE THE "GREAT CIRCLE ROUTE". ALLOW A 3/4" SPACE BETWEEN BATTENS AT THE AFT END AND TAPER THE SPACE RUNNING FORWARD.

THAT'S IT. NOW STAND BACK AND LOOK AT THE IMPROVEMENT. WASN'T THAT WORTH IT ?

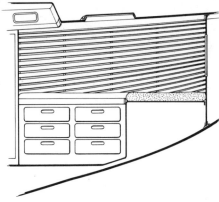

THE FINISHED CEILING

The Jones Plug

I OWE MY GRATITUDE TO ELSTON SWANSON FOR INTRODUCING ME TO THE 'JONES PLUG'. WITHOUT A DOZEN OF THEM, MY BOAT WOULD PROBABLY CEASE TO FUNCTION!

IT IS SIMPLY A SMALL, INEXPENSIVE ELECTRICAL PLUG WITH MATCHING SOCKET DESIGNED FOR POLARIZED, DIRECT CURRENT. OF THE PAIR OF PRONGS AND SOCKETS, ONE IS LARGER, PREVENTING YOU FROM INADVERTENTLY REVERSING NEGATIVE AND POSITIVE.

WHEN YOU THINK OF ALL THE 12-VOLT APPLIANCES YOUR BOAT MIGHT HAVE (MOST OF THEM PORTABLE) YOU CAN UNDERSTAND HOW HANDY IT IS TO PLUG THEM IN AT WILL AT VARIOUS LOCATIONS:

SEARCH LIGHT
TELEVISION
HI FI
LORAN AND R.D.F.
TROUBLE LIGHT
NAV. INSTRUMENTS
VACUUM CLEANER
RAZOR , 12-V TOOLS
LAMPS
AUTO PILOT
FANS

INDEED, ALMOST EVERY ELECTRICAL GADGET ABOARD CAN BE UN-PLUGGED, MOVED ABOUT, TAKEN HOME OR SERVICED WITHOUT HAVING TO MONKEY WITH WIRES.

JONES PLUGS ARE MUCH SMALLER AND FAR LESS COSTLY THAN CIGARETTE-LIGHTER ADAPTERS AND CAN BE PURCHASED AT ANY ELECTRONICS STORE.

BULKHEAD SOCKET

OR

IN-LINE SOCKET

B.P. Bingham

THE IN-LINE SOCKET IS WIRED AND ASSEMBLED EXACTLY LIKE THE PLUG BELOW.

EITHER THE LARGE OR SMALL TERMINAL MAY BE NEGATIVE, BUT THE CHOICE MUST BE APPLIED CONSISTENTLY TO ALL SOCKETS AND PLUGS.

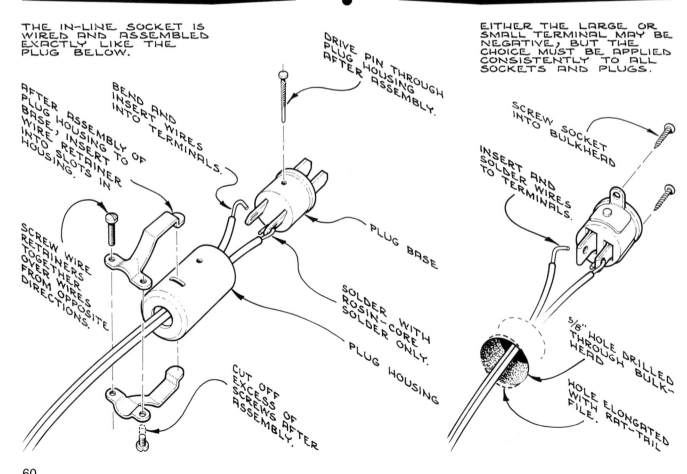

AFTER ASSEMBLY OF PLUG HOUSING TO BASE, INSERT WIRE RETAINER INTO SLOTS IN HOUSING.

BEND AND INSERT WIRES INTO TERMINALS.

DRIVE PIN THROUGH PLUG HOUSING AFTER ASSEMBLY.

SCREW WIRE RETAINERS TOGETHER OVER WIRES FROM OPPOSITE DIRECTIONS.

PLUG BASE

SOLDER WITH ROSIN-CORE SOLDER ONLY.

PLUG HOUSING

CUT OFF EXCESS OF SCREWS AFTER ASSEMBLY.

SCREW SOCKET INTO BULKHEAD

INSERT AND SOLDER WIRES TO TERMINALS.

5/8" HOLE DRILLED THROUGH BULK-HEAD

HOLE ELONGATED WITH RAT-TAIL FILE.

CHAPTER 4 Tender Topics

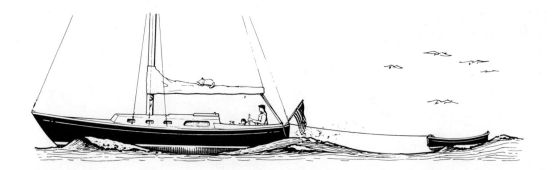

The Boat Boom

VERY OFTEN, I FIND THAT I HAVE TO ANCHOR IN AN AREA WITH CURRENTS. MY PERMANENT MOORING IN OYSTER BAY WAS CURRENT-SWEPT FOR THE BETTER PART OF EACH DAY, AND I'VE ENCOUNTERED STRONG CURRENTS IN ALMOST EVERY PLACE I'VE CRUISED.

NOW, IT ISN'T REALLY THE CURRENTS ALONE THAT I MIND. AFTER ALL, THEY DEVELOP ROWING PROFICIENCY. WHAT BOTHERS ME IS THE WIND THAT OCCASIONALLY BLOWS AGAINST THE CURRENT. IT INVARIABLY CREATES A NASTY LITTLE CHOP THAT SENDS THE GLASSES TO RATTLING IN THEIR RACKS. MORE IRRITATING IS THE INEVITABLE "CLUNK, SLAM, BANG" AS THE DINGHY CRASHES AGAINST MY SHINY TOPSIDES.

WELL, HAVING HAD TOO MANY NIGHTS OF SLEEP INTERRUPTED BY THIS GUNWALE SYMPHONY, I DECIDED TO SOLVE THIS PROBLEM ONCE AND FOR ALL.

THE FIRST APPROACH WAS SIMPLY TO TRAIL A SMALL SEA ANCHOR FROM THE DINK'S TRANSOM. THIS WORKED FINE ONLY AS LONG AS THE CURRENT WAS INDEED RUNNING. "SLAM, BANG" WOULD STILL OCCUR DURING SLACK WATER. I ALSO TRIED USING A BUCKET AS A DROGUE BUT IT DIDN'T WORK VERY WELL.

THE ULTIMATE SYSTEM FOR DINGHY TRAILING RESULTED IN THE USE OF A BOAT BOOM. IF SHIPS CAN USE 'EM, WHY CAN'T I?

THE BOAT BOOM ALLOWS THE DINGHY TO LIE IN WHATEVER DIRECTION SHE CHOOSES, REGARDLESS OF THE HEADING OF THE MOTHER SHIP. IT IS QUICKLY SET UP USING YOUR SPINNAKER POLE AND IS A PRACTICAL METHOD FOR REDUCING YOUR SWINGING ROOM IN TIGHT ANCHORAGES. ADDITIONALLY, IT IS VERY PROPER AND A MARK OF A YACHT.

MANY TIMES, ANCHORED IN STRANGE HARBORS WITH THE DINGHY ABOOM, THE BOATS AROUND ME SEEMED TO SPROUT SPINNAKER POLES. IT MUST SOLVE A COMMON PROBLEM.

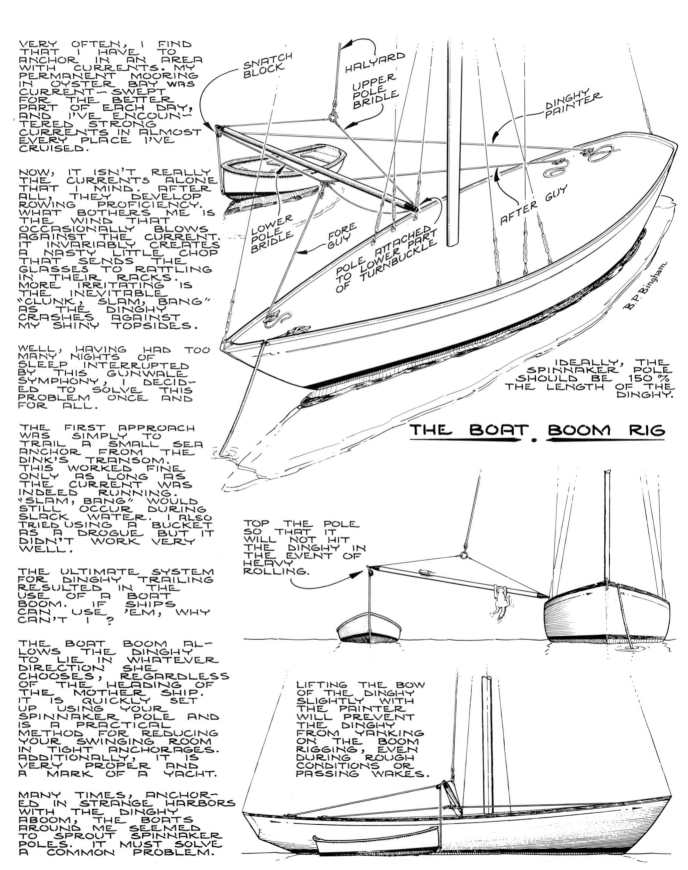

SNATCH BLOCK

HALYARD

UPPER POLE BRIDLE

DINGHY PAINTER

AFTER GUY

LOWER POLE BRIDLE

FORE GUY

POLE ATTACHED TO LOWER PART OF TURNBUCKLE

B.P. Bingham

IDEALLY, THE SPINNAKER POLE SHOULD BE 150% THE LENGTH OF THE DINGHY.

THE BOAT BOOM RIG

TOP THE POLE SO THAT IT WILL NOT HIT THE DINGHY IN THE EVENT OF HEAVY ROLLING.

LIFTING THE BOW OF THE DINGHY SLIGHTLY WITH THE PAINTER WILL PREVENT THE DINGHY FROM YANKING ON THE BOOM RIGGING, EVEN DURING ROUGH CONDITIONS OR PASSING WAKES.

Stepping Up

IF YOU ARE SHORT-LEGGED, HAVE BACK PROBLEMS, OR OWN A BOAT WITH VERY HIGH FREEBOARD, YOU MAY FIND IT DIFFICULT TO BOARD YOUR BOAT FROM A DINGHY. YOU MAY HAVE FREQUENT NON-SAILING GUESTS (PARTICULARLY OF THE LONG-SKIRTED VARIETY) THAT JUST CAN'T STEP OVER THE TOERAIL WITHOUT A HELPING HAND. PERHAPS YOU OWN A PET THAT IS TOO SMALL OR FRIGHTENED TO SUCCESSFULLY CLEAR THE BULWARK WITHOUT DESTROYING THE TEAK.

AN EASY SOLUTION TO THIS DILEMMA COULD BE AN ACCOMMODATION STEP OR PLATFORM. THEY'RE EASILY INSTALLED, INEXPENSIVE AND UNOBTRUSIVE. BEST OF ALL, THEY MAKE LIFE AFLOAT MUCH MORE CONVENIENT, ESPECIALLY IN A HEAVY CHOP.

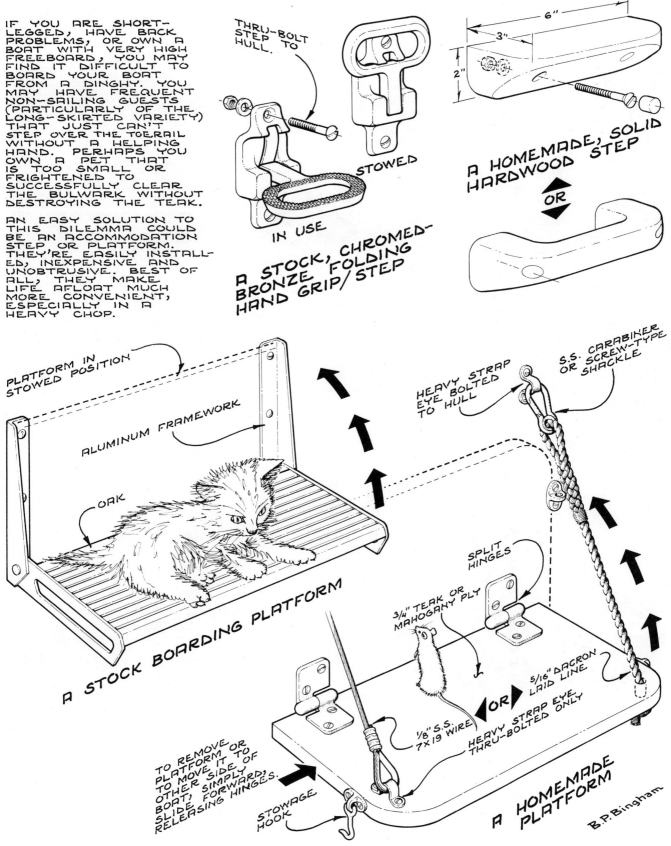

THRU-BOLT STEP TO HULL.

STOWED

IN USE

A STOCK, CHROMED-BRONZE FOLDING HAND GRIP/STEP

6"

3"

2"

A HOMEMADE, SOLID HARDWOOD STEP

OR

PLATFORM IN STOWED POSITION

ALUMINUM FRAMEWORK

OAK

A STOCK BOARDING PLATFORM

HEAVY STRAP EYE BOLTED TO HULL

S.S. CARABINER OR SCREW-TYPE SHACKLE

SPLIT HINGES

3/4" TEAK OR MAHOGANY PLY

5/16" DACRON LAID LINE

1/8" S.S. 7X19 WIRE

OR

HEAVY STRAP EYE THRU-BOLTED ONLY

TO REMOVE PLATFORM OR TO MOVE IT TO OTHER SIDE OF BOAT, SIMPLY SLIDE FORWARD, RELEASING HINGES.

STOWAGE HOOK

A HOMEMADE PLATFORM

B.P. Bingham

Tender Towing

BEFORE I BOUGHT *SAGA* (EQUIPPED WITH DAVITS), I'D SAILED AND POWERED 18,000 MILES AND EVERY INCH OF IT WHILE TOWING MY LITTLE, EIGHT-FOOT *TRINKA* DINGHY. ALTHOUGH A GOOD PART OF THIS WAS, INDEED, ON PROTECTED WATERS, ALMOST 9,000 MILES WERE RACKED UP ON OPEN OCEAN.

THE MOST HAIR-RAISING TRIP OF ALL OCCURRED WHILE SAILING OVER THE TOP OF *HURRICANE BELLE* IN 1976 ON A BROAD REACH ABOARD MY SCHOONER, *AT LAST*. SHE HAD ALL HER LOWERS SET AND AVERAGED TEN KNOTS FOR A SIX-HOUR PERIOD.

DURING THAT PASSAGE, THE TREMENDOUS SPEED CAUSED SUCH HIGH PRESSURES INSIDE THE CENTERBOARD TRUNK THAT THE CENTERBOARD COVER WAS BLOWN RIGHT OUT OF THE DINGHY. THE WATER POURED INTO HER AND SHE WAS SOON RIDING WITH HER BOW IN THE AIR. LUCKILY, SHE DIDN'T BROACH OR TURN TURTLE.

WITHIN THE WEEK, I INSTALLED AN AUTOMATIC TRANSOM BAILER OF THE RUBBER-VALVE TYPE. IT WORKED LIKE A CHARM AND I BELIEVE IT IS A MINIMUM REQUIREMENT.

THERE ARE, OF COURSE, OTHER TYPES OF BAILERS THAT WILL WORK EQUALLY WELL BUT MAY NOT BE AUTOMATIC-SHUTTING.

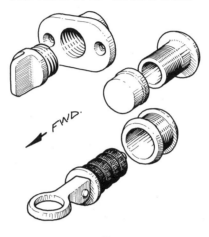

FWD.

OR

THIS TYPE OF MANUAL-SHUTTING BAILER MAY BE USED BUT MUST BE LOCATED AT THE AFTERMOST, LOWEST PART OF THE HULL. THIS MAY BE DIFFICULT.

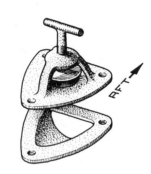

AFT

THEN THERE'S THE SEMIAUTOMATICALLY CLOSING, SMALL-BOAT, RACING BAILER. IT MUST ALSO BE PLACED ALL THE WAY AFT TO WORK.

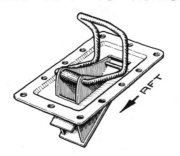

AFT

THE BAILERS I'VE SHOWN SO FAR ARE CAPABLE OF COMPLETELY PURGING AN EIGHT-FOOT DINGHY OF ALL WATER IN LESS THEN TEN MINUTES FROM A TOTAL SWAMPING. THIS IS ASSUMING THAT THE TOWING YACHT CAN MAINTAIN FIVE KNOTS WHEN THE DINGHY IS IN ITS DRY CONDITION.

THOSE TEN MINUTES ARE EXTREMELY LONG AND CRITICAL BECAUSE THE DINGHY WILL BE VERY TENDER AND THE PROGRESS OF THE YACHT VERY SLOW AT FIRST. FOR THE THREE OR FOUR MINUTES IMMEDIATELY FOLLOWING THE SWAMPING, THE DINGHY WILL BE IN DANGER OF CAPSIZING IF THE SEAS ARE ROUGH.

I RECOMMEND INSTALLING A RACING-DINGHY, TRAP-DOOR BAILER IN THE TRANSOM, AN INCH OR TWO ABOVE HER LOADED WATERLINE. THIS WILL RELIEVE THE DINGHY OF HUNDREDS OF POUNDS OF WATER IN LESS THAN A MINUTE.

A SMALL BAILER SHOULD ALSO BE USED TO DRAIN OFF THOSE LAST TEN GALLONS OR SO.

MOUNT BAILER AS LOW AS POSSIBLE IN TRANSOM.

Sabrina

AFT

Sabrina

B.P. Bingham

YOUR DINGHY'S NOT READY FOR OFFSHORE WORK YET. IF SHE'S A SAILING DINK, SECURELY PLUGGING THE CENTERBOARD TRUNK IS A MUST. THESE ARE THE METHODS I WOULD RECOMMEND:

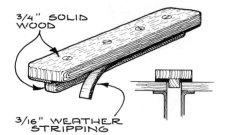

3/4" SOLID WOOD

3/16" WEATHER STRIPPING

OR BETTER

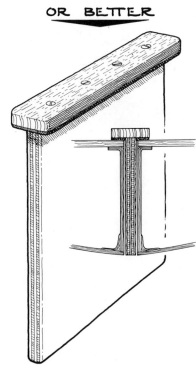

NOW, SECURE THE PLUG SO THAT IT CANNOT BECOME DISLODGED.

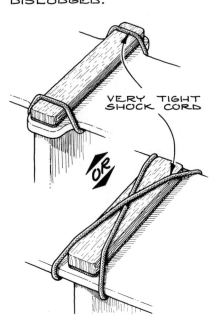

VERY TIGHT SHOCK CORD

OR

BEFORE TOWING YOUR DINGHY IN THE BIG STUFF, YOU'LL HAVE TO DO SOME WORK ON THE BOW EYE.

I HAVE SEEN VERY FEW BOW EYES THAT I WOULD REALLY TRUST FOR OPEN-OCEAN TOWING, INSOMUCH AS THE DINK MAY BE COMPLETELY FULL OF WATER FROM TIME TO TIME, CAPSIZED AT HIGH SPEEDS OR SURGING ON ITS PAINTER WITH HUNDREDS OF POUNDS OF FORCE. IF YOU EXPECT TO SEE YOUR DINGHY FROLICKING SAFELY ASTERN AT SUNRISE AFTER A STORMY NIGHT'S RIDE, CONSIDER THE FOLLOWING INSTALLATIONS:

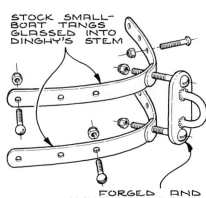

STOCK SMALL-BOAT TANGS GLASSED INTO DINGHY'S STEM

FORGED AND WELDED HEAVY-DUTY PAD EYE.

OR

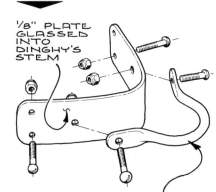

1/8" PLATE GLASSED INTO DINGHY'S STEM

STOCK, FORGED BOOM BALE BENT TO FIT DINGHY'S STEM

OR

5/16" S.S. ROD BENT, CUT AND THREADED

1½" HARDWOOD GLASSED INTO DINGHY'S STEM.

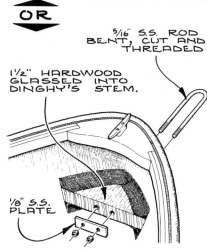

1/8" S.S. PLATE

THE FOREGOING EYE ARRANGEMENTS ARE OBVIOUSLY DESIGNED FOR FIBERGLASS DINGHIES. ALL OF THE PARTS ARE STAINLESS STEEL AND ONLY LOCK NUTS ARE USED.

BUT WHAT ABOUT THE TOWING EYE FOR A WOODEN DINGHY? WELL, THE EYE MUST NOT BE FASTENED TO THE STEM ALONE, (OR THE BOW PIECE ONLY IN THE CASE OF A PRAM). THIS COULD LOOSEN THE STEM TIMBER FROM THE HULL PLANKING OR TEAR THE BOW RIGHT OUT OF THE BOAT.

LET'S LOOK AT SOME SOLUTIONS:

WASHER PLATE

FORGED TIE RODS

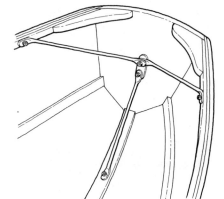

OR

WHATEVER THE TYPE OF DINGHY OR INSTALLATION YOU USE, THE TOWING EYE MUST BE OF A LARGE ENOUGH INSIDE DIAMETER TO RECEIVE TWO 3/8" PAINTERS OR TWO FORGED SNAP HOOKS OR SHACKLES.

WHILE I'M ON THE TOPIC OF TOWING EYES, I SHOULD VOICE MY OPINION THAT EVERY EYE I'VE EVER SEEN HAS BEEN IN- STALLED TOO LOW. THE IDEA MUST BE TO HELP LIFT THE DINGHY'S BOW WHEN UNERWAY.

WELL, MOST DINGHYS RIDE TOO BOW-HIGH WHEN THEY'RE FORCED BEYOND THEIR HULL SPEEDS. TOWING RESISTANCE IN THIS ATTITUDE CAN BE TREMENDOUS, AND STABILITY RE- DUCED SIGNIFIGANTLY.

EYE TOO LOW

TOWING RESISTANCE CAN BE REDUCED BY AS MUCH AS FIFTY PERCENT AND STABILITY INCREASED BY ENCOURAGING THE DINK TO RIDE NEAR ITS NATURAL FLOTATION PLANE. THIS IS PARTICULARLY TRUE WHEN SAILING VERY FAST OR RUN- NING IN PROTECTED WATERS. RAISING THE TOWING EYE WILL ACCOMPLISH THIS.

EYE JUST RIGHT

WHEN I AM SAILING OR MOTORING IN CALM CONDITIONS, I WILL REDUCE DINGHY DRAG EVEN FURTHER BY PASSING THE PAINTER UP AND AROUND THE BOW CLEAT, THUS LOWERING THE BOW EVEN MORE. THE BREAST HOOK AND CLEAT MUST BE VERY STRONGLY IN- STALLED TO WITH- STAND HEAVY JERKING.

PAINTER AROUND CLEAT

IF YOU DON'T THINK RAISING THE PAINT- ER'S POSITION WILL MAKE A DIFFERENCE, NOTE YOUR SPEED WITH IT IN ITS USUAL POSITION THEN MOVE IT TO THE CLEAT AND CHECK YOUR SPEED AGAIN. SURPRISE!

CERTAINLY, THE DAY WILL COME WHEN YOUR DINGHY WILL BE CAPSIZED, WHETH- ER BY HEAVY SEAS OR A LARGE WAKE. CHANCES ARE, IT WILL HAPPEN WHILE RUN- NING DOWNWIND OR ON A BROAD REACH.

NOT TO WORRY (TOO MUCH, ANYWAY)! A LOT CAN BE DONE BEFOREHAND TO MIN- IMIZE THE PROBLEM. YOU SURELY WOULD NOT TRY TO BRING HER ALONGSIDE OR GET INTO HER TO BAIL HER OUT. SHE'D JUST KEEP FILLING UP AGAIN. THE REMEDY IS TO LASH YOUR DOCKING FEND- ERS AMIDSHIP, ON TOP OF THE CEN- TER THWART. THIS WILL PROVIDE A LOW CENTER OF BUOYANCY (HENCE NEGATIVE STABILITY) WHEN THE DINGHY IS INVERTED. THE NEGATIVE STABILITY WILL CAUSE HER TO ROLL UPRIGHT, AND KEEP HER THERE WHILE SHE BAILS HERSELF OUT.

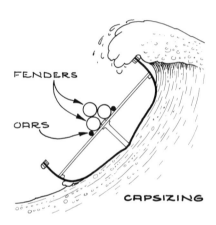

FENDERS

OARS

CAPSIZING

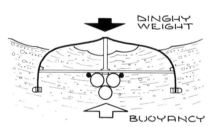

DINGHY WEIGHT

BUOYANCY

NEGATIVE STABILITY

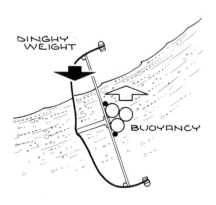

DINGHY WEIGHT

BUOYANCY

RIGHTING

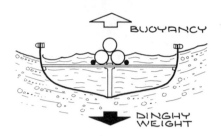

BUOYANCY

DINGHY WEIGHT

POSITIVE STABILITY REGAINED

THE ENTIRE CAPSIZE/ RIGHTING SEQUENCE TAKES ABOUT THREE MINUTES (TO THE POINT WHEN THE DINGHY IS BONE DRY). DURING THIS PERIOD, STEER A BEAM REACH FOR MAXIMUM POWER AND TO PREVENT NEW BREAKERS FROM ROLLING INTO THE DINKS STERN.

YOU ARE BEST TO TRUST IN THE DINGHY'S DYNAMICS UNDERWAY TO KEEP HER UPRIGHT WHILE SHE BAILS. BEAR OFF ONLY WHEN SHE'S EMPTY.

THE MOST DANGER- OUS CONDITION FOR TOWING A DINGHY IS DEAD DOWNWIND.

ONE SECOND THE DINGHY MAY COME SURFING DOWN A WAVE AT YOU AT SPEEDS IN EXCESS OF FIFTEEN KNOTS WHILE YOU STALL ON THE BACKSIDE OF THE PRECEDING WAVE. IF THE DINGHY SLAMS INTO YOUR TRANSOM... IT COULD BE CURTAINS FOR THE DINGHY. THIS PROBLEM CAN BE REPEATED AS MANY AS SEVERAL HUNDRED TIMES EVERY HOUR!

THE NEXT SECOND, YOUR YACHT BEGINS TO REGAIN HER SPEED AND, PERHAPS, SURF. THE DINGHY, ON THE OTHER HAND, NOW STALLS. THE TWO BOATS SEPARATE AT A TERRIFYING RATE UNTIL... WHAM! THE DINK FETCHES UP ON THE PAINT- ER AND IS YANKED FROM ZERO TO TEN KNOTS IN LESS THAN A WINK. THE FORCE OF THIS ACCELERATION CAN WRING THE WATER RIGHT OUT OF THE LINE, TEAR OUT HARD- WARE AND REDUCE YOUR DINGHY TO SPLINTERS.

DINGHY FREE-SURFING MUST BE ARRESTED AND THE PAINTER'S STRAIN STABILIZED. LET'S DISCUSS THIS IN DETAIL.

THERE ARE TWO BASIC ELEMENTS OF DOWNWIND DINGHY-SURGE CONTROL: THE USE OF DROGUES AND WAVE/PAINTER LENGTH ADJUSTMENT.

A DROGUE IS SIMPLY ANYTHING THAT CAN BE STREAMED BEHIND THE DINGHY TO INCREASE RESISTANCE TO THE DINGHY'S FORWARD MOTION. THE IDEA IS TO PREVENT THE DINGHY FROM TAKING OFF ON A WILD PLANE AS IT BEGINS TO HEAD DOWN THE FACE OF A WAVE. IT ALSO DECREASES THE TENDENCY OF THE DINGHY TO BROACH. A RELATIVELY UNIFORM STRAIN IS KEPT ON THE PAINTER AT ALL TIMES REGARDLESS OF OTHER INFLUENCES.

THE YACHT STALLS.

THE DINGHY SURFS. PAINTER GOES SLACK.

THE YACHT PICKS UP SPEED BUT...

THE DINGHY WALLOPS THE YACHT.

THE YACHT TAKES OFF ON A SURF.

THE DINGHY STALLS; LOOSENS THE YACHT'S TRANSOM; DISLODGES HELMSMAN.

YACHT/DINGHY INTERACTION WITHOUT DROGUE

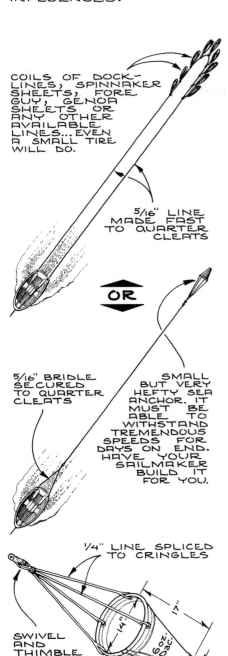

COILS OF DOCKLINES, SPINNAKER SHEETS, FORE GUY, GENOA SHEETS OR ANY OTHER AVAILABLE LINES...EVEN A SMALL TIRE WILL DO.

5/16" LINE MADE FAST TO QUARTER CLEATS

OR

5/16" BRIDLE SECURED TO QUARTER CLEATS

SMALL BUT VERY HEFTY SEA ANCHOR. IT MUST BE ABLE TO WITHSTAND TREMENDOUS SPEEDS FOR DAYS ON END. HAVE YOUR SAILMAKER BUILD IT FOR YOU.

1/4" LINE SPLICED TO CRINGLES

17"

14"

6 oz. Dac.

3"

SWIVEL AND THIMBLE

WELDED 1/4" STEEL-ROD HOOP

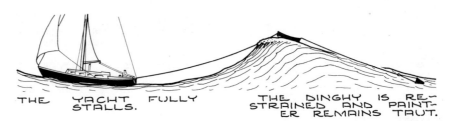

THE YACHT FULLY STALLS.

THE DINGHY IS RESTRAINED AND PAINTER REMAINS TAUT.

THE YACHT SURFS; HELMSMAN PRAYS.

DINGHY PLANES ON A TIGHT PAINTER.

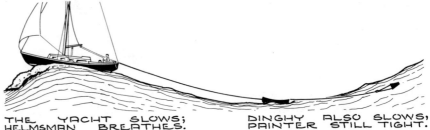

THE YACHT SLOWS; HELMSMAN BREATHES.

DINGHY ALSO SLOWS; PAINTER STILL TIGHT.

THE YACHT STALLS AGAIN.

THE DINGHY IS PREVENTED FROM SURFING FORWARD.

YACHT/DINGHY INTERACTION WITH DROGUE

WAVE/PAINTER LENGTH ADJUSTMENT CAN HAVE A GREAT EFFECT ON YOUR DINGHY'S SAFETY WHEN RUNNING DOWN-WIND IN ROUGH SEAS. THE PAINTER LENGTH HAS VERY LITTLE BEARING ON OTHER POINTS OF SAIL, HOWEVER.

THE TRICK IS TO ADJUST THE PAINTER LENGTH SO BOTH THE YACHT AND THE DINGHY SURF AND STALL AT THE SAME TIME. BY DOING SO, A RELATIVELY CONSTANT DISTANCE AND SPEED WILL BE MAINTAINED BETWEEN BOTH OF THE BOATS. IT WILL ALSO RETARD ALTERNATING SHOCKS AND SAGS OF YOUR PAINTER. AS YOU CAN SEE, A FULL WAVE LENGTH MUST BE KEPT BETWEEN THE YACHT AND DINGHY ON THE OPEN OCEAN. THIS COULD MEAN A TWO-HUNDRED FOOT PAINTER (OR PAIR OF PAINTERS).

WHEN SAILING OR RUNNING UNDER POWER IN PROTEC-TED WATERS, I'VE FOUND THAT YACHT SPEED CAN BE IN-CREASED AND FUEL SAVED IF THE DINGHY IS POSITION-ED SO THAT IT RIDES CONSTANTLY ON THE FORWARD SIDE OF THE YACHT'S STERN WAVE. THIS CAUSES THE DINGHY TO SURF BUT NOT QUITE FAST ENOUGH TO CATCH THE YACHT, THUS TOWING RE-SISTANCE IS MINIMAL.

ONLY NYLON SHOULD BE USED FOR PAINT-ERS BECAUSE OF ITS STRETCH CHARACTER-ISTICS: IT ACTS LIKE A SHOCK ABSORBER. 3/8" SEEMS TO BE THE IDEAL SIZE.

WHEN THE GOING GETS TOUGH, TWO PAINT-ERS SHOULD BE USED, EACH BEING MADE FAST TO THE OPPOSITE QUARTERS OF THE YACHT. THIS NOT ONLY PROVIDES A BACK-UP IF ONE OF THE PAINTERS GOES, BUT ALSO ENCOUR-AGES THE DINK TO TOW STRAIGHT.

ATTACHMENT TO THE DINGHY SHOULD BE BY LARGE BRONZE OR STAINLESS SNAP HOOKS, EYE-SPLICED AROUND THIMBLES TO THE PAINTERS.

CHAFING GEAR, CHOCKS OR POLISHED RUB RAILS SHOULD PROTECT THE PAINT-ERS WHERE THEY PASS OVER THE YACHT'S STERN.

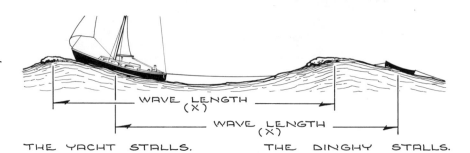

WAVE LENGTH (X)

WAVE LENGTH (X)

THE YACHT STALLS.   THE DINGHY STALLS.

THE YACHT SURFS.   THE DINGHY SURFS.

WAVE / PAINTER LENGTH ADJUSTMENT AT SEA

PEAK OF STERN WAVE

WAVE / PAINTER LENGTH ADJUSTMENT IN SMOOTH WATER

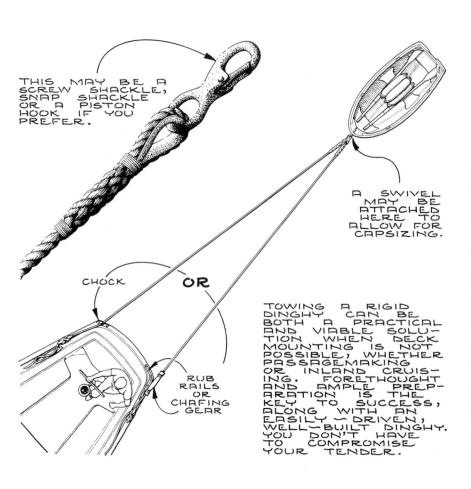

THIS MAY BE A SCREW SHACKLE, SNAP SHACKLE OR A PISTON HOOK IF YOU PREFER.

A SWIVEL MAY BE ATTACHED HERE TO ALLOW FOR CAPSIZING.

CHOCK   OR

RUB RAILS OR CHAFING GEAR

TOWING A RIGID DINGHY CAN BE BOTH A PRACTICAL AND VIABLE SOLU-TION WHEN DECK MOUNTING IS NOT POSSIBLE, WHETHER PASSAGEMAKING OR INLAND CRUIS-ING. FORETHOUGHT AND AMPLE PREP-ARATION IS THE KEY TO SUCCESS, ALONG WITH AN EASILY-DRIVEN, WELL-BUILT DINGHY. YOU DON'T HAVE TO COMPROMISE YOUR TENDER.

Boat Dangles

STERN DAVITS ARE ONE OF THE MOST LOGICAL SOLUTIONS TO DINGHY STOWAGE. I'VE SEEN THEM SUCCESSFULLY USED ON BOATS AS SMALL AS 27 FEET.

BUT, THERE'S MORE TO DAVITS THAN JUST BUYING A PAIR AND STICKING THEM ON. THERE ARE SOME QUESTIONS THAT SHOULD BE ADDRESSED AND SOLVED BEFORE SPENDING YOUR MONEY OR DRILLING BOLT HOLES:

- THE DAVITS MUST NOT STRAIN THEIR FASTENINGS OR THE DECK IF THE DINGHY SHOULD BECOME FILLED WITH WATER. SUCH MIGHT OCCUR WHEN POOPED BY A LARGE SEA OR DELUGED BY HEAVY RAIN.
- THE DAVITS MUST NOT BEND NOR MUST ANY OF THE LIFTING HARDWARE FAIL UNDER THE SAME CONDITIONS.
- DAVITS MUST NOT INTERFERE WITH SAILING OPERATIONS SUCH AS MAIN OR MIZZEN SHEETING.
- WILL DAVITS PRECLUDE A SELF-STEERING VANE?
- WILL DAVITS INTERFERE WITH DOCKING OR BOARDING? THEY MAY REQUIRE MOVING SOME EXISTING HARDWARE.
- WILL THE INSTALLATION OF DAVITS TURN THE BOAT'S STERN INTO AN UNMANAGEABLE MAZE OF PIPE AND CASTINGS TO THE DETRIMENT OF SAFE WORKING OR FOOTING?
- CAN THE DINGHY BE RAISED ENOUGH TO BE CLEAR OF THE QUARTER WAVE WHEN UNDER SAIL IN FOLLOWING SEAS?
- PROVISIONS MUST BE MADE TO PREVENT EVEN THE SLIGHTEST DINGHY MOVEMENT ON ALL PLANES DURING THE VERY WORST SEA CONDITIONS.
- IS THE SYSTEM STRONG ENOUGH TO ALLOW YOUR CRAWLING OUT TO SECURE DINGHY GEAR OR EMERGENCY BAIL?
- WILL YOUR BOAT LOOK ATTRACTIVE WITH DAVITS?

KEEP THESE POINTS IN MIND WHILE YOU LOOK AT THESE IDEAS.

MODERN BOATS WITH "STRAIGHTISH" LINES LOOK BEST WITH DAVITS CONSTRUCTED OF STRAIGHT LINES.

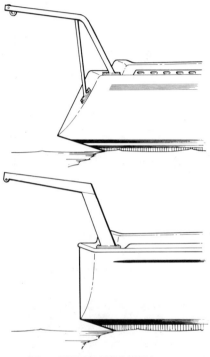

BUT, TRADITIONAL BOATS AND BOATS WITH MANY PRONOUNCED CURVES LOOK BETTER WITH CURVED DAVITS.

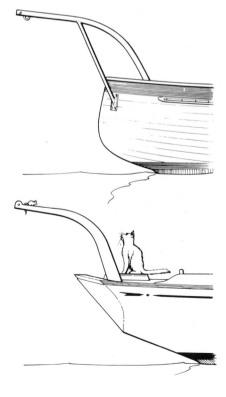

DAVITS MAY BE CONSTRUCTED OF BENT AND WELDED STAINLESS PIPE. YOU DO SEE DAVITS OF ORDINARY STEEL PIPE (GALVANIZED), BUT THAT STUFF IS PRETTY SOFT AND NOT VERY ELASTIC.

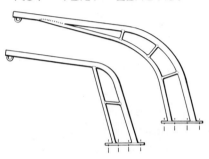

MOST STOCK DAVITS ARE OF CAST ALUMINUM. THAT'S OKAY.

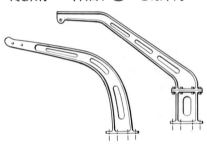

AND LAMINATED OR STEAMED WOOD CAN MAKE FINE DAVITS. ASH IS THE BEST BECAUSE IT TAKES GLUE WELL, DOESN'T BECOME BRITTLE LIKE OAK, WON'T TURN BLACK IF BARED AND IS VERY STRONG. ASH AND HONDURAS MAHOGANY ARE A GOOD COMBINATION BUT TEAK SHOULD BE AVOIDED. DON'T CONSIDER SOFT WOODS AT ALL.

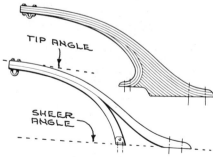

TIP ANGLE

SHEER ANGLE

THE ANGLE AT THE TIPS OF THE DAVITS SHOULD EQUAL OR EXCEED THE UPWARD RISE OF THE SHEER LINE. OTHERWISE THE DAVITS WILL APPEAR TO DROOP AS IF READY TO FALL OFF.

DAVITS MIGHT BE DE-
SIGNED OR MODIFIED
TO SERVE AS, AND
THUS ELIMINATE,
YOUR EXISTING STERN
PULPIT. THIS CAN GO
A LONG WAY TOWARD
KEEPING YOUR AFTER-
DECK CLEAN, CLEAR
AND FUNCTIONAL.

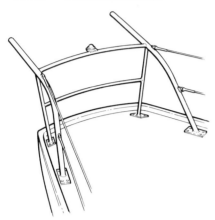

STOCK, CAST DAVITS
CAN ALSO SERVE A
DUAL FUNCTION AS
A PULPIT.

REGARDLESS OF THE
TYPE OF DAVITS YOU
INSTALL, BE SURE
THE TRICED-UP
DINGHY DOES NOT
OBSCURE THE STERN
LIGHT.

THE STRENGTH OF
DAVITS SHOULD NEVER
DEPEND ON DECK
FLANGES ALONE.
SOMETHING FAR MORE
SUBSTANTIAL MUST
BE DONE TO SUPPORT
EXTREME LOADING
AND WRENCHING THAT
MAY OCCUR.

ONE MEASURE IS
TO PROVIDE COM-
PRESSION STANCHIONS
UNDER THE DAVITS.

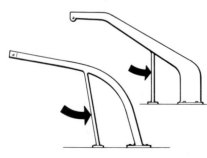

ANOTHER STEP THAT
WILL INCREASE DAVIT
STRENGTH GREATLY
IS TO CONNECT THE
OUTER DAVIT ENDS TO
THE MASTHEAD. THIS
IS DONE WITH 5/32",
1 X 19, STAINLESS RIG-
GING WIRE.

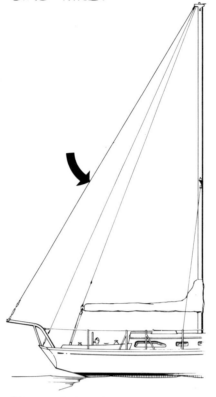

THE DAVIT STAYS MAY BE
TWO SEPARATE WIRES OR
MAY BE A "SPLIT BRIDLE".
NICOPRESS EYES OR
SWAGED TERMINALS MAY
BE USED. A TURNBUCKLE
SHOULD BE INSTALLED
AT EACH DAVIT.

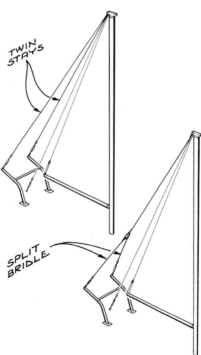

TWIN
STAYS

SPLIT
BRIDLE

DAVIT STAYS MAY, OF
COURSE, BE USED WITH
COMPRESSION STANCHIONS.

THE PERSON WHO SAID
"IF YOU HAVE DAVITS,
YOU CAN'T HAVE A
SELF-STEERING VANE,"
WAS SIMPLY LACKING
INGENUITY. IT DOES
REQUIRE ENGINEERING,
BUT IT CAN BE DONE.

NOW YOU'VE GOT YOUR
DAVITS INSTALLED, SO
LET'S MOVE ON TO THE
LIFTING HARDWARE.
LIFTING EYES MUST BE
FITTED TO THE DINGHY
AND THERE IS A SELEC-
TION OF SPECIAL AND
EXPENSIVE HARDWARE
ON THE MARKET JUST
FOR THIS PURPOSE.

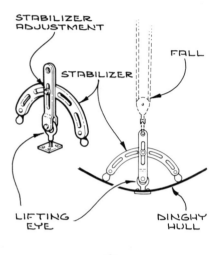

STABILIZER
ADJUSTMENT

FALL

STABILIZER

LIFTING
EYE

DINGHY
HULL

OR

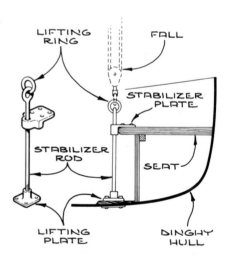

LIFTING
RING

FALL

STABILIZER
PLATE

STABILIZER
ROD

SEAT

LIFTING
PLATE

DINGHY
HULL

THE PURPOSE OF THE
STABILIZERS IS TO
PROVIDE A RIGID LIFT
POINT WELL ABOVE
THE DINGHY'S CENTER
OF GRAVITY, THUS
PREVENTING TIPPING
AND CAPSIZING ONCE
THE DINGHY IS OUT
OF THE WATER. THIS
IS ONE REASON THAT
SIMPLE EYE BOLTS
SHOULD NOT BE USED
AS LIFTING EYES.
THEY ALSO CONCEN-
TRATE THE DINGHY'S
LOAD ON TOO SMALL
AN AREA, RISKING
LOCAL HULL FRACTURE.

WHATEVER HARD-
WARE YOU USE, IT
SHOULD BE PROVIDED
WITH 1/8" (MINIMUM)
STAINLESS BACKING
PLATES... NOT JUST
WASHERS.

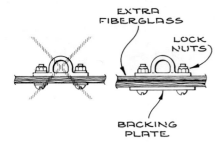

EXTRA
FIBERGLASS

LOCK
NUTS

BACKING
PLATE

A TWO-POINT LIFT SYS-
TEM MIGHT BE ALL
RIGHT IF YOU'RE ONLY
CRUISING INLAND AND ARE
SURE TO KEEP THE
DINGHY'S BILGE DRAIN
OPEN WHILE IT'S
TRICED UP.

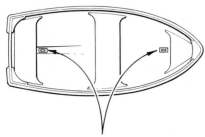

TWO-POINT LIFT
FOR LIGHT DUTY

BUT I STRONGLY RE-
COMMEND A FOUR-POINT
LIFT SYSTEM FOR
OFFSHORE SAILING. IT
GREATLY REDUCES THE
LOAD ON EACH OF THE
LIFTING EYES AND THE
SYSTEM CAN BE IN-
STALLED VERY INEX-
PENSIVELY BECAUSE NO
EXOTIC OR SPECIALLY
DESIGNED HARDWARE IS
USED. INSOMUCH AS
THE FOUR-POINT SYS-
TEM IS INHERENTLY
STABLE, THE DINGHY
WILL HAVE NO TENDENCY
TO CAPSIZE. AND, IF
ONE OF THE POINTS
SHOULD FAIL, THE
DINGHY WILL STILL BE
SUPPORTED BY BOTH
DAVITS.

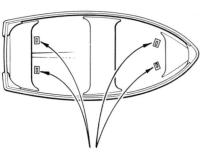

FOUR-POINT LIFT
FOR HEAVY DUTY

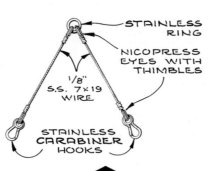

STAINLESS
RING

NICOPRESS
EYES WITH
THIMBLES

1/8"
S.S. 7x19
WIRE

STAINLESS
CARABINER
HOOKS

OR

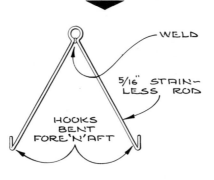

WELD

5/16" STAIN-
LESS ROD

HOOKS
BENT
FORE'N'AFT

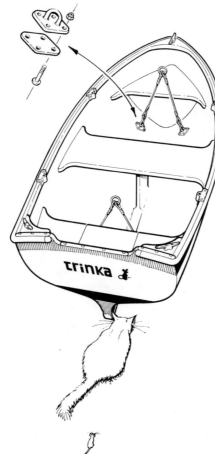

trinka

MOST DAVIT FALLS
(TACKLES) I'VE SEEN
ARE ONLY A 2:1 PUR-
CHASE CONSISTING OF
A PAIR OF SINGLE
BLOCKS. I THINK THIS
IS INADEQUATE, CON-
SIDERING THE WEIGHT
OF A FULLY EQUIPPED
DINGHY (FLOOR BOARDS,
OUTBOARD OR SAILING
GEAR, OARS, LIFE
JACKETS OR CUSHIONS,
BAILER, PAINTER AND

STERN LINE, ANCHOR,
FLARES, LANTERN,
FENDERS, ETC., ETC.).
SO, I PREFER A 4:1 OR
5:1 PURCHASE USING
DOUBLE BLOCKS, TOP
AND BOTTOM. ANYONE
CAN HOIST THE HEAV-
IEST DINGHY SINGLE
HANDED WITH THIS
MUCH POWER.

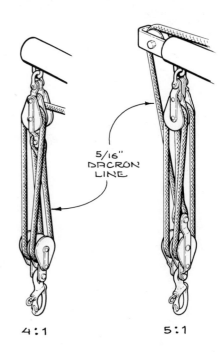

5/16"
DACRON
LINE

4:1   5:1

YOU'LL NOTICE THAT
THE SNAP SHACKLE IS
ALIGNED PERPENDIC-
ULARLY TO THE DAVIT.
DO NOT USE A CAST
SNAP HOOK... AND DO
NOT USE SWIVELING
BLOCKS OR SHACKLES
AS THESE WILL CAUSE
THE LINES TO TWIST
TOGETHER. OVER-AND-
UNDER FIDDLE BLOCKS
DON'T BELONG ON
DAVIT FALLS BECAUSE
THEY USE UP TOO
MUCH VERTICAL SPACE.

YOU CAN INSTALL CAM-
ACTION CLEATS OR
CLAMCLEATS® TO SUP-
PLEMENT THE FIXED TEE
CLEATS. THESE WILL
ALLOW YOU TO PAUSE
EASILY DURING THE
LIFTING. BUT DON'T
DEPEND ON THEM FOR
FINAL DINGHY SECURITY.
USE THE TEE CLEATS.

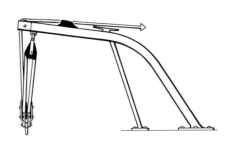

NOW, LET'S HOIST THE DINGHY AND SECURE IT FOR SEA. THE LATTER INVOLVES A COMBINATION OF MEASURES THAT PREVENT THE DINGHY FROM SWINGING WHEN THE SHIP ROLLS, PITCHES AND HEELS.

THE FIRST MEASURE IS TO SECURE THE DINGHY'S GUNWALE TO THE INBOARD REACHES OF THE DAVITS.

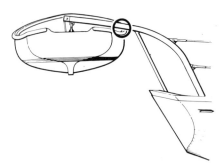

ONE VERY SIMPLE METHOD IS TO DRILL HOLES JUST BELOW THE DINGHY GUNWALE AT EACH DAVIT POSITION TO ALLOW THE PASSING OF LASHINGS.

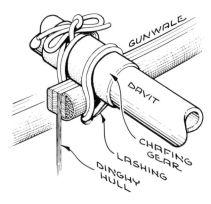

GUNWALE

DAVIT

CHAFING GEAR

LASHING

DINGHY HULL

ANOTHER APPROACH IS TO ATTACH STRAP EYES OR PAD EYES TO THE DINGHY HULL TO RECEIVE LASHINGS.

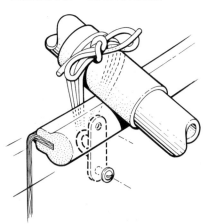

THESE LASHINGS SHOULD BE CINCHED UP VERY TIGHTLY WITH AS MANY PASSES AS PRACTICAL. THEY WILL HELP ABSORB SOME OF THE WEIGHT IF THE DINGHY TAKES ON WATER.

ANOTHER METHOD OF SECURING THE DINGHY GUNWALE TO THE DAVITS IS TO INSTALL STOCK OR CUSTOM FABRICATED DAVIT/GUNWALE CLAMPS. THEY ARE EXPENSIVE AND REALLY NO BETTER THAN LASHINGS, BUT YOU STILL MIGHT PREFER THEM.

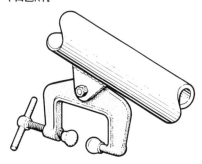

THE SECOND MEASURE FOR TRICING THE DINGHY UP TIGHT IS TO PASS TWO WIDE NYLON STRAPS (SUCH AS SAFETY-BELT WEBBING) OR 3/8" NYLON LINE UNDER THE DINGHY.

THESE STRAPS ARE PERMANENTLY FASTENED TO THE DAVIT ENDS, CRISS-CROSSED UNDER THE DINGHY, PULLED TIGHT, THEN SECURED TO CLEATS AT THE INBOARD ENDS OF THE DAVITS. THE STRAPS WILL ASSUME A LARGE PORTION OF THE DINGHY LOAD, RELIEVING THE FALLS AND RELATED FASTENINGS AND HARDWARE.

A COMPLETE DAVIT SYSTEM

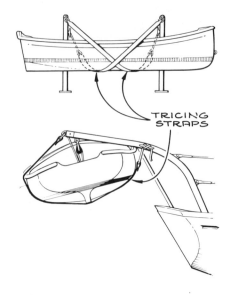

TRICING STRAPS

SOME ADDITIONAL POINTS:

● WHEN ATTACHING THE FALLS TO THE DINGHY, FASTEN THE FORWARD ONE FIRST.
● KEEP THE DINGHY'S BAILER OPEN WHENEVER THE DINGHY IS HOISTED.
● LOWER THE DINGHY'S STERN SLIGHTLY WHEN YOU LEAVE YOUR BOAT FOR A DAY OR MORE AND DURING RAINS. THIS WILL HELP IT DRAIN.
● A HEAVY, TIGHT, CANVAS DINGHY COVER WILL HELP KEEP OUT "THE BIG WATER".
● KEEP THE KIDDIES OUT OF THE HOISTED DINGHY. CATS ARE O.K!

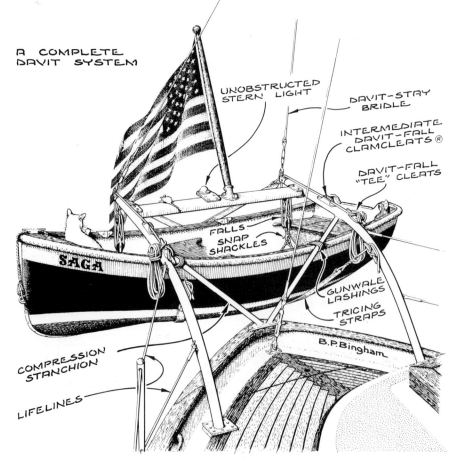

UNOBSTRUCTED STERN LIGHT

DAVIT-STAY BRIDLE

INTERMEDIATE DAVIT-FALL CLAMCLEATS®

DAVIT-FALL "TEE" CLEATS

FALLS SNAP SHACKLES

SAGA

GUNWALE LASHINGS

TRICING STRAPS

B.P.Bingham

COMPRESSION STANCHION

LIFELINES

CHAPTER 5 Hooks and Harbors

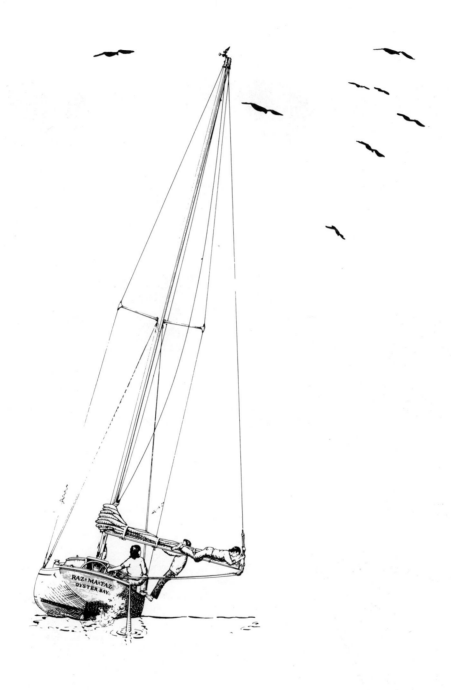

A Chain-Hook Pendant

IF YOUR BOAT HAS A BOWSPRIT, YOU HAVE PROBABLY BEEN JOLTED AWAKE BY THE SICKENING GRINDING SOUND OF THE ANCHOR CHAIN SAWING AWAY AT THE BOBSTAY.

RARELY IS ANY REAL HARM INCURRED, BUT IN A HARD BLOW WITH THE BOAT SAILING MADLY BACK AND FORTH, THE BOBSTAY TURNBUCKLE OR WIRE MAY BE DAMAGED. WORSE YET, A FIBER ANCHOR RODE COULD CHAFE THROUGH WITH DEVASTATING RESULTS.

A SOLUTION COULD BE THE USE OF A CHAIN-HOOK PENDANT.

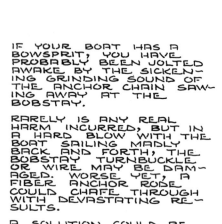

PAY OUT CHAIN TO CORRECT SCOPE AND DIG IN. PASS THE CHAIN-HOOK PENDANT THROUGH A BLOCK OR CHOCK AT THE END OF BOWSPRIT.

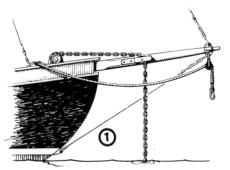

ATTACH THE CHAIN HOOK TO THE ANCHOR CHAIN; THEN MAKE THE PENDANT FAST TO A MOORING CLEAT.

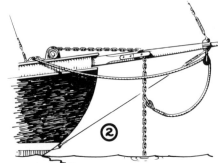

THIS MAY BE AT THE CHAIN-TO-RODE SHACKLE.

PAY OUT CHAIN, PLACING ALL OF THE STRAIN ON THE PENDANT.

CHAIN HOOK

CARABINER

◀ OR ▶

MAY BE PARCELED THEN SERVED WITH LEATHER AT POSITION OF ROLLER OR CHOCK.

SAME SIZE AS ANCHOR RODE

MAKE PENDANT AS LONG AS NECESSARY.

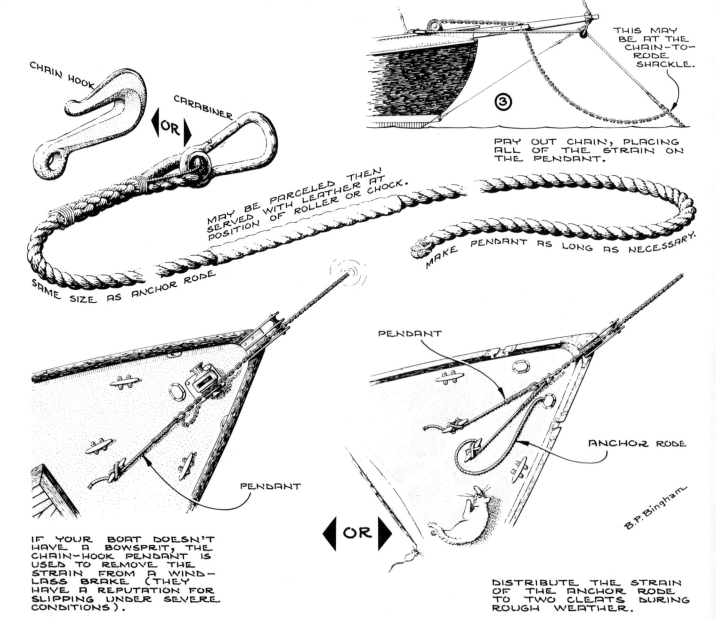

PENDANT

ANCHOR RODE

PENDANT

B.P. Bingham

IF YOUR BOAT DOESN'T HAVE A BOWSPRIT, THE CHAIN-HOOK PENDANT IS USED TO REMOVE THE STRAIN FROM A WINDLASS BRAKE (THEY HAVE A REPUTATION FOR SLIPPING UNDER SEVERE CONDITIONS).

◀ OR ▶

DISTRIBUTE THE STRAIN OF THE ANCHOR RODE TO TWO CLEATS DURING ROUGH WEATHER.

The Riding Sail

WHEN YOU LIVE PERPETUALLY ON THE HOOK AS I DO, YOU FULLY APPRECIATE THE STRAINS ON GROUND TACKLE AND ASSOCIATED DECK GEAR, ESPECIALLY WHILE RIDING OUT THOSE AWFUL WINTER GALES SO FREQUENT ALONG THE EAST COAST. THE ANCHOR RODE MOANS 'N' GROANS ALL NIGHT LONG. IT'S A WONDER I GET ANY SLEEP AT ALL.

BUT I HAVEN'T DONE BADLY. IT'S THE OTHER BOATS THAT WORRY ME, WHAT WITH THEIR SAILING BACK AND FORTH ON THEIR MOORINGS DURING A BLOW LIKE POOR CAGED ANIMALS WAITING FOR THE SLIGHTEST CHANCE TO BREAK FREE. I OFTEN WATCH THROUGH A PORT, AGHAST, AS EACH NEW WIND BLAST SHIFTS THE ANCHORED MASSES ONTO THE OPPOSITE TACK. ONCE IN A WHILE A BOAT CAN'T TAKE ANOTHER JOLTING YANK AND GOES RACING SHOREWARD.

IT DOESN'T HAVE TO BE THIS WAY. USE ADEQUATE TACKLE, KEEP IT IN GOOD SHAPE, APPLY CHAFING GEAR AND... HOIST YOUR RIDING SAIL.

KETCHES, SCHOONERS AND YAWLS ARE THE TRUE LADIES WHILE MOORED OR ANCHORED BUT EVEN THE MOST SUBDUED OF THEM IS TEMPTED TO GAD ABOUT A LITTLE ONCE IN A WHILE.

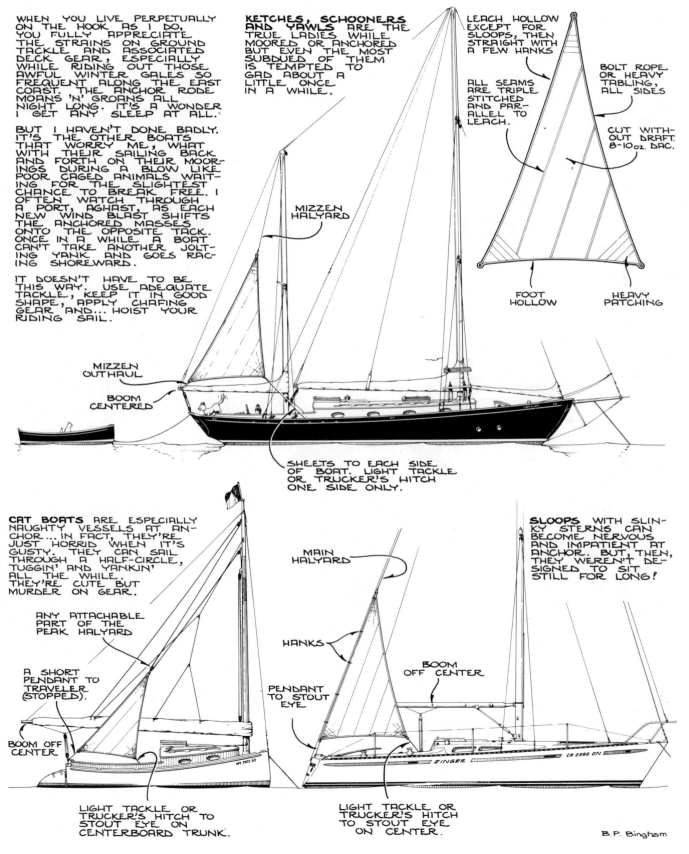

LEACH HOLLOW EXCEPT FOR SLOOPS, THEN STRAIGHT WITH A FEW HANKS

ALL SEAMS ARE TRIPLE STITCHED AND PARALLEL TO LEACH.

BOLT ROPE OR HEAVY TABLING, ALL SIDES

CUT WITHOUT DRAFT. 8-10 oz. DAC.

FOOT HOLLOW

HEAVY PATCHING

MIZZEN HALYARD

MIZZEN OUTHAUL

BOOM CENTERED

SHEETS TO EACH SIDE OF BOAT. LIGHT TACKLE OR TRUCKER'S HITCH ONE SIDE ONLY.

CAT BOATS ARE ESPECIALLY NAUGHTY VESSELS AT ANCHOR... IN FACT, THEY'RE JUST HORRID WHEN IT'S GUSTY. THEY CAN SAIL THROUGH A HALF-CIRCLE, TUGGIN' AND YANKIN' ALL THE WHILE. THEY'RE CUTE BUT MURDER ON GEAR.

ANY ATTACHABLE PART OF THE PEAK HALYARD

A SHORT PENDANT TO TRAVELER (STOPPED).

BOOM OFF CENTER

LIGHT TACKLE OR TRUCKER'S HITCH TO STOUT EYE ON CENTERBOARD TRUNK.

MAIN HALYARD

HANKS

PENDANT TO STOUT EYE

BOOM OFF CENTER

LIGHT TACKLE OR TRUCKER'S HITCH TO STOUT EYE ON CENTER.

SLOOPS WITH SLINKY STERNS CAN BECOME NERVOUS AND IMPATIENT AT ANCHOR. BUT, THEN, THEY WEREN'T DESIGNED TO SIT STILL FOR LONG!

B.P. Bingham

Safer Rafting Rules

RAFTING CAN BE A MISERABLE EXPERIENCE, HOWEVER PLEASANT THE INTENTIONS. IT CAN RESULT IN SQUEAKING FENDERS, VIOLENTLY CLASHING MASTS AND RIGGING, BROKEN SPREADERS, GRINDING OF TONS OF HULLS, SPLINTERED TOERAILS AND GOUGED TOPSIDES. AN ERSTWHILE PLEASANT EVENING CAN BECOME

A RESTLESS NIGHT WITH AN UNSCHEDULED VOYAGE DOWNSTREAM, TERMINATING ABRUPTLY ON THE NEAREST LEE SHORE.

ON THE OTHER HAND, RAFTING CAN BE A JOYOUS OR ROMANTIC RENDEZVOUS ACCOMPANIED BY CLOSENESS, COMFORT AND CONFIDENCE.

THE DIFFERENCE BETWEEN DEVASTATING AND SUCCESSFUL RAFTING CAN BE THE ATTENTION PAID TO A FEW SIMPLE DETAILS. I HATE TO USE THE WORD "RULES", BUT IT'S APPROPRIATE HERE.

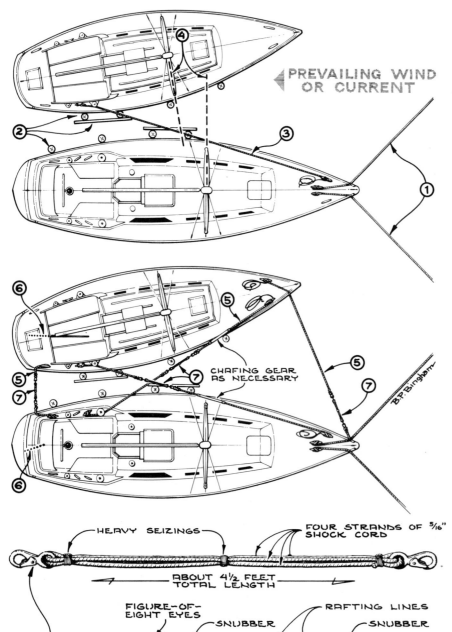

PREVAILING WIND OR CURRENT

CHAFING GEAR AS NECESSARY

B.P.Bingham

HEAVY SEIZINGS — FOUR STRANDS OF 5/16" SHOCK CORD

ABOUT 4½ FEET TOTAL LENGTH

NO. 2 BRONZE SNAP HOOK OR 3/16" STAINLESS CARABINER HOOK AT EACH END

FIGURE-OF-EIGHT EYES

RAFTING LINES

SNUBBER   SNUBBER

◀ OR ▶

① CHECK THE LATEST LOCAL WEATHER FORECAST TO ANTICIPATE WIND SHIFTS AND STRENGTHS DURING THE RAFTING PERIOD. IF THE CONDITIONS ARE FAVORABLE, THE LARGEST VESSEL SETS **TWO** ANCHORS FOR THE STRONGEST WIND/CURRENT DIRECTION.

② BOTH VESSELS RIG FENDERS **AND** FENDER BOARDS IN ALTERNATING POSITIONS. EACH FENDER BOARD SHOULD BE "SANDWICHED" BETWEEN THE FENDERS OF EACH VESSEL. THIS WILL DOUBLE THE GAP BETWEEN THE VESSELS AT TIMES OF CLOSE ENCOUNTERS.

③ THE MOST IMPORTANT LINE, A SPRING LINE FROM THE QUARTER OF THE SMALLER VESSEL TO THE BOW OF THE LARGER VESSEL, IS MADE FAST.

④ ADJUST THIS SPRING LINE SO THAT THE RIGGING AND MASTS CANNOT HIT OR TANGLE EACH OTHER.

⑤ SECURE THE BOW, STERN, AND SECOND SPRING LINES SO THE VESSELS DIVERGE AT 10°–15°. THIS WILL HELP KEEP THE VESSELS SEPARATE.

⑥ SECURE THE HELMS OF EACH VESSEL TO STEER THEMSELVES AWAY FROM EACH OTHER. IT ONLY TAKES ONE UNEXPECTED WAKE TO CAUSE SERIOUS DAMAGE, SO **KEEP THE VESSELS APART!**

⑦ ATTACH SHOCK CORD OR RUBBER SNUBBERS TO ALL LINES TO ABSORB ROLL, PITCH AND SURGE LOADS. THIS WILL ELIMINATE JERKS AND STRAINS.

Clear The Foredeck!

THE CONVENIENCE OF AN ON-DECK ANCHOR WELL GOES UNQUESTIONED. FLUSH STOWAGE PREVENTS THE SNAGGING OF SHEETS, SAILS AND HALYARDS. IT ALSO HELPS TO CLEAR THE FOREDECK OF DANGEROUS MECHANICAL OBSTACLES THAT HAVE BEEN KNOWN TO FOUL THE BEST CREWMAN AT NIGHT OR DURING NASTY GOING.

BUT AN ANCHOR WELL NEED NOT BE ONLY FOR GROUND TACKLE. IT MAY SERVE AS A STOWAGE PLACE FOR THE SEA ANCHOR AND ITS RODE, DOCK LINES OR BUMPERS, A TURTLE FOR THE SPINNAKER, A NEST FOR SCUBA EQUIPMENT OR A HANDY NOOK FOR SAIL COVERS AND GASKETS.

HENCE, A FOREDECK WELL MAY JUST TAKE ADVANTAGE OF OTHERWISE WASTED SPACE, THUS MAKING YOUR BOAT A MITE BIT LARGER. AND WHO CAN'T USE THAT?

REMOVE THE BOW PULPIT, CLEATS OR ANY OTHER HARDWARE THAT WOULD IMPAIR THE USE OF A SABER SAW OR THE INSTALLATION OF THE WELL HATCH SILLS.

FROM UNDER THE DECK, DRILL A VERY SMALL HOLE 4" FORWARD OF THE FORE-MOST BULKHEAD. THIS WILL LOCATE THE AFTER-MOST WELL CUT-LINE ON DECK.

NOW DRAW THE WELL OPENING ON THE DECK. ALLOW AT LEAST 2½" FROM THE OPENING TO ANY HARDWARE FASTENINGS. ROUND ALL CORNERS LIBERALLY.

CUT THE OPENING USING A SABER SAW WITH A FINE-TOOTH BLADE. REMOVE THE NEW HATCH TOP.

ON THE INSIDE OF THE HULL, ESTABLISH THE BOTTOM OF THE WELL. IT MAY BE SLANTED OR HORIZONTAL. MARK THE WELL BOTTOM ON THE HULL AND THE FORWARD BULKHEAD. DRAW A CONTINUOUS LINE ½" BELOW THE MARKS TO SHOW THE POSITION OF THE "CLEATING".

REMOVE ALL GELCOAT OR PAINT 2" ABOVE AND 3½" BELOW THE CLEAT POSITIONS AS IT WILL BE RECEIVING FIBERGLASS A LITTLE LATER.

CUT LENGTHS OF FIR CLEATING SUCH AS THOSE SHOWN BELOW. THE UPPER SURFACES MUST BE HORIZONTAL. THE LENGTHS MAY BE CUT INTO SMALLER PIECES TO ACCOMMODATE THE CURVE OF THE HULL.

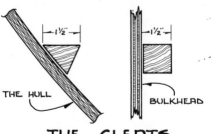

THE HULL

BULKHEAD

THE CLEATS

GLUE THE SQUARE CLEAT TO THE BULKHEAD AND SCREW FASTEN IT FROM BEHIND. "TACK" THE HULL CLEATS INTO POSITION WITH "MINUTE" EPOXY. COVER THEM WITH A LAYER OF 1oz GLASS MAT AND 18oz ROVING. USE POLYESTER BONDING RESIN. OVERLAP THE FIBERGLASS 2" ONTO THE HULL.

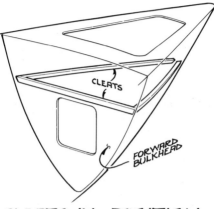

CLEATS

FORWARD BULKHEAD

CLEATS IN POSITION

FROM ½" PLYWOOD, FASHION THE BOTTOM OF THE WELL. IT MAY BE NECESSARY TO CUT THE BOTTOM INTO TWO PIECES IN ORDER TO GET IT THROUGH THE WELL OPENING. IN SUCH A CASE, YOU WILL HAVE TO "BUTT BLOCK" THE JOINT WITH A 6" WIDE PIECE OF PLY APPLIED FROM THE UNDERSIDE. USE GLUE AND SCREWS AFTER THE BOTTOM HAS BEEN FASTENED TO THE CLEATS.

FASTEN THE WELL BOTTOM TO THE CLEATS WITH FLAT HEAD SCREWS.

FILL THE GAPS BETWEEN THE WELL BOTTOM AND HULL WITH A POLYESTER "PUTTY".

NOW APPLY A LAYER OF 1½ oz GLASS MAT TO THE WELL BOTTOM AND THE EXPOSED BULKHEAD PLY. ALLOW THE GLASS TO OVERLAP ONTO THE HULL ABOUT 2½". USE POLYESTER RESIN.

FASHION THE "SILL" FROM ½" x 2" SOLID FIR OR FIR PLY. THE SILL SHOULD EXTEND INBOARD OF THE OPENING ½". THE OUTBOARD EDGE OF THE SILL MUST BE BEVELED 45° TO ACCOMMODATE FIBERGLASS TAPING MORE EASILY.

APPLY THICKENED EPOXY TO THE UPPER SIDE OF THE SILL. THEN CLAMP IT TO THE UNDERSIDE OF THE DECK. WITH THE SAME EPOXY, SEAL THE EXPOSED EDGES OF THE DECK LAMINATE AS WELL AS THE HATCH COVER.

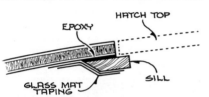

HATCH TOP

EPOXY

SILL

GLASS MAT TAPING

THE HATCH SILL

DRILL SEVERAL ⅜" HOLES THROUGH THE HULL AT THE WELL BOTTOM FOR DRAINAGE. NOW AFFIX TWO HARDWOOD HATCH TOGGLES ON THE DECK ON EACH SIDE OF THE OPENING. USE BOLTS, LOCK NUTS AND LARGE WASHERS UNDER THE TOGGLES.

A STOCK CHAIN PIPE FITTING MAY BE FASTENED THROUGH THE WELL BOTTOM OR A SHORT SECTION OF PIPE MAY BE FIBERGLASSED THROUGH THE PLYWOOD LEADING TO THE CHAIN LOCKER.

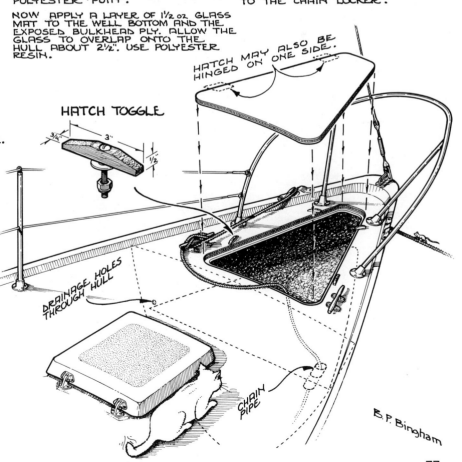

HATCH MAY ALSO BE HINGED ON ONE SIDE.

HATCH TOGGLE

DRAINAGE HOLES THROUGH HULL

CHAIN PIPE

B.P. Bingham

Anchors Away

THIS ISN'T A LESSON ON "PROPER" ANCHORING TECHNIQUES NOR A LECTURE ON THE SUPERIORITY OF ONE TYPE OF ANCHOR OVER ALL OTHERS. I'LL LEAVE SUCH RANTING TO THOSE MORE QUALIFIED SEAMEN ENDOWED BY THE **GREAT DESIGNER** WITH FLAWLESS INSIGHT AND NAUTICAL OMNISCIENCE.

MY OWN BOAT CARRIES THREE DIFFERENT TYPES, AND I LOVE THEM ALL, BUT USUALLY ONE MORE THAN THE OTHERS AS THE CIRCUMSTANCES CHANGE. I'VE FOUND THAT THE ANCHORS AND METHODS THAT WORK IN ROCKY MAINE DON'T NECESSARILY WORK IN MUDDY MISSISSIPPI, SANDY FLORIDA OR THE GRASSY GREAT LAKES. FURTHER, THE WEEKEND SAILOR WHO JUST WANTS TO KEEP HIS BOAT IN PLACE LONG ENOUGH TO ENJOY A COOLING SWIM, DOESN'T GIVE A HOOT ABOUT RIDING OUT A GALE IN 30 FATHOMS OFF A LEE SHORE.

SOONER OR LATER, HOWEVER, ALL SAILORS MUST PULL THEIR HOOKS AND STOW THEM SECURELY.

CLEARING THE DECK OF GROUND-TACKLE SNAGS THAT ORDINARILY TEAR SAILS, BREAK TOES AND CATCH SHEETS. THEY MIGHT ALSO BE USED TO STOW DOCK LINES AND POSSIBLY FENDERS. AN ANCHOR WELL MAKES AN EXCELLENT SPINNAKER LAUNCHER WHEN CLEARED OF OTHER GEAR.

UNFORTUNATEY, FEW STOCK-YACHT WELLS CAN RECEIVE ANYTHING LARGER THAN A MODERATE "LUNCH HOOK".

PULPIT ANCHOR BRACKETS

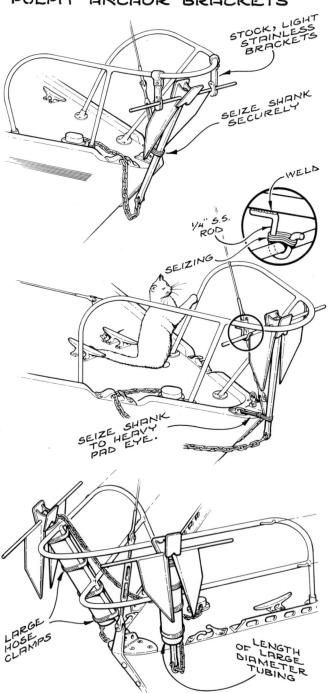

STOCK, LIGHT STAINLESS BRACKETS

SEIZE SHANK SECURELY

WELD

1/4" S.S. ROD

SEIZING

SEIZE SHANK TO HEAVY PAD EYE.

LARGE HOSE CLAMPS

LENGTH OF LARGE DIAMETER TUBING

ANCHOR WELLS

ANCHOR WELLS ARE USUALLY DESIGNED TO ACCOMMODATE LIGHTWEIGHT ANCHORS ONLY. THEY HAVE THE ADVANTAGE OF

CHAIN PIPE MAY BE INSIDE WELL.

NOTCH FOR RODE EXIT WITH HATCH CLOSED

WELL MUST HAVE OVERBOARD DRAINS.

INSTALL-IT-YOURSELF, STOCK, VERTICAL WELL FROM SAILING SPECIALTIES, Inc. FOR SMALL LIGHTWEIGHT ANCHORS

THE DYNAMICS OF A BOW-PULPIT HUNG
ANCHOR SLAMMING INTO WAVES ARE SO
FORMIDABLE THAT THEY LEAVE LITTLE
DOUBT THAT, SOONER OR LATER,
DAMAGE TO THE PULPIT OR DISLODGING
OF THE ANCHOR WILL OCCUR. THEREFORE,
BOW-PULPIT BRACKETS SHOULD BE CON-
SIDERED ONLY FOR LIGHT CRUISING AND
WEEKENDING. THE STOCK BRACKETS,
ESPECIALLY, SHOULD NOT BE USED IF
ROUGH, OFFSHORE WAVES ARE TO BE
ENCOUNTERED. ALTERNATIVELY, THE
ANCHOR SHOULD BE SECURED SAFELY
ELSEWHERE DURING QUESTIONABLE
WEATHER. HOW ABOUT STOWAGE AFT?

DECK STOWAGE

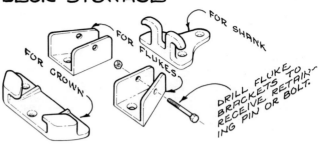

FOR SHANK

FOR FLUKES

FOR CROWN

DRILL FLUKE
BRACKETS TO
RECEIVE RETAIN-
ING PIN OR BOLT.

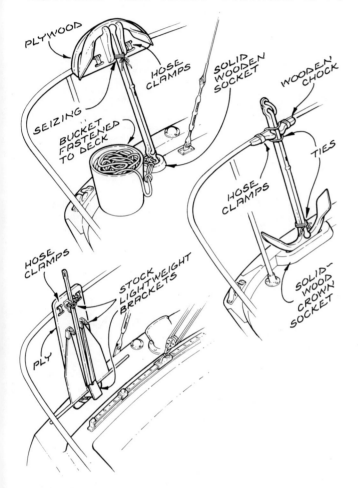

PLYWOOD

SEIZING

HOSE
CLAMPS

SOLID WOODEN
SOCKET

WOODEN
CHOCK

BUCKET
FASTENED
TO DECK

TIES

HOSE
CLAMPS

HOSE
CLAMPS

STOCK
LIGHTWEIGHT
BRACKETS

PLY

SOLID-
WOOD
CROWN
SOCKET

STOCK, LIGHT-
WEIGHT ANCHOR
BRACKETS

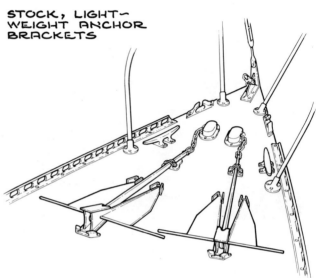

ANCHORS BRACKETED FLAT ONTO THE
FOREDECK IS ONE OF THE MOST
POPULAR STOWAGE METHODS. IT IS
CERTAINLY A CONVENIENT SETUP.
BUT, THERE IS A DANGER OF
SNAGGING SAILS AND IT MAKES
FOOTING EXTREMELY AWKWARD.

LIFELINE MOUNTING

WITH ALL OF THE FOREGOING PULPIT
MOUNTING METHODS, YOU MUST KEEP
AN EYE ON SHEETS AND SAILS SO
THEY WILL NOT GET HUNG UP. IF
THIS SEEMS VERY LIKELY, YOU'D
BETTER CONSIDER ANOTHER SYSTEM.

IT'S POSSIBLE TO BRACKET A LIGHT-
WEIGHT ANCHOR TO THE LIFELINE.

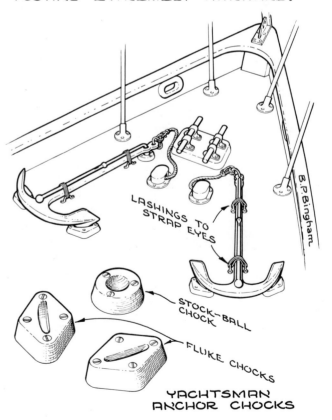

LASHINGS TO
STRAP EYES

B.P.Bingham

STOCK-BALL
CHOCK

FLUKE CHOCKS

YACHTSMAN
ANCHOR CHOCKS

OF COURSE, THERE'S NO RULE THAT
SAYS YOU CAN'T MIX THE TYPES OF
ANCHORS ON YOUR FOREDECK!

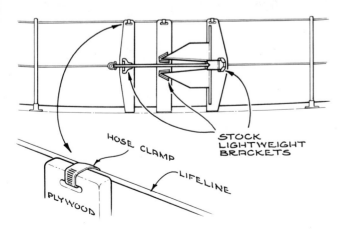

HOSE CLAMP

STOCK
LIGHTWEIGHT
BRACKETS

LIFELINE

PLYWOOD

CABIN-TOP STOWAGE

THE STOWAGE OF A SECOND OR THIRD ANCHOR ON THE CABIN TOP DOES MAKE SENSE. IT HELPS TO CLEAR THE FOREDECK, IT CENTRALIZES ITS POSITION IN CASE IT MIGHT BE USED AS A STERN KEDGE AND IT'S READILY AVAILABLE FOR PORT OR STARBOARD USE. THE DRAWBACKS ARE THAT IT NOW CLUTTERS THE CABIN TOP, MAY CATCH HEADS'L SHEETS AND HALYARDS AND RAISES THE CENTER OF GRAVITY.

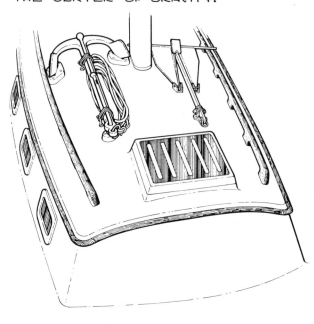

TO HELP PREVENT HALYARDS AND SHEETS FROM FOULING CABIN-TOP OR FOREDECK-MOUNTED ANCHORS, YOU MIGHT CONSIDER SNAP-DOWN CANVAS ANCHOR COVERS.

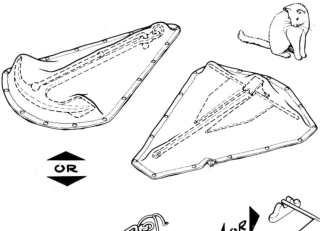

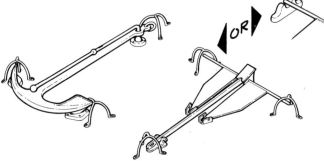

COMPASS-TYPE, STAINLESS CAGES CAN BE INSTALLED TO COVER PRO-TRUDING ANCHOR PARTS...THE USUAL SNAG POINTS. WOODEN BLOCKS MAY ALSO BE FASHIONED TO SERVE THE SAME PURPOSE.

BOW ROLLERS

THERE ARE SO MANY STYLES OF BOW-ROLLER SYSTEMS THAT I'VE CHOSEN TO BREAK THEM DOWN INTO CLASSES. THE FIRST IS **STEM ROLLERS**. STEM ROLLERS ARE NOT INSTALLED INTO A PLATFORM OR BOWSPRIT AND ARE USUALLY POSITIONED ON ONE OR BOTH SIDES OF THE STEMHEAD/JIB-TACK FIT-TING ON MANY STOCK BOATS.

STEM ROLLERS ARE NOT A CURE-ALL, NOR ARE THEY COMPATIBLE WITH ALL SIZES AND TYPES OF ANCHORS. IN FACT, SOME DESIGNS ARE USELESS, PARTICULARLY THOSE INSTALLED ON MANY STOCK YACHTS.

MOST OFTEN, TWO ROLLERS ARE FABRICATED AS AN INTEGRAL PART OF THE STEMHEAD FITTING. THE ROLLERS ARE USUALLY VERY SMALL, THE SIDE PLATES TOO CLOSE TO-GETHER TO ALLOW THE PASSAGE OF SHACKLES AND THIMBLES, AND ARE OF TOO LIGHT A MATERIAL TO WITHSTAND ANCHORING STRAINS. RARELY IS AN ANCHOR/RODE RE-TAINING SYSTEM PROVIDED, AND SHARP METAL CHAFING EDGES SEEM TO BE THE RULE.

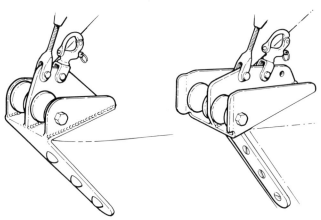

YOU CAN CLEARLY SEE THAT THESE STOCK STEMHEAD/ROLLER FITTINGS WILL SURELY CAUSE THE ANCHORS TO HIT THE HULL. THE ROLLERS ARE JUST TOO FAR AFT...

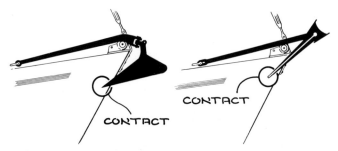

AND, THE ROLLERS ARE TOO CLOSE TOGETHER FOR TWO ANCHORS!

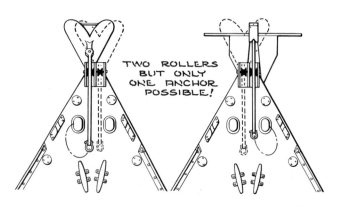

TWO ROLLERS BUT ONLY ONE ANCHOR POSSIBLE!

ONE SOLUTION MIGHT BE TO SETTLE WITH THE ROLLER STOWAGE OF ONLY ONE ANCHOR, HOUSED FAR ENOUGH FORWARD SO AS NOT TO GOUGE THE BOAT'S STEM. THIS MAY ENTAIL A CUSTOM FABRICATION SPECIFICALLY DESIGNED FOR YOUR BOAT AND THE ANCHOR.

IF YOU INTEND TO HOUSE TWO AN-CHORS IN TWIN STEM ROLLERS, THEY MUST BE WELL SEPARATED. WHEN LAYING OUT SUCH AN ARRANGEMENT CONSIDER THE LEADS OF ANCHOR RODES AND DOCK LINES AND THE POSITIONS OF OTHER HARDWARE.

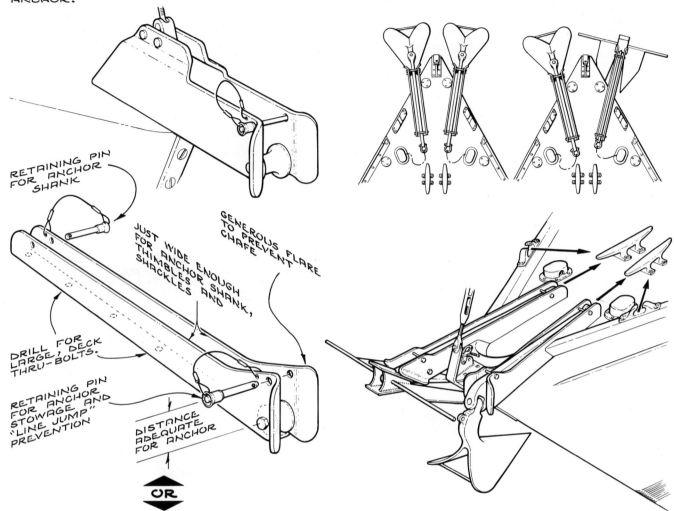

RETAINING PIN FOR ANCHOR SHANK

JUST WIDE ENOUGH FOR ANCHOR SHANK, THIMBLES AND SHACKLES AND

GENEROUS FLARE TO PREVENT CHAFE

DRILL FOR LARGE, DECK THRU-BOLTS.

RETAINING PIN FOR ANCHOR STOWAGE AND "LINE JUMP" PREVENTION

DISTANCE ADEQUATE FOR ANCHOR

OR

YOU MIGHT GET AWAY WITH A HEAVY, WELL-BUILT, STOCK ROLLER UNIT. TAKE YOUR ANCHOR AND SHACKLES WITH YOU WHEN PURCHASING TO MAKE SURE EVERYTHING FITS.

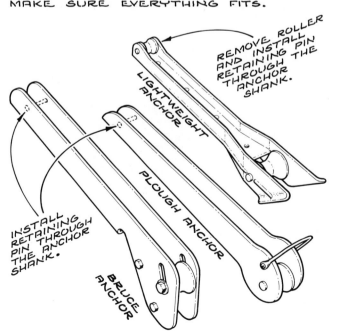

REMOVE ROLLER AND INSTALL RETAINING PIN THROUGH THE ANCHOR SHANK.

LIGHTWEIGHT ANCHOR

PLOUGH ANCHOR

INSTALL RETAINING PIN THROUGH THE ANCHOR SHANK.

BRUCE ANCHOR

ROLLER PLATFORMS

ANOTHER SOLUTION TO STEM-ROLLER PROBLEMS IS TO INSTALL A ROLLER PLATFORM. IF THE PLATFORM IS KEPT RELATIVELY SHORT, THERE WILL BE NO STRUCTURAL JINX. BUT, IF YOU GET GREEDY BY IN-STALLING A LONG PLATFORM, YOU WILL RISK STRAINING THE DECK, PLATFORM FASTENINGS AND THE PLATFORM ITSELF. THE LONGER THE PLATFORM, THE GREATER WILL BE THE LOADS ON IT, HENCE THE NEED FOR STIFFENING.

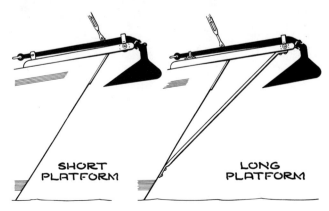

SHORT PLATFORM

LONG PLATFORM

IF A PLATFORM IS TO BE BUILT OF WOOD, USE ONLY THE BEST LUMBER YOU CAN BUY: NO KNOTS, NO SQUIRRELLY GRAIN, NO CHECKS OR SAP POCKETS. A HARDWOOD IS PREFERRED SUCH AS ASH, OAK OR TEAK, BUT HONDURAS MAHOGANY IS ALSO GOOD. **DON'T** USE GENERAL-CONSTRUCTION LUMBER.

THE LONGER THE PLATFORM, THE WIDER THE AFT END SHOULD BE TO SPREAD OUT AND ACCOMMODATE MORE FASTENINGS.

RELOCATE EXISTING DECK HARDWARE AS NECESSARY TO INSTALL A REALLY GOOD PLATFORM. YOUR BOAT'S SAFETY WILL HANG ON IT SO DON'T COMPROMISE.

AN ANCHOR-ROLLER PLATFORM MAY ALSO BE BUILT WITH A STOCK ROLLER FABRICATION.

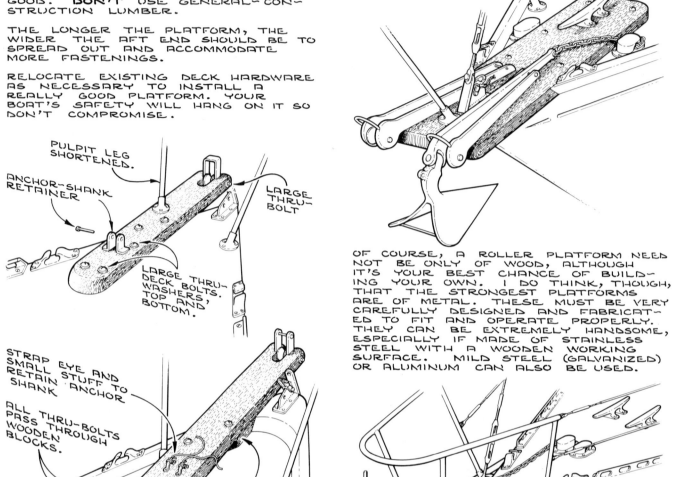

PULPIT LEG SHORTENED.

ANCHOR-SHANK RETAINER

LARGE THRU-BOLT

LARGE THRU-DECK BOLTS. WASHERS, TOP AND BOTTOM.

STRAP EYE AND SMALL STUFF TO RETAIN ANCHOR SHANK

ALL THRU-BOLTS PASS THROUGH WOODEN BLOCKS.

SOLID WOODEN BLOCKS TO RAISE PLATFORM TO TOERAIL

OF COURSE, A ROLLER PLATFORM NEED NOT BE ONLY OF WOOD, ALTHOUGH IT'S YOUR BEST CHANCE OF BUILDING YOUR OWN. I DO THINK, THOUGH, THAT THE STRONGEST PLATFORMS ARE OF METAL. THESE MUST BE VERY CAREFULLY DESIGNED AND FABRICATED TO FIT AND OPERATE PROPERLY. THEY CAN BE EXTREMELY HANDSOME, ESPECIALLY IF MADE OF STAINLESS STEEL WITH A WOODEN WORKING SURFACE. MILD STEEL (GALVANIZED) OR ALUMINUM CAN ALSO BE USED.

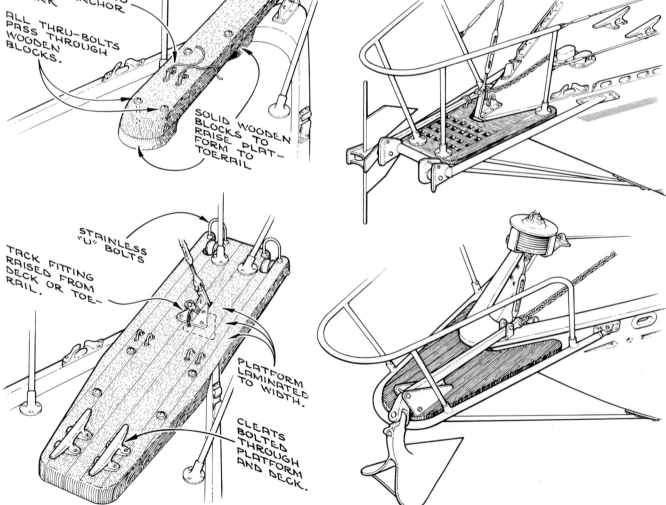

STAINLESS "U" BOLTS

TACK FITTING RAISED FROM DECK OR TOE-RAIL.

PLATFORM LAMINATED TO WIDTH.

CLEATS BOLTED THROUGH PLATFORM AND DECK.

BOWSPRIT ROLLERS

BOWSPRITS ARE AS USEFUL FOR STOWING ANCHORS AS THEY ARE FOR HANGING HEADSTAYS. ANY BOAT WITH A BOWSPRIT HAS A BUILT-IN GROUND-TACKLE ASSET THAT CAN BE USED TO THE FULLEST.

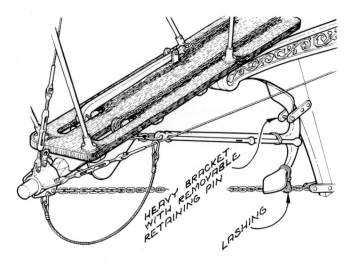

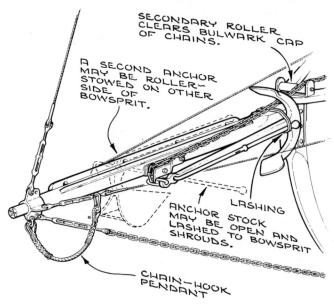

SECONDARY ROLLER CLEARS BULWARK CAP OF CHAINS.

A SECOND ANCHOR MAY BE ROLLER-STOWED ON OTHER SIDE OF BOWSPRIT.

ANCHOR STOCK MAY BE OPEN AND LASHED TO BOWSPRIT SHROUDS.

LASHING

CHAIN-HOOK PENDANT

HEAVY BRACKET WITH REMOVABLE RETAINING PIN

LASHING

THERE ARE AS MANY BOWSPRIT-ROLLER ARRANGEMENTS AS THERE ARE TYPES OF BOWSPRITS. WHATEVER STYLE YOU CHOOSE, THE SAME PREMISES HOLD AS FOR ALL OTHER ROLLER SYSTEMS: AVOID POSSIBLE CHAFE ON THE ROLLER EDGES OR METAL FABRICATIONS; PROVIDE FOR AN ANCHOR RETAINING MECHANISM; INSTALL ROLLERS FAR ENOUGH APART SO THAT TWO ANCHORS WON'T INTERFERE WITH EACH OTHER; MAKE YOUR SYSTEM STRONG ENOUGH TO WITHSTAND REPEATED SLAMMING INTO VIOLENT SEAS. ADDITIONALLY, PROVIDE A METHOD OF CHAFE PROTECTION TO PREVENT DAMAGE TO THE RODE BY THE BOBSTAY.

OF COURSE, NOT ALL BOWSPRITS ARE OF A TRADITIONAL TYPE OR OF ONLY WOOD. AS WITH PLATFORMS, THEY MAY BE OF METAL OR OF METAL/WOOD COMPOSITE.

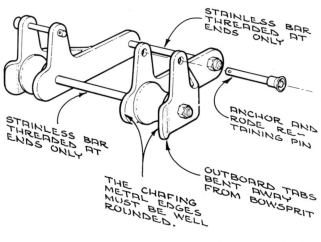

STAINLESS BAR THREADED AT ENDS ONLY

STAINLESS BAR THREADED AT ENDS ONLY

ANCHOR AND RODE RETAINING PIN

OUTBOARD TABS BENT AWAY FROM BOWSPRIT

THE CHAFING METAL EDGES MUST BE WELL ROUNDED.

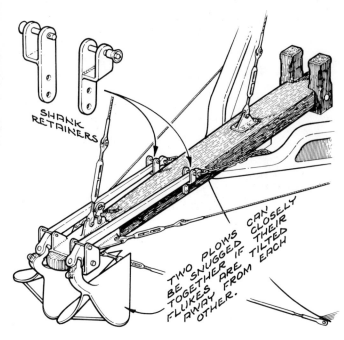

SHANK RETAINERS

TWO PLOWS CAN BE SNUGGED CLOSELY TOGETHER IF THEIR FLUKES ARE TILTED AWAY FROM EACH OTHER.

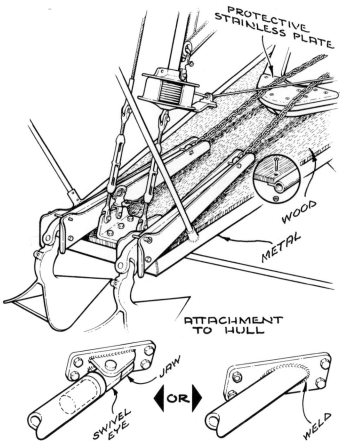

PROTECTIVE STAINLESS PLATE

WOOD

METAL

ATTACHMENT TO HULL

JAW

OR

SWIVEL EYE

WELD

STOWAGE ALTERNATIVES

HERE ARE A FEW MORE IDEAS TO CONSIDER.

HOW ABOUT INSTALLING HAWSE PIPES?

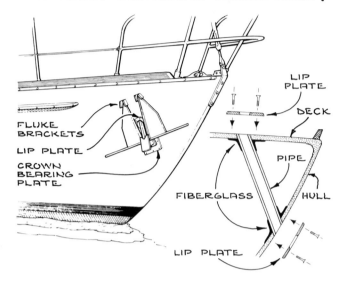

FLUKE BRACKETS
LIP PLATE
CROWN BEARING PLATE
FIBERGLASS
LIP PLATE
DECK
PIPE
HULL
LIP PLATE

YOUR TRANSOM MIGHT BE A HANDY PLACE FOR A SECOND OR STERN ANCHOR.

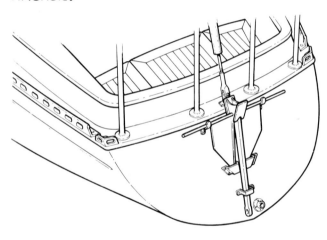

A SECOND ANCHOR MIGHT ALSO FIND A PLACE SUSPENDED FROM THE UNDER-SIDE OF YOUR FOREDECK, A SPACE OF LITTLE VALUE FOR ANYTHING ELSE.

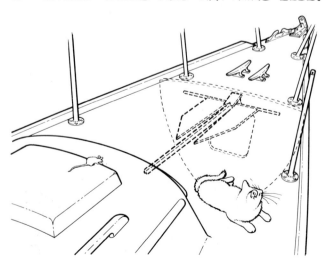

IF YOU'RE LUCKY, YOU MIGHT RUN ACROSS A "HERRESHOFF" ANCHOR. IF YOU DO, GRAB IT, EVEN IF IT NEEDS REGALVANIZING. THESE WONDERFUL ANCHORS LOOK AND HOLD LIKE A "YACHTSMAN" ANCHOR BUT CAN BE DISASSEMBLED AT THE CROWN. THIS ALLOWS THE ARMS AND FLUKES TO BE ALIGNED WITH THE STOCK AND SHANK OR SEPARATED FOR EASY STOWAGE INSIDE THE BOAT.

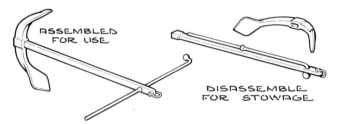

ASSEMBLED FOR USE

DISASSEMBLE FOR STOWAGE

ONE OF THE PROBLEMS WITH DECK OR BELOW-DECK STOWAGE OF LIGHTWEIGHT ANCHORS IS THAT THE STOCK (CROSS PIPE) TAKES UP A LOT OF SPACE AND CAUSES SNAGS. WITH A LITTLE BIT OF WORK, THE STOCK MAY BE MADE REMOVABLE.

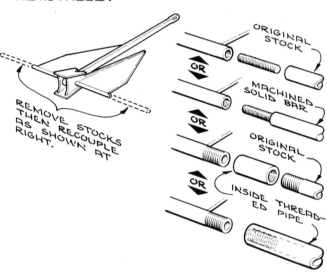

REMOVE STOCKS THEN RECOUPLE AS SHOWN AT RIGHT.

ORIGINAL STOCK
MACHINED SOLID BAR
ORIGINAL STOCK
INSIDE THREAD-ED PIPE

AN ANCHOR SHOULD BE KEPT IN YOUR DINGHY, BUT IT DOESN'T HAVE TO BOUNCE AROUND, CLUTTER OR GET UNDER FOOT. TRY THESE IDEAS:

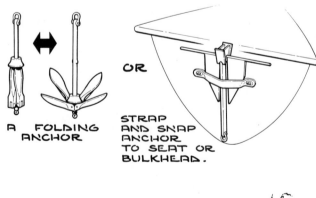

A FOLDING ANCHOR

OR

STRAP AND SNAP ANCHOR TO SEAT OR BULKHEAD.

Bumper Boards

ANYONE WHO'S EVER DONE THE WATERWAY KNOWS THE SCARCITY OF FLOATING DOCKS IN TIDAL AREAS. ON THE I.C.W., BUMPER BOARDS ARE AN ABSOLUTE NECESSITY TO PREVENT HULL SCARRING FROM ROUGH PILINGS. FOR THAT MATTER, BUMPER BOARDS (ALSO CALLED FENDER BOARDS) ARE DESIRABLE ON ANY BOAT THAT FREQUENTLY DOCKS AGAINST VERTICAL TIMBERS.

THE SIMPLE BUMPER BOARDS SHOWN HERE CAN BE FABRICATED IN LESS THAN AN HOUR. EVERY BOAT OUGHT TO HAVE A PAIR.

BOARDS MAY BE OF TEAK OR MAHOGANY BUT A GOOD GRADE OF KNOT-FREE, KILN-DRIED FIR 2×4 WORKS JUST AS WELL AT A FRACTION OF THE COST.

ALL EDGES OF THE BOARDS SHOULD BE WELL ROUNDED.

THE LOWER PENDANT KNOTS MAY BE "LET IN" FLUSH BY COUNTERBORING THE PENDANT HOLE WITH A 1" BIT.

A VARNISHED BOARD LOOKS BETTER THAN A PAINTED ONE AND DOESN'T SHOW GRIME AS READILY.

BOARDS SHOULD BE 4-5 FEET FOR USE WITH TWO BUMPERS BUT MAY BE LONGER IF THREE BUMPERS ARE USED.

BE SURE THAT NO SHARP SCREW HEADS PROTRUDE THAT MIGHT CAUSE SCRATCHES WHEN BEING STOWED. FILE DOWN THE FASTENINGS IF NECESSARY.

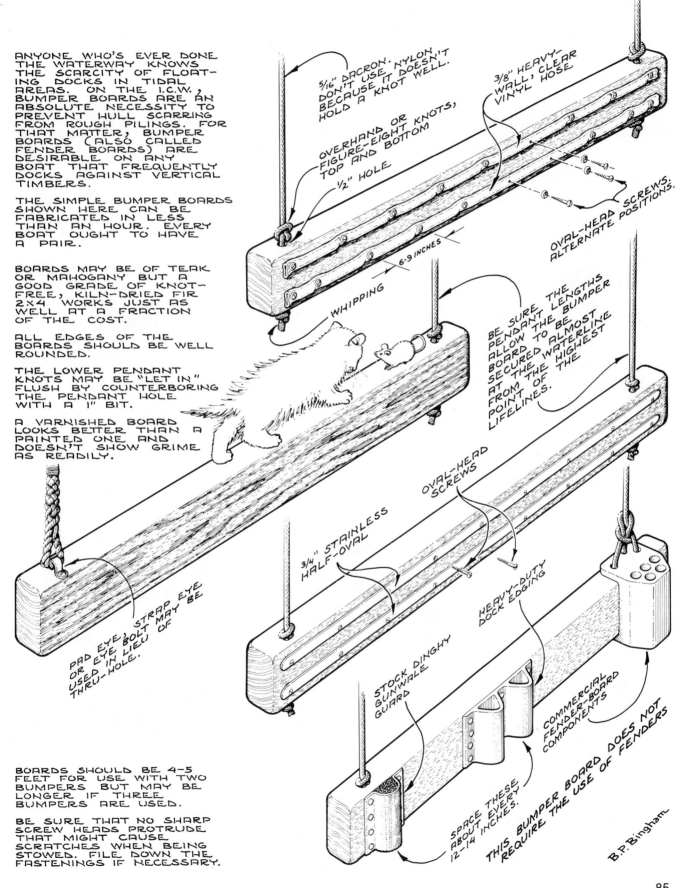

5/16" DACRON. DON'T USE NYLON BECAUSE IT DOESN'T HOLD A KNOT WELL.

3/8" HEAVY-WALL, CLEAR VINYL HOSE

OVERHAND OR FIGURE-EIGHT KNOTS, TOP AND BOTTOM

1/2" HOLE

OVAL-HEAD SCREWS; ALTERNATE POSITIONS.

6-9 INCHES

WHIPPING

BE SURE THE PENDANT LENGTHS ALLOW THE BUMPER BOARD TO BE SECURED ALMOST AT THE WATERLINE FROM THE HIGHEST POINT OF THE LIFELINES.

PAD EYE, STRAP EYE OR EYE BOLT MAY BE USED IN LIEU OF THRU-HOLE.

3/4" STAINLESS HALF-OVAL

OVAL-HEAD SCREWS

HEAVY-DUTY DOCK EDGING

STOCK DINGHY GUNWALE GUARD

COMMERCIAL FENDER-BOARD COMPONENTS

SPACE THESE ABOUT EVERY 12-14 INCHES.

THIS BUMPER BOARD DOES NOT REQUIRE THE USE OF FENDERS

B.P.Bingham

An "Earth-Shaking" Idea

EVERY SUNDAY, FRIENDS AND I WOULD SPEND SOME LEISURELY TIME IN A RESTAURANT AT THE OPENING OF THE SANTA BARBARA HARBOR. IF WE WERE LUCKY, WE COULD WATCH AS MANY AS THREE OR FOUR GROUNDINGS IN AN HOUR, AS THE AFTERNOON SAILING TRAFFIC ATTEMPTED TO NAVIGATE THE MUCKY SHOALS AT THE CHANNEL'S BEND.

SOME OF THE GROUNDINGS WERE ACTUALLY HILARIOUS AS SAILORS REVVED THEIR ENGINES IN REVERSE AND RAN TO AND FRO ON DECK AMIDST CLOUDS OF SMOKE AND FOUL LANGUAGE. THE GREATEST COMEDIES OCCURRED DURING THE PANIC OF AN EBBING TIDE.

BUT I REALIZE THAT GROUNDING IS NOT MUCH OF A LAUGHING MATTER, HAVING BEEN THOROUGHLY STUCK IN THE WATERWAY AT LEAST A GROSS OF TIMES MYSELF.

SO, TO THOSE SOULS IN SANTA BARBARA (AND ELSEWHERE) WHO REGULARLY BECOME CAPTIVES OF THEIR OWN DEEP DRAFT, I OFFER THE FOLLOWING SUGGESTIONS:

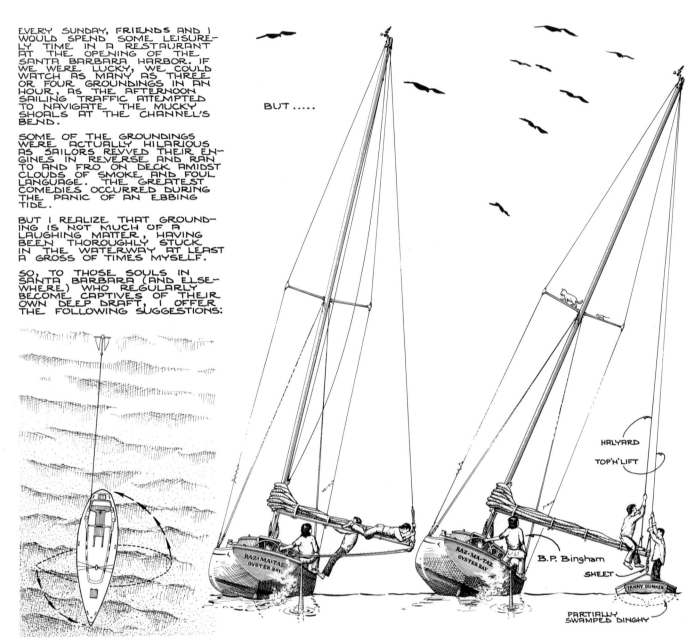

BUT.....

HALYARD

TOP'N'LIFT

B.P. Bingham

SHEET

PARTIALLY SWAMPED DINGHY

RAZ-MA-TAZ OYSTER BAY

FANNY DUNKER

SET OUT A KEDGE ANCHOR AS FAR AS POSSIBLE INTO THE DIRECTION OF THE SWELLS OR WAVES (WHICHEVER HAVE THE MOST INFLUENCE ON THE BOAT'S MOTION). LEAD THE WARP TO A BOW CHOCK THEN TO YOUR MOST POWERFUL WINCH. TAKE UP ON THE WARP, TRYING TO PULL THE BOW UP-SEA (YOUR ENGINE WILL PRODUCE MORE POWER IN FORWARD GEAR). IF YOU JUST CAN'T SWING THE BOW, DON'T WASTE TIME. TRANSFER THE WARP TO A QUARTER CHOCK AND HORSE THE STERN UP-SEA.

WITH YOUR ENGINE IN GEAR AND REVVING AT A SAFE SPEED, WINCH A HEAVY STRAIN ONTO THE WARP, KEEPING YOUR RUDDER 'MIDSHIP. THE BOAT WILL PROBABLY SLIDE OFF THE BAR.

IF SHE DOESN'T BUDGE:

PUT YOUR HEAVIEST CREWMAN ATOP THE EXTREME END OF THE BOOM AND SWING HIM OUTBOARD. CONTINUE REVVING THE ENGINE WHILE TAKING A STRAIN ON THE KEDGING WARP. ROLL THE BOAT IF POSSIBLE. SHE SHOULD WORK HER WAY OFF NOW.

BUT....

IF SHE'S STILL STUCK FAST, UNSHACKLE THE LOWER END OF THE MAIN SHEET AND FASTEN IT TO A ROPE BRIDLE SLUNG UNDER YOUR DINGHY. PLACE YOUR CREW INTO THE DINGHY. SWING THE BOOM OUTBOARD THEN HAUL AWAY ON THE SHEET. NOW REV THE ENGINE WHILE TAKING UP ON THE WARP. THIS TIME YOUR BOAT SHOULD SLIDE FREE.

BUT.... IF SHE DOESN'T GO:

FLOOD THE DINGHY! (HOPE YOU HAVE A STRONG TOP'N'LIFT. IT MAY BE SUPPLEMENTED WITH THE MAIN HALYARD PASSED AROUND THE BOOM'S END.) NOW, HAUL AWAY AGAIN.

YEA! I THINK SHE'S MOVIN'! THERE SHE GOES! YEA, YEA!

FOLLOWING THESE STEPS, YOU WILL BE ABLE TO ROLL A 35 FOOTER RIGHT ONTO HER BEAMS, REDUCING DRAFT BY WELL OVER A FOOT OR MORE.

THE "BOOM ROUTINE" HAS BEEN SUCCESSFUL IN 100 PERCENT OF MY OWN GROUNDINGS, EVEN SNAGGING A BOAT OFF A FLORIDA SURF BEACH, ONCE. BUT, **WORK FAST**. IT'S THE KEY.

CHAPTER 6 Gingerbread

Charlie Tinker's New Boat

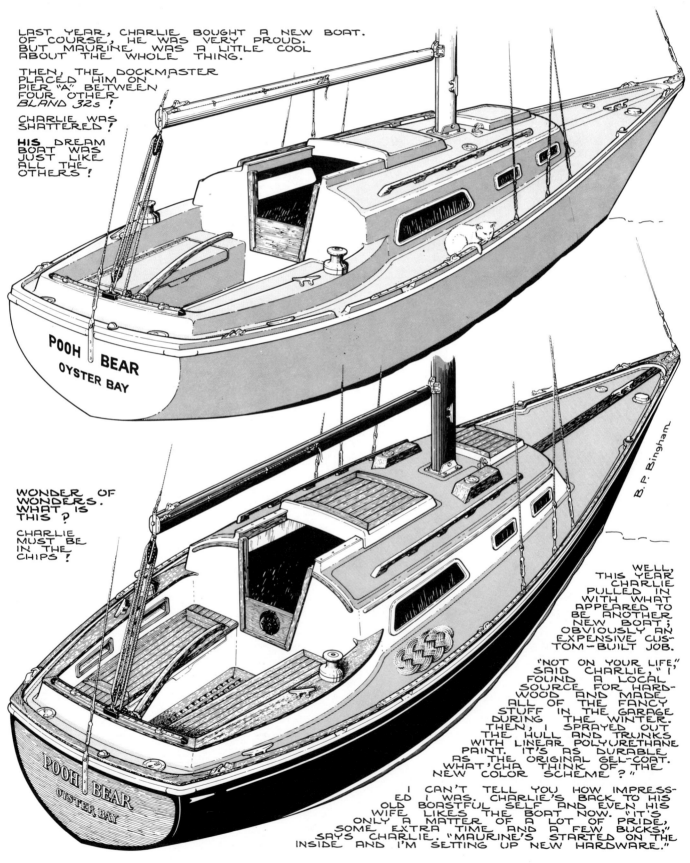

LAST YEAR, CHARLIE BOUGHT A NEW BOAT. OF COURSE, HE WAS VERY PROUD. BUT MAURINE WAS A LITTLE COOL ABOUT THE WHOLE THING.

THEN, THE DOCKMASTER PLACED HIM ON PIER "A" BETWEEN FOUR OTHER BLAND 32s!

CHARLIE WAS SHATTERED!

HIS DREAM BOAT WAS JUST LIKE ALL THE OTHERS!

POOH BEAR
OYSTER BAY

WONDER OF WONDERS. WHAT IS THIS?

CHARLIE MUST BE IN THE CHIPS!

POOH BEAR
OYSTER BAY

WELL, THIS YEAR CHARLIE PULLED IN WITH WHAT APPEARED TO BE ANOTHER NEW BOAT; OBVIOUSLY AN EXPENSIVE CUSTOM-BUILT JOB.

"NOT ON YOUR LIFE," SAID CHARLIE, "I FOUND A LOCAL SOURCE FOR HARDWOOD AND MADE ALL OF THE FANCY STUFF IN THE GARAGE DURING THE WINTER. THEN, I SPRAYED OUT THE HULL AND TRUNKS WITH LINEAR POLYURETHANE PAINT. IT'S AS DURABLE AS THE ORIGINAL GEL-COAT. WHAT'CHA THINK OF THE NEW COLOR SCHEME?"

I CAN'T TELL YOU HOW IMPRESSED I WAS. CHARLIE'S BACK TO HIS OLD BOASTFUL SELF AND EVEN HIS WIFE LIKES THE BOAT NOW. "IT'S ONLY A MATTER OF A LOT OF PRIDE, SOME EXTRA TIME AND A FEW BUCKS," SAYS CHARLIE. "MAURINE'S STARTED ON THE INSIDE AND I'M SETTING UP NEW HARDWARE."

B.P. Bingham

Showin' Off

IF YOU HADN'T ALREADY SURMISED, I AM A LITTLE BIT OF A SHOWOFF. NAY, I AM A LOT OF SHOWOFF! BUT THERE'S REALLY NO DISTINCTION IN BEING ONE... EVERY YACHTSMAN I KNOW IS A SHOWOFF TO SOME DEGREE.

I MET TWO VERY UNUSUAL AND UNIQUE SHOWOFFS AS THEY CRUISED DOWN THE WATERWAY IN THEIR LITTLE VENTURE 23 CUTTER *VOYAGEUR* FROM DETROIT. WHILE BEING A PRETTY BOAT, IT WAS HER SAIL COVER THAT DREW MY FOCUS. IT WAS COVERED WITH EM-BROIDERED PATCHES NOT UNLIKE THE ONES SKIERS SEW ONTO THEIR JACKETS. *VOYAGEUR'S* SAIL COVER PATCHES, HOWEVER, REPRE-SENTED THE MANY PLACES THAT LINDA AND RICK WOODARD HAD BEEN ON THEIR JOURNIES. LINDA SAYS THE PATCHES CAN BE PURCHASED AT SOUVENIR SHOPS, DIME STORES AND EVEN LARGE DRUG STORES. SHE SAYS THAT EVERY COUNTRY, EVERY PROVINCE, EVERY STATE AND ALMOST EVERY CITY AND TOWN HAS THEM. THEY COST FROM ONE TO TWO DOLLARS.

I THOUGHT THAT THE EFFECT WAS SO ATTRACTIVE AND THE STORY OF THE BOAT'S TRAVELS SO INTER-ESTING THAT I DE-CIDED TO DRESS UP *SABRINA'S* SAIL COVER IN MUCH THE SAME MANNER. BEING ARTISTICALLY INCLINED, HOWEVER, I PREFERRED TO HAND LETTER THE NAMES OF THE PORTS I HAD VISITED. I USED MODEL AIRPLANE ENAMEL (SLIGHTLY THINNED) APPLIED BY BRUSH. IT'S THE ONLY SYSTEM I CAN ABSO-LUTELY GUARANTEE NOT TO RUN OR FADE. EACH PORT WAS LETTERED IN A DIFFERENT COLOR WHILE THE SIZE VARIED WITH THE IMPORTANCE OF THE HARBOR. THE DESIGNS OF THE LETTERING ALSO CHANGED FROM PLACE TO PLACE AND WERE COPIED FROM A BOOK OF LETTERING STYLES PURCHASED AT AN ARTIST'S SUPPLY STORE. OCCA-SIONALLY, I DREW AN ADJOINING PIC-TURE REPRESENTING THE PORT.

IT WAS GREAT FUN AND VERY REWARDING, ESPECIALLY WHEN DOCKSIDERS CAME OVER JUST TO READ THE SAIL COVER!

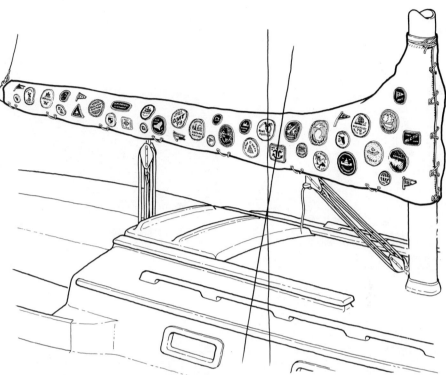

VOYAGEUR'S SAIL COVER

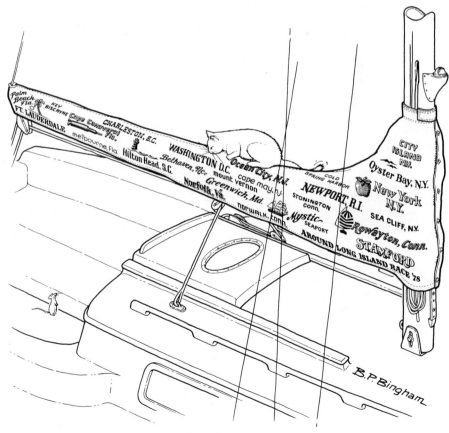

SABRINA'S SAIL COVER

Salty Signatures

IN THE DAYS OF YORE,
DRAWING, PAINTING OR
CARVING SCROLLS WAS
A RESPECTED PRO-
FESSION, A LOVING ART
THAT REFLECTED A
SHIP OWNER'S PRIDE
AND INDIVIDUALITY.

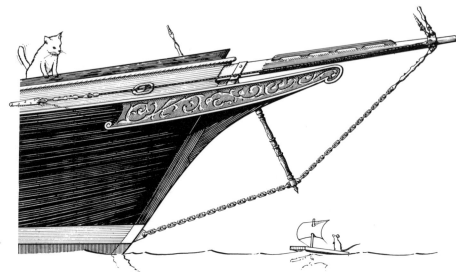

TODAY, SADLY, THE FEEL-
ING FOR SCROLLS SEEMS
TO HAVE BECOME LOST.
THEY HAVE DEGENERATED
INTO SIMPLY A SERIES OF
INTERCONNECTED LOOPS,
"CEES" AND CURLIQUES.
REPETITIOUS SWIRLS DO
NOT A SCROLL MAKE!
WHAT HAS HAPPENED TO
THE CLUSTERS OF FRUIT;
ENTWINED STALKS AND
SPRIGS; GARLANDS OF
HEATHER, HOLLY OR MINT?
THEY HAVE GONE THE WAY
OF MODERN IMAGINATIONS!

I OFFER THESE STEMS,
LEAVES AND PIROUETTES
OF BRANCHES FOR YOUR
INSPIRATION. DO WITH
THEM AS YOU WILL.
COPY THEM TO ANY
SCALE OR CREATE YOUR
OWN WITH AN EYE
TOWARD MOTION.

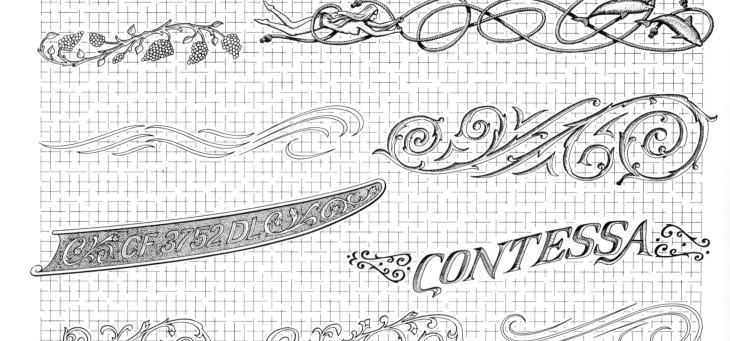

THESE SCROLLS MAY BE
ENLARGED TO ANY SIZE
USING THE CROSS-GRID
PROVIDED OR THEY MAY
BE PHOTOSTATED TO DE-
SIRED SCALE.

THESE SCROLLS MAY BE
MODIFIED TO FIT YOUR
WHIMS. LET YOURSELF GO.

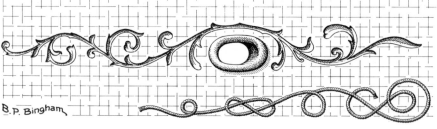

B.P. Bingham

Remembering Sailing Friends

ON TOP OF EVERYTHING ELSE A BOAT GIVES US, IT CERTAINLY PROVIDES AN ENVIRONMENT, A COMMON LANGUAGE AND PHILOSOPHY, A BOND OF UNIVERSAL CIRCUMSTANCES, A SENSE OF BROTHERHOOD THAT PROMOTES THE GROWTH OF FRIENDSHIPS.

WHILE PEOPLE ASHORE LOCK THEIR DOORS AND ARE AFRAID TO WALK THE STREETS, AVOID ALL CONTACT WITH STRANGERS AND INSULATE THEMSELVES FROM FOREIGN INTRUSIONS, SAILORS GRAVITATE TOWARDS EACH OTHER MAGNETICALLY.

ALTHOUGH THEY MAY NEVER HAVE MET BEFORE, SAILORS LEND EACH OTHER A HAND WHEN IT'S NEEDED, WATCH OUT FOR EACH OTHER WHEN DANGER IS SENSED, WISH EACH OTHER WELL ON A DEPARTURE AND JOIN IN SONG AT A VOYAGE'S END.

SAILORS ARE FOREVER EAGER TO SHARE THEIR EXPERIENCES, THEIR FOOD, THEIR BOOZE, THEIR TOOLS, THEIR TIME AND, MOST IMPORTANTLY, THEMSELVES WITH OTHER SAILORS.

BANKERS DRINK WITH PLUMBERS, STOCK BROKERS GAM WITH BRICK LAYERS, THE WEALTHY BRUSH WITH THE NOT-SO-WEALTHY, THE BIG WELCOME THE SMALL. WHEN SAILORS MEET, ALL OTHER DIFFERENCES BECOME TOTALLY IRRELEVANT; ONLY BEING SAILORS MATTERS. FRIENDSHIPS THAT MAY LAST A DAY OR A LIFETIME BUT ARE NEVER FORGOTTEN.

THAT'S HOW WE WERE INVITED ABOARD LOVELY *QUICKSTEP* BY RUTH AND LARRY PENN TO SHARE COCKTAILS AND A SUNSET IN *NO NAME HARBOR*. ONE STORY LED TO OTHERS, EACH DRINK WAS FOLLOWED BY MORE AND THE TIME SECRETLY FADED INTO THE EVENING. IN ONLY THE FIRST HOUR, WE FELT WE'D KNOWN EACH OTHER FOR YEARS.

AFTER A CASUAL DINNER, WE WERE HONORED TO SIGN THE GUEST LOG. IT WAS THE TABLE CLOTH, HAND EMBROIDERED IN VARIOUS COLORS BY RUTH WITH THE SIGNATURES AND NOTATIONS OF ALL THE FRIENDS THAT HAD PRECEEDED US: FRIENDS ALWAYS REMEMBERED.

AFTER THE TABLE CLOTH HAS BEEN SIGNED WITH PENCIL, GO OVER IT WITH EMBROIDERY FLOSS USING "STEM" OR "OUTLINE" STITCHING.

B.P. Bingham.

"Uncle Al" Reviore
6-17-78
ROCINANTE
OYSTER BAY, N.Y.

Plush, Practical Pillows

ADMITTEDLY, I'M REALLY A RAGAMUFFIN AT HEART. I WON'T WEAR A TIE AND EVEN AVOID YACHT CLUBS THAT REQUIRE THEM.

BUT I ALSO LIKE MY LITTLE TOUCHES OF CLASS: FINE CHINA, ETCHED GLASSWARE AND A DISPLAY OF PROPER FLAGS. MOST IMPORTANTLY, I ESPECIALLY ENJOY NICETIES THAT CANNOT BE PURCHASED...THOSE PRODUCTS OF CRAFTSMANSHIP AND PATIENCE FROM OUR OWN HANDS AND TOIL. THESE THINGS, MORE THAN ANYTHING, ARE OUTWARD SYMBOLS OF OUR BRAND OF SEAMANSHIP. THEY LABEL OUR VESSEL "A YACHT AMONG BOATS": A FLAWLESS COAT OF VARNISH, A TIDY DECK, GOLD-LEAF WORK, A TURK'S HEAD HERE OR THERE.

NOW I'VE ADDED PERSONALIZED PILLOW COVERS MADE BY A FRIEND. THEY ARE BOLT-ROPED WITH LAID DACRON AND EMBROIDERED IN BLACK AND GOLD YARN.

THE PILLOWS ON BOARD HAVE TO LIVE SOMEWHERE WHEN THEY'RE NOT BEING USED TO SLEEP UPON; SO RATHER THAN DRESSING THE SHIP WITH DECORATOR "THROW PILLOWS," DURING THE DAY I SIMPLY KEEP THE BERTH PILLOWS COVERED, THUS SERVING AN ATTRACTIVE DUAL PURPOSE.

IT TOOK QUITE A BIT OF TIME TO MAKE EACH COVER, BUT IT WASN'T RUSH WORK SO IT DIDN'T MATTER. MY FRIEND DID THE SEWING AND EMBROIDERY (ABOUT FIVE HOURS WHILE WATCHING TELEVISION). I ATTACHED THE VELCRO BUTTONS AND BOLT ROPE AND LAID OUT THE DESIGN.

THE BEST MATERIAL FOR THE COVERS IS "SAIL CLOTH" FROM YOUR LOCAL FABRIC STORE...NOT FROM A SAILMAKER. DOMESTIC SAIL CLOTH IS AVAILABLE IN A WIDE VARIETY OF SOFT AND BRIGHT COLORS AND IS VERY INEXPENSIVE.

WHEN THE COVERS WERE FINISHED, I SPRAYED THEM WITH SCOTCHGUARD®. THEY ARE FOUR YEARS OLD AND STILL LIKE NEW.

B.P.Bingham

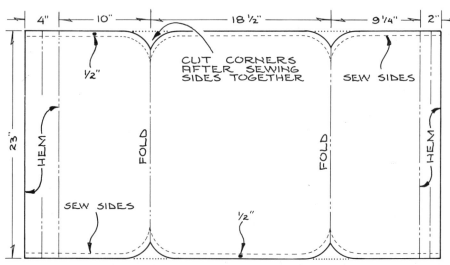

THE FABRIC LAYOUT

① AFTER LAYING OUT AND CUTTING YOUR CLOTH, SEW THE HEMS AT EACH END.

② SEW THREE PAIR OF 3/4" VELCRO BUTTONS ONTO THE HEMS AS SHOWN. MAKE SURE THAT THEIR POSITIONS MATCH. THE BUTTONS ARE AVAILABLE IN COLORS TO COMPLEMENT YOUR COVER FABRIC.

THESE BUTTONS MUST BE ON THE OPPOSITE SIDE

11½"

4½"

③ FOLD THE FABRIC WITH THE HEMS TOWARD THE OUT- SIDE THEN CLOSE THE VELCRO BUTTONS. WHEN LAID FLAT, THERE MUST BE NO SIGN OF WRINKLES.

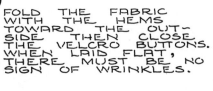

④ SEW THE EDGES OF THE COVER. ROUND THE CORNERS LIBER- ALLY WITH THE STITCHING THEN CUT AWAY THE EXCESS.

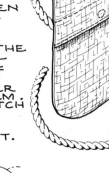

⑧ COMPLETE THE ROPING AT THE JOINT AREA.

⑨ CAREFULLY DRAW OUT YOUR PILLOW DESIGN OR LETTERING ON TISSUE PAPER.

⑩ ACCURATELY TRANSFER THE DESIGN TO THE COVER FABRIC USING TAILOR'S CARBON PAPER.

⑪ LARGE AREAS TO BE COLORED SOLIDLY ARE EMBROIDERED WITH TAPESTRY YARN USING "SATIN" STITCHING.

⑤ TURN THE COVER RIGHT SIDE OUT. BOLT ROPE YOUR COVERS WITH 3/8" LAID DACRON LINE USING DOUBLE STRANDS OF WHITE BUTTON OR CARPET THREAD. START ROPING AT THE BOTTOM EDGE THEN PASS ONE SPIRAL STITCH THROUGH EACH STRAND OF THE LINE. WHEN STITCHING, OPEN THE LAY OF THE LINE SLIGHTLY SO THE NEEDLE WILL NOT PENETRATE THE STRANDS BUT RATHER PASS BETWEEN THEM. LINE UP EACH STITCH WITH THE LAY OF THE LINE SO IT WILL DISAPPEAR WHEN PULLED TIGHT.

CENTER
2" 2"

ALLOW AMPLE TAIL ON ENDS FOR SAFETY

⑫ FINE LINES ARE "STEM" OR "OUTLINE" STITCHED.

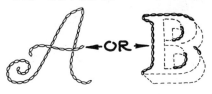

A ← OR → B

⑥ WHEN YOU'VE ROPED TO WITHIN FOUR INCHES OF THE STARTING POINT, PLACE THE ENDS SIDE BY SIDE AND CUT THEM SLOWLY WITH A RED-HOT KNIFE. KEEP THE KNIFE HOT THROUGH THE ENTIRE CUTTING AS THIS WILL FUSE THE ENDS.

⑦ HOLD THE TWO ENDS TOGETHER SO THE LAYS MATCH. WITH THE HOT KNIFE AGAIN MELT THE STRANDS SLIGHTLY AND SCULPT THE ENDS TOGETHER SO THAT THE JOINT LOOKS LIKE A CON- TINUOUS PIECE OF LINE.

JOINT

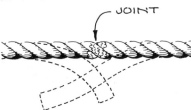

THE STITCHES COM- BINED LOOK LIKE THIS:

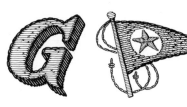

Boat Lettering

GOOD LETTERING ISN'T EASY... EVEN FOR A PROFESSIONAL. FOR AN AMATEUR, IT'S ALMOST IMPOSSIBLE. GOOD LETTERING IS THAT FINAL TOUCH FOR A FINE BOAT BUT SLOPPY LETTERING CAN BE ITS RUIN. CONSIDER THAT ONE OF THE FIRST THINGS YOU LOOK AT ON A PASSING BOAT IS HER NAME AND PORT OF HAIL. IF IT'S POORLY PRESENTED, IT CASTS A SHADOW OVER THE ENTIRE VESSEL, REGARDLESS OF HOW PROPER SHE MIGHT BE IN ALL OTHER RESPECTS.

A GOOD LETTERING MAN IS WORTH HIS WEIGHT IN GOLD (EVEN AT TODAY'S PRICES). WHEN COMMISSIONING YOUR BOAT, TRY TO SET ASIDE A REASON-ABLE AMOUNT OF MONEY TO HAVE THE NAME PAINTING DONE WELL. BUT, IF YOU JUST CAN'T WORK IT INTO YOUR BUDGET, HERE ARE SOME TIPS THAT CAN HELP YOU.

① DON'T TRY TO DESIGN YOUR OWN LETTERING. IT HAS TAKEN CENTURIES FOR STYLES TO EVOLVE AND YEARS FOR ARTISTS TO LEARN. EVEN THE SIMPLEST BLOCK LETTERING IS COM-POSED OF SUBTLE CURVES AND VARYING THICKNESSES. TRY FINDING ATTRACTIVE TYPESTYLES IN MAGA-ZINE AND NEWSPAPER HEADLINES, ADS, PRODUCT LABELING OR TYPESTYLE BOOKS.

Letraset reg. TM.
Letraset Corp.

B.P.Bingham

② ENLARGE THE LETTERING BY USING A SQUARE-GRID SYSTEM. DRAW THE PENCIL GRID OVER YOUR CHOSEN TYPE (SAY, 1/8" SQUARES), USING IT AS A GUIDE WHEN TRANSPOSING THE LETTERS TO YOUR ENLARGED TISSUE GRID.

ONCE YOUV'E DRAWN A LETTER OR A PART OF A LETTER THAT WILL BE REPEATED, MAKE A TRACING OF THAT LETTER OR PART. USE THE TRACINGS AS TEMPLATES FOR CREATING PERFECT REPEATS. THIS WILL SAVE MUCH TIME AND ASSURE CONTINUITY.

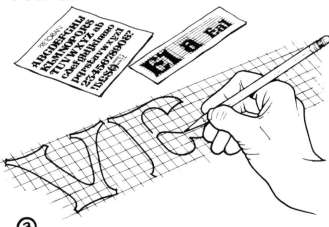

③ DRAW YOUR FINAL LETTERING ON TRAC-ING TISSUE. USE GUIDELINES FOR THE TOPS OF CAPITALS AND ASCENDERS, TOPS OF LOWERCASE, BOTTOMS OF DESCENDERS, AND BASE OF CAPS AND LOWERCASE LETTERS. ROUNDS AND POINTS SHOULD JUST EXCEED THE LINES.

Bright
———— ASCENDERS / CAPS
———— LOWERCASE
———— BASE
———— DESCENDERS

④ LETTERS ARE RARELY SPACED EVENLY. ROUNDED LETTERS NEXT TO EACH OTHER SHOULD BE CLOSER TOGETHER THAN STRAIGHT-SIDED LETTERS. LETTERS WITH OPENINGS ARE ALSO SPACED MORE CLOSELY. ALSO, CLOSE UP SLANTED LETTERS.

A SIMPLE TRICK USED BY TYPESETTERS TO ACHIEVE CORRECT SPACING IS TO ARRANGE THE LETTERS SO THE SAME NUMBER OF MARBLES CAN BE FITTED BETWEEN THEM.

Evening Star

OR

EVENING

LETTERS WITH SLANTED OR CUTAWAY
SIDES CAN ACTUALLY OVERHANG OTHER
SUCH LETTERS TO PROVIDE THE
CORRECT SPACING. THEY CAN EVEN
TOUCH OR JOIN EACH OTHER IF THE
SPACE WOULD OTHERWISE BE SEVERE.

LIGATURES

5

ADJUSTING THE SPACING CAN BE DONE
BY CUTTING AND RETAPING THE TIS-
SUE OR BY ADDING THIN TISSUE
STRIPS BETWEEN LETTERS.

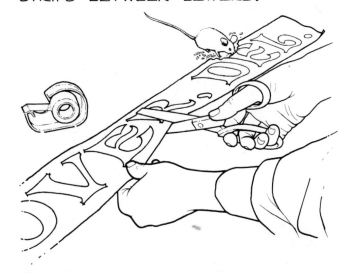

6

AVOID THE USE OF SCRIPT LETTERING.
IT IS THE MOST DIFFICULT OF ALL
LETTER FORMS TO DRAW AND PAINT.
FURTHER, IT IS NOT PERMITTED ON
DOCUMENTED YACHTS (AS WELL AS
ITALICS), OR AS REGISTRATION NUMBERS.

7

TO FIND THE CENTER OF YOUR WORD
OR NAME, DON'T COUNT CHARAC-
TERS... FOLD THE TISSUE IN HALF.

8

PROFESSIONAL LETTERERS AND GUILDERS
USE A PATTERN WHEEL AND CHALK BAG
TO TRANSFER LETTERING TO THE WORK-
ING SURFACE. EASIER FOR YOU IS TO
BLACKEN THE LETTER OUTLINES ON
THE BACKSIDE OF THE TISSUE WITH
A BLACK EBONY PENCIL, THUS FORM-
ING A CARBON SURFACE.

9

WITH THE TISSUE TAPED TO THE
WORKING SURFACE, GO OVER THE
LETTERS WITH A BALLPOINT PEN.
THE CARBON LETTERS WILL TRANSFER
TO THE WORKING SURFACE, EVEN
VARNISH AND BLACK GEL COAT.

10

IF YOU ARE GOING TO PAINT YOUR
LETTERING (THERE'S AN ALTERNATIVE),
USE STRIPING ENAMEL PURCHASED
FROM AN ARTIST-SUPPLY OR SIGN-
SUPPLY STORE. DON'T USE ANY
PAINT MANUFACTURED AS A RUST
INHIBITOR AS ITS PIGMENT IS TOO
THIN, IT TACKS TOO QUICKLY AND
NEVER DRIES TO A SUPER-HARD
FINISH. SIGN STRIPING STROKES
OUT BEAUTIFULLY, COVERS ON THE
FIRST SHOT AND GIVES YOU PLENTY
OF TIME TO WORK.

STRAIGHT LINES MAY BE MASKED. EVEN THE BEST SIGN PAINTERS OFTEN MASK THE TOPS AND BOTTOMS OF SQUARE LETTERS AT THE GUIDELINES.

USE A SIGN BRUSH, NOT AN "ARTIST'S" BRUSH. SIGN BRUSHES ARE DESIGNED TO HOLD A LARGE AMOUNT OF PAINT TO REDUCE RE-DIPPING IN MID STROKE. THEY ALSO PRODUCE A VERY SHARP PAINT EDGE AND SQUARE CORNERS. GOOD LETTERING JUST CAN'T BE DONE WITH A CHEAP, DIME-STORE BRUSH.

⑪

TO PRODUCE A SHADOWED LETTER, TRACE THE ORIGINAL LETTER OUT-LINE ONTO A SECOND TISSUE.

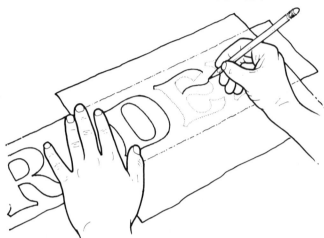

THEN SHIFT THEIR POSITIONS 45° UP OR DOWNWARD.

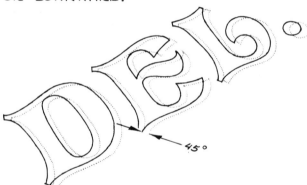

FOR A THREE-DIMENSIONAL EFFECT, CONNECT THE TANGENTS AND POINTS OF THE TWO LETTERS WITH 45° STRAIGHT LINES.

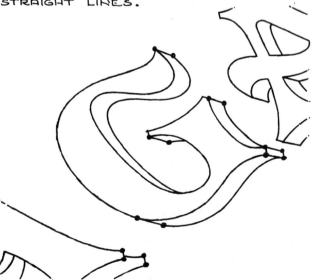

⑫

PRIOR TO TRANSFERRING YOUR LETTER-ING TO A FIBERGLASS HULL, BE SURE TO WIPE THE AREA WITH PREP SOLVENT TO REMOVE ALL TRACES OF WAX, GRIME AND OIL. FOR WOODEN BOATS (OR WOODWORK), WIPE THE AREA WITH A LIQUID SANDING SOLU-TION OR DULLING AGENT. DON'T SAND. DON'T TOUCH SYNTHETIC LIFERINGS WITH ANYTHING BUT SOAP (OR DETERGENT) AND WATER.

⑬

IF YOU'RE NOT UP TO PAINTING YOUR LETTERING, THERE ARE SEVERAL ALTERNATIVES THAT WILL GIVE YOUR BOAT'S NAME A NICE FLARE. THE VERY EASIEST APPROACH IS TO APPLY TWO DIFFERENT COLORS OF STOCK, STICK-ON LETTERS (SAY, GOLD ON TOP OF BLACK) SHIFTED 45° FOR A SHADOWED EFFECT. THE FIRST COLOR DOWN BECOMES THE SHADOW; THE SECOND COLOR BECOMES THE LETTER.

Scotch Cal reg.T.M.
3M Company

⑭

AN ALTERNATIVE TO STOCK LETTERS IS TO MAKE YOUR OWN, CUSTOM, STICK-ON LETTERS. PROCEED IN THE PRESCRIBED MANNER FROM STEPS 1 TO 8. LAY THE TISSUE ONTO A SHEET OF SCOTCH CAL IT'S AVAILABLE IN MANY COLORS AND YOU'LL PROBABLY BE ABLE TO BUY A SMALL AMOUNT FROM YOUR SAIL-MAKER (HE USES IT FOR SAIL NUMBERS).

ONCE YOU HAVE TRANSFERRED YOUR LETTERING TO THE SCOTCH CAL, CUT

THROUGH THE SCOTCH CAL WITH AN EXACTO KNIFE, USING A NO. 11 BLADE. BE CAREFUL NOT TO CUT THROUGH THE BACKING SHEET.

⑮ USING THE SAME TISSUE AS BEFORE, TRANSFER THE LETTER LOCATIONS ONTO THE HULL (OR WHATEVER). BEING SURE THE HULL IS CLEAN, SIMPLY REMOVE YOUR CUT LETTERS FROM THE BACKING SHEET AND APPLY LIKE ANY OTHER STICK-ON LETTERING.

A SHADOWED, TWO-COLOR, CUSTOM, STICK-ON LETTERFORM MAY BE CREATED AS DESCRIBED IN STEP 13. JUST CUT TWO SETS OF CONTRAST-ING SCOTCH CALS.

⑯ IF YOU LIKE GOLD LEAF BUT FIND THE PRICE A LITTLE DEAR, TRY THE GOLD SCOTCH CAL. IT'S AVAILABLE IN BOTH BRIGHT AND DULL FINISHES. IT ACTUALLY LOOKS MORE LIKE GOLD THAN GOLD AND CAN WITHSTAND ABUSE FAR BETTER THAN THE REAL THING. YOUR SAILMAKER WON'T HAVE IT SO TRY CALLING YOUR LOCAL 3M BUSINESS PRODUCTS REPRESENTATIVE FOR A LINE ON WHERE TO FIND IT.

TAKE YOUR TIME WITH YOUR LETTERING. DON'T TRY TO BE TOO CLEVER OR TOO HUMOROUS. STICK TO ESTABLISHED FORMS. AGAIN, CONSIDERING THE IN-VESTMENT YOU'VE MADE IN YOUR BOAT, ISN'T SHE WORTH THE COST OR TIME OF A REALLY FINE LETTERING JOB? HIRE A PRO IF YOU'RE NOT CONFIDENT THAT YOU CAN DO IT CRISPLY YOURSELF.

FELICITY

Rag Doll

VENTURE

gazelle

ROSINANTE

Sabrina

Oyster Bay, N.Y.

SuperStar

AT LAST

Fiberglass "Stained, Leaded Windows"

NOW, HERE'S A PROJECT WITH ABSOLUTELY NO REDEEMING FUNCTIONAL VALUE (BUT THEY ARE ALWAYS THE MOST FUN). THE "LEADED GLASS" PANELS SHOWN HERE ARE EASY TO MAKE AND CAN ADD A DISTINCTIVE, CLASSY TOUCH TO EVEN A COLD STOCK YACHT. THE PANELS CAN RANGE FROM THE VERY SIMPLE, ONE COLOR DIAMOND PATTERN (BEST FOR YOUR FIRST ATTEMPT) TO THE VERY COMPLICATED MULTI-COLORED DESIGNS.

THE TIME INVOLVED CAN RANGE BETWEEN A SINGLE AFTERNOON TO SEVERAL DAYS. COST MAY BE AS LITTLE AS $10 TO AS MUCH AS $20. IN ANY EVENT, THE RESULT WILL BE REWARDING AND WORTHY OF ENVY.

FOR A 2 SQUARE FOOT PANEL YOU WILL NEED:

① ONE PIECE OF ¾ OUNCE FIBERGLASS MAT AND TWO PIECES OF 8 OUNCE FIBERGLASS CLOTH. EACH PIECE MUST BE LARGE ENOUGH TO COVER THE INTENDED PANEL PLUS A 2" MARGIN.

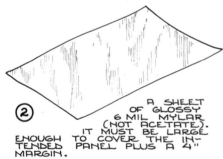

② A SHEET OF GLOSSY 6 MIL MYLAR (NOT ACETATE). IT MUST BE LARGE ENOUGH TO COVER THE INTENDED PANEL PLUS A 4" MARGIN.

③ TWO QUARTS OF POLYESTER CASTING RESIN AND CATALYST

④ A QUART OF ACETONE FOR CLEANING HANDS AND BRUSHES.

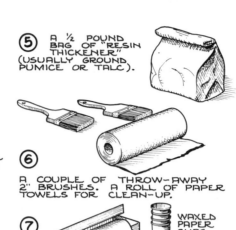

⑤ A ½ POUND BAG OF "RESIN THICKENER" (USUALLY GROUND PUMICE OR TALC).

⑥ A COUPLE OF THROW-AWAY 2" BRUSHES. A ROLL OF PAPER TOWELS FOR CLEAN-UP.

⑦ WAXED PAPER CUPS. A ROLL OF WAX PAPER.

⑧ A TUBE OF CONDENSED BLACK RESIN DYE.

⑨ AND, FINALLY, AN ASSORTMENT OF RESIN COLOR DYES OF YOUR OWN CHOICE AND NUMBER IF YOU WISH TO STAIN YOUR "LEADED" PANELS.

LET'S BEGIN

Ⓐ LAY OUT THE PERIMETER OF THE DESIRED PANEL ON WHITE PAPER, USING A FELT-TIP MARKER. WITHIN THIS PERIMETER, DESIGN THE "LEADING" FOR THE PANEL. KEEP THE SPACES BETWEEN THE LEADING OPEN AND SIMPLE. I WOULD SUGGEST LOOKING THROUGH SOME BOOKS ABOUT STAINED GLASS IN ORDER TO HELP GIVE YOURSELF MORE OF A FEEL FOR IT. WHEN YOU HAVE ACHIEVED A SATISFACTORY DESIGN, DARKEN IT IN WITH THE FELT TIP PEN. YOU MAY ALSO COLOR THE DESIGN WITH CRAYON.

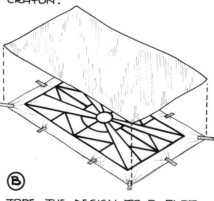

Ⓑ TAPE THE DESIGN TO A FLAT, HORIZONTAL SURFACE, THEN COVER IT WITH THE MYLAR GLOSSY SIDE UP.

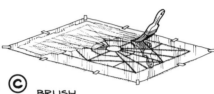

Ⓒ BRUSH A HEAVY COAT OF CATALIZED RESIN (SEVEN DROPS OF CATALYST FOR EACH OUNCE OF RESIN) ONTO THE MYLAR.

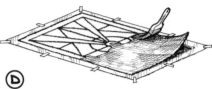

Ⓓ IMMEDIATELY LAY DOWN A LAYER OF GLASS CLOTH. BRUSH ON A HEAVY COAT OF CATALIZED RESIN USING A SQUEEGEEING MOTION WITH THE BRUSH TO INSURE FULL PENETRATION OF THE RESIN INTO THE CLOTH. THE CLOTH WILL BECOME TOTALLY CLEAR AS RESIN SATURATION IS ACHIEVED. AIR TRAPPED IN THE CLOTH WILL APPEAR AS WHITE DOTS OR BUBBLES. THEY MUST BE SQUEEGEED OUT.

NOW, LET THE RESIN "KICK OFF" (HARDEN). THIS WILL TAKE ABOUT 40 MINUTES FROM THE TIME YOU MIXED THE RESIN.

Ⓔ FOLLOWING STEPS C AND D, APPLY A LAYER OF MAT THEN A FINAL LAYER OF CLOTH.

WHEN SATURATING THE GLASS YOU NEED NOT ACHIEVE A GLOSSY SURFACE.

IMMEDIATELY AFTER EACH GLASSING APPLICATION, CLEAN YOUR BRUSH AND HANDS WITH ACETONE.

Ⓕ YOU MUST NOW MAKE ABOUT A DOZEN RESIN SQUEEZERS OUT OF WAX PAPER. START WITH PAPER SQUARES CUT TO 10"x 10". FOLD AS SHOWN:

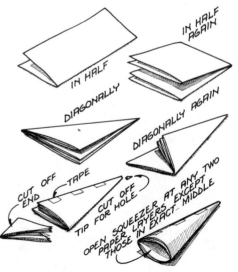

IN HALF

IN HALF AGAIN

DIAGONALLY

DIAGONALLY AGAIN

CUT OFF END

TAPE

CUT OFF TIP FOR HOLE

OPEN SQUEEZER AT ANY TWO PAPER LAYERS EXCEPT THOSE IN EXACT MIDDLE

YOU HAVE NOW COMPLETED THE PRE-LAMINATED FIBER-GLASS PANEL. IT WILL BE VERY STRONG AND PERFECTLY CLEAR. ALLOW IT TO CURE FOR A FULL DAY. YOU MAY NOW BEGIN "LEADING" THE WINDOW.

(G) MIX THE LEADING AS FOLLOWS:

3 OUNCES RESIN, 14 DROPS CATALYST, ENOUGH THICKENER TO ALTER RESIN TO THE VISCOSITY OF TOOTHPASTE. ABOUT A QUARTER INCH OF CONCENTRATED BLACK DYE FROM THE TUBE. STIR ALL ELEMENTS THOROUGHLY.

(H) PLACE ONE TABLESPOON OF THE LEADING MIX INTO A RESIN SQUEEZER. ROLL UP THE LARGE, OPEN END UNTIL THE LEADING BEGINS TO OOZE FROM THE TIP.

(I) VERY SLOWLY, VERY CAREFULLY SQUEEZE THE THICKENED BLACK RESIN ONTO THE FIBERGLASS PANEL.

FOLLOW YOUR LEADED DESIGN FAITHFULLY. BUILD UP A BEAD OF RESIN MEASURING ABOUT 3/16" X 3/16". YOU MAY HAVE TO GO OVER YOUR LEADING TWICE TO ACHIEVE THE DESIRED LEADING WEIGHT. I WOULD SUGGEST PRACTICING LEADING ON A PIECE OF CARDBOARD BEFORE COMMITTING THE THICKENED RESIN TO YOUR FIBERGLASS PANEL. TAKE YOUR TIME.

FOLLOW STEPS **G, H** and **I** AS MANY TIMES AS NECESSARY TO COMPLETE THE LEADING OF THE DESIGN.

(J) ALLOW THE LEADING TO EXTEND 1" BEYOND THE DESIGN.

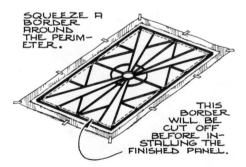

SQUEEZE A BORDER AROUND THE PERIMETER.

THIS BORDER WILL BE CUT OFF BEFORE INSTALLING THE FINISHED PANEL.

(K) NOW, IT'S TIME TO MIX THE RESIN FOR THE "GLASS" INLAYS. QUANTITY WILL DEPEND ON THE AREA OF EACH COLOR. SAY, FOR EACH SIX OUNCES OF RESIN, USE 42 DROPS OF CATALYST. THEN SQUEEZE IN THE RESIN DYE.

MIX YOUR COLOR ALMOST TWICE AS DARK IN THE CUP THAN YOU'LL WANT FOR THE FINISHED WINDOW. IT WILL BECOME MUCH LIGHTER IN ITS FINAL FORM, ESPECIALLY IF NATURAL LIGHT IS TO PASS THROUGH THE WINDOW.

(K)

(L) ONCE MIXED, POUR THE RESIN ONTO THE WINDOW, KEEPING THE FLOW WITHIN THE BOUNDARIES OF COLOR DELINEATED BY THE LEADING. FILL THE AREAS OF COLOR ALMOST TO THE TOP OF THE LEADING.

IF THE COLORED RESIN LEAKS UNDER THE LEADING A LITTLE, DON'T WORRY ABOUT IT. YOU WILL BE ABLE TO SCRAPE IT OUT OF THE UNDESIRED LEADED SECTION WHEN THE RESIN REACHES THE GEL STATE.

(M) CONTINUE STEPS **K** and **L** UNTIL YOU HAVE FILLED IN ALL LEADED SECTIONS OF THE WINDOW DESIGN WITH CLEAR OR COLORED RESIN. ALLOW ALL RESIN TO CURE BEFORE ATTEMPTING TO REMOVE THE WINDOW FROM THE WORKING SURFACE.

(N) INVERT THE WINDOW AND CAREFULLY PEEL OFF THE MYLAR SHEET.

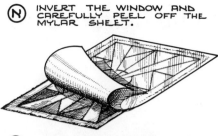

(O) SAND THE BACKSIDE OF THE WINDOW THOROUGHLY THEN GIVE IT ONE COAT OF CLEAR, CATALIZED RESIN.

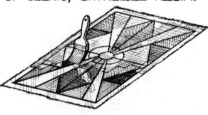

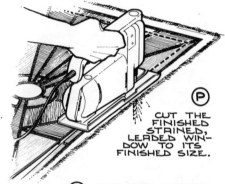

(P) CUT THE FINISHED STAINED, LEADED WINDOW TO ITS FINISHED SIZE.

(Q) CUT THE OPENING IN THE WOODWORK 1/2" SMALLER THAN THE FINISHED WINDOW. RABBET THE OPENING EDGE TO 1/4" X 1/2". SET IN THE WINDOW, THEN FINISH OFF WITH A BRIGHT MOLDING. USE BRASS ESCUTCHEON PINS FOR FASTENING.

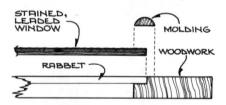

STAINED, LEADED WINDOW

MOLDING

WOODWORK

RABBET

R.P. Bingham

The Three-Strand Turk's Head

by **K.M. Burke**

THE TURK'S HEAD HAS LONG BEEN A FAVORITE AMONG SAILORS, MOSTLY AS A WAY OF IMPRESSING THEIR LANDLUBBER FRIENDS. TO THE UNINITIATED, IT'S A MYSTERIOUS KNOT, APPEARING TO HAVE NO BEGINNING AND NO END. IT'S A ROMANTIC KNOT...THE VERY NAME CONJURES UP VISIONS OF TEA PACKETS BATTLING THE ELEMENTS TO DELIVER THEIR EXOTIC CARGOES OF SPICES, SILKS AND JADE TO A LUSTING NEW WORLD FROM THE FAR-FLUNG PORTS OF SINGAPORE, HONG KONG AND BOMBAY. WE CAN PICTURE THE PIGTAILED TARS SWAGGERING DOWN THE GANGPLANK TO TEMPT A FAIR MAIDEN WITH TRINKETS FROM THE ORIENT. LOOK AT A TURK'S HEAD AND YOU CAN SMELL THE OPIUM DENS, TASTE THE SUGARY SWEETNESS OF MOON CAKE, AND HEAR THE RICKSHAWS CLATTERING ALONG NARROW, CONGESTED ALLEYWAYS AMID FAST-TALKING SING-SONG MERCHANTS.

IT'S A FUN KNOT AND I THINK ONE OF THE PRETTIEST, YET IT DOES HAVE SOME PRACTICAL APPLICATIONS AS WELL AS BEING SIMPLY GORGEOUS. A TURK'S HEAD TRADITIONALLY MARKS THE KING SPOKE OF THE SHIP'S WHEEL. SEVERAL LARGE ONES MARCHING ALONG THE BOWSPRIT GIVE SURER FOOTING THAN SLIPPERY VARNISH. I TIED ONE ON THE END OF *SABRINA'S* TILLER, PRIMARILY FOR DECORATION, ALTHOUGH IT DID MAKE A FIRM HAND GRIP. *SABRINA'S* THERMOS JUG FITTED INTO A HOLE IN THE COUNTER BEHIND THE SINK, AND A TURK'S-HEAD COLLAR PREVENTED IT FROM FALLING THROUGH. TURK'S HEADS ARE FREQUENTLY USED AS FINISHING KNOTS TO COVER THE ENDS OF OTHER ROPE WORK AND ARE ADDED TO THE TOPS AND BOTTOMS OF COACH-WHIPPED STANCHIONS. THE JUDICIOUS PLACEMENT OF TURK'S HEADS CAN GIVE A CUSTOM TOUCH TO ABSOLUTELY ANY STOCK BOAT AND CERTAINLY A FLAVOR OF TRADITION TO A YACHT THAT IS, OTHERWISE, SOMEWHAT MODERN.

I HAD THE PLEASURE RECENTLY OF MEETING *MR. AND MRS. BEAUDOIN* OF MYSTIC, CONNECTICUT. IN HIS YOUTH, *MR. BEAUDOIN* SIGNED ON AS BOSUN'S MATE ABOARD THE FULL-RIGGED SHIP, *JOSEPH CONRAD* DURING HER WORKING DAYS UNDER SAIL (THE *JOSEPH CONRAD* IS NOW PART OF THE *MYSTIC SEAPORT MUSEUM*, A SHORT WALK DOWN *GREENMANVILLE AVENUE* FROM THE *BEAUDOINS' ROPE LOCKER*). THE TOBACCO-CHAWING *MR. BEAUDOIN* IS CONSIDERED ONE OF THE FOREMOST AUTHORITIES ON MARLINSPIKE SEAMANSHIP IN THE COUNTRY. HIS ROPEWORK GRACES MUSEUMS AND SHIPS THROUGHOUT THE WORLD AND THE *BEAUDOIN'S* HOME IS ALMOST A MUSEUM IN ITSELF. INCREDIBLY INTRICATE PICTURE FRAMES, KNOT BOARDS, BELL ROPES, LANYARDS AND TURK'S HEADS ARE EVERYWHERE. EVEN THE WINDOW CURTAINS ARE DELICATE LACE-LIKE MACRAME. *MR. BEAUDOIN* SHOWED ME ONE

KNOT BOARD WITH SEVERAL DOZEN VARIATIONS OF *BOWLINE EYES* (I HAVE TROUBLE REMEMBERING JUST ONE!). HAVE YOU EVER WONDERED WHO TIES ALL THOSE TURK'S-HEAD BRACELETS YOU SEE IN MARINAS AND NAUTICAL GIFT STORES? *MR. AND MRS. BEAUDOIN* SUPPLY THE MAJORITY OF THEM. WHEN THEY TRAVEL, JUST TO THE GROCERY STORE, THE ONE NOT DRIVING TIES TURK'S HEADS.

MRS. BEAUDOIN TOLD ME THAT SHE MAKES AND SELLS OVER 3,000 BRACELETS PER YEAR! IN FACT, WHILE WE WERE TALKING, SHE WHIPPED UP A PAIR FOR ME BEFORE I COULD BAT AN EYE. SHE SCARCELY EVEN GLANCED AT HER NIMBLE FINGERS AS SHE WOVE THE INTRICATE PATTERN OF THE KNOT.

B.P. Bingham

THERE ARE NUMEROUS VARIETIES OF
TURK'S-HEAD KNOTS, SOME OF THEM
EXTREMELY COMPLICATED. THE ONE
I'M SHOWING HERE IS A SIMPLE
THREE-STRAND, FIVE-BIGHT TURK'S
HEAD. IT WORKS WELL ON SMALL
ITEMS UP TO ABOUT 2-INCH DIAMETER
SUCH AS TILLERS, OARS AND STAN-
CHIONS. IN LARGER DIAMETERS THE
TURK'S HEAD GETS TOO STRETCHED
OUT AND LANKY, SO YOU'D PROB-
ABLY WANT TO ADD ADDITIONAL
BIGHTS (I'LL SHOW YOU HOW).

TYING A TURK'S HEAD ON YOUR
HAND FIRST IS THE EASIEST WAY.
THEN YOU CAN SLIP IT ONTO THE
TILLER, OR WHATEVER, AND SNUG
IT UP. OBVIOUSLY, YOU CAN'T
ALWAYS DO THIS SUCH, AS IF YOU
WANT ONE AROUND THE MAST, OR IF
THE FINISHED KNOT WILL BE LARG-
ER THAN YOUR FIST. BUT IF IT'S
YOUR FIRST TRY, PRACTICE TYING
SEVERAL SMALL ONES ON YOUR
HAND UNTIL YOU GET USED TO THE
OVER/UNDER SEQUENCE. THEN YOU
CAN TRY TACKLING A BIG PROJECT.

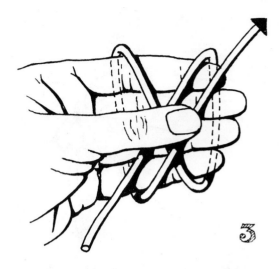

NOW WRAP IT AROUND ONCE AGAIN
AND BRING IT ACROSS THE SECOND
PASS, CREATING ANOTHER X JUST
BELOW THE FIRST ONE. SHIFT YOUR
THUMB SLIGHTLY TO HOLD ALL OF
THE PASSES IN POSITION.

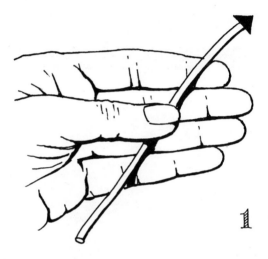

HOLD THE LINE IN YOUR LEFT HAND
SO THAT IT CROSSES YOUR FINGERS
AT ABOUT A 45° ANGLE, WITH THE
STANDING END AT THE BOTTOM AND
THE WORKING END LEADING OFF TO
THE RIGHT.

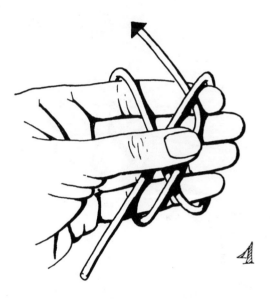

PASS THE WORKING END UNDER THE
ORIGINAL PASS, LEADING OFF TOWARD
THE LEFT.

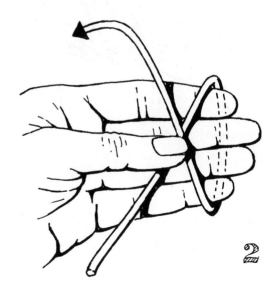

WRAP THE LINE AROUND YOUR HAND
AND BACK ACROSS THE FIRST PASS,
FORMING AN "X".

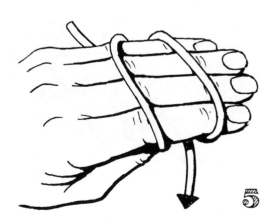

TURN YOUR HAND OVER. YOU'LL
SEE TO LINES RUNNING IN PARALLEL
ACROSS THE BACKS OF YOUR FINGERS.

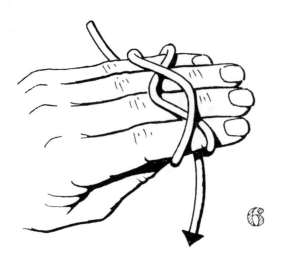

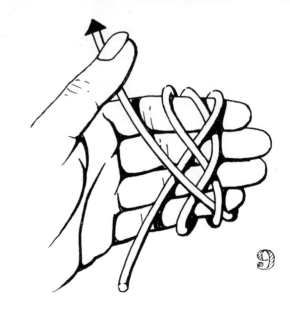

BEING CAREFUL NOT TO LET GO OF
THE PASSES HELD BY YOUR THUMB,
LIFT THE LEFT STRAND UP AND OVER
THE RIGHT STRAND, FORMING A
DIAMOND. NOW I'LL TEST YOUR
DEXTERITY !

PASS THE WOKING END UNDER THE
STRAND AT THE LOWER RIGHT, COMING
OUT OVER THE LOWER LEFT STRAND.

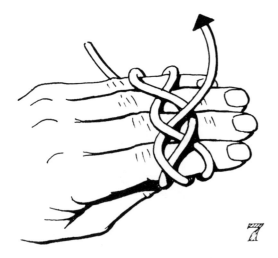

PASS THE WORKING END OVER THE
STRAND AT THE BOTTOM LEFT OF YOUR
HAND AND BRING IT UP THROUGH THE
DIAMOND SO THAT IT LEADS OFF TO
THE RIGHT.

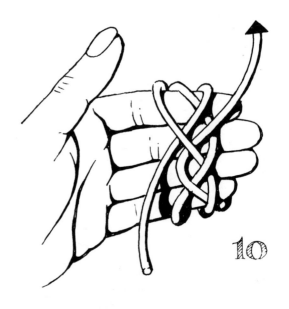

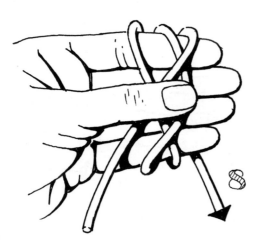

TURN YOUR HAND OVER ONCE AGAIN,
THUMB FACING YOU. BE CAREFUL NOT
TO LET THE DIAMOND PATTERN ON
THE BACK OF YOUR HAND COME APART.

NOW BRING THE WORKING END UNDER
THE NEXT STRAND ALONGSIDE THE
STANDING END, KEEPING THE LINE TO
THE RIGHT OF THE STANDING END
(OR THE ORIGINAL PASS). YOU HAVE
JUST COMPLETED THE FIRST "ROUND"
OR "PASS" OF THE TURK'S HEAD.
NOTE THAT THE STANDING END AND
WORKING END ARE NOW PARALLEL,
BOTH PASSING UNDER A BIGHT
TOGETHER.

11

AT THIS POINT, IT'S SAFE TO TAKE
THE KNOT OFF YOUR HAND IF YOU
WISH. TO MAKE A SECOND PASS,
FOLLOW THE ORIGINAL PASS COMPLETE-
LY AROUND THE TURK'S HEAD USING
THE WORKING END AND TAKING CARE
TO FOLLOW THE OVER/UNDER SEQUENCE.
GO AROUND A THIRD TIME AND YOU
HAVE THE MOST COMMONLY SEEN
THREE-PASS, THREE-STRAND
TURK'S-HEAD KNOT.

NOW COMES THE FUN PART...TIGHTEN-
ING UP. START AT THE BEGINNING
AND WORK SLOWLY, OVER AND UNDER,
ROUND AND ROUND, KEEPING THE
BIGHTS EVENLY SPACED UNTIL THE
TURK'S HEAD FITS SNUGLY AND
SMOOTHLY. CUT THE ENDS OFF SO
THEY'RE HIDDEN BENEATH THE
KNOT.

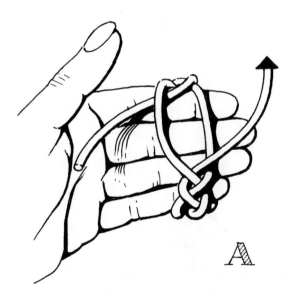

A

AS I'VE ALREADY MENTIONED, THIS
MAKES A RATHER SMALL TURK'S
HEAD. YOU CAN ENLARGE ITS
DIAMETER BY ADDING ADDITIONAL
BIGHTS. TO DO THIS, COMPLETE
STEPS 1 THROUGH 10. THEN...

PUSH APART THE WORKING END AND
STANDING END. NOTICE THAT YOU
ARE ONCE AGAIN SEEING TWO LINES
PARALLEL TO ONE ANOTHER, SIMI-
LAR TO STEP 5.

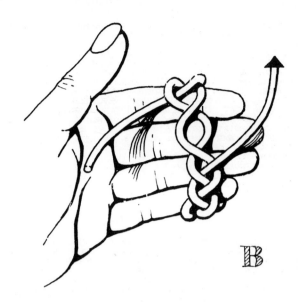

B

BRING THE LEFT STRAND UNDER THE
RIGHT STRAND, FORMING ANOTHER
DIAMOND.

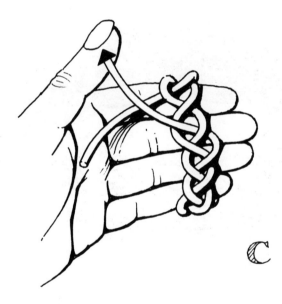

C

PASS THE WORKING END UNDER THE
STRAND ON THE RIGHT, COMING UP
THROUGH THE CENTER OF THE DIA-
MOND AND OUT OVER THE STRAND
ON THE LEFT.

REPEAT STEP 10, BRINGING THE
WORKING END UNDER THE NEXT
STRAND ALONGSIDE THE STANDING
END, KEEPING THE LINE TO THE
RIGHT. THEN PROCEED TO STEP 11
AND TIGHTENING UP.

YOU CAN CONTINUE STEPS A-C
AS MANY TIMES AS YOU'D LIKE,
DEPENDING ON THE SIZE OF THE
FINISHED KNOT. REMEMBER THAT
EACH TIME YOU REPEAT THE SE-
QUENCE, THE LEFT STRAND GOES
UNDER THE RIGHT STRAND.

TO MAKE THE SMALL TURK'S HEAD SHOWN AT THE BEGINNING, SEVEN OR EIGHT FEET OF LINE WILL BE REQUIRED (NO ADDITIONAL BIGHTS). I GENERALLY LIKE TO USE A SMOOTH LINE, LIKE A HARD, WOVEN COTTON SIMILAR TO THAT USED FOR BACK-YARD CLOTHESLINE, ONLY SMALLER. YOU CAN FIND IT IN SEVERAL SIZES AT GENERAL HARDWARE STORES (RARELY IN MARINE HARD-WARE OUTLETS). IF YOU USE A LAID LINE, WRAP THE ENDS WITH A BIT OF MASKING TAPE TO PREVENT THEM FROM UNRAVELING WHILE YOU WORK. I ACTUALLY DON'T RECOMMEND LAID LINE SINCE IT TENDS TO BLUR THE BASIC BEAUTY OF THE KNOT. A SMOOTH LINE WILL SHOW IT BEST.

IF THE KNOT IS INTENDED TO STAND ALONE AS A BRACELET, NAPKIN RING, OR PERHAPS A SLIDING RING AROUND THE LANYARDS OF A DITTY BAG, PUT A DOLLOP OF GLUE ON THE CUT-OFF ENDS TO PREVENT THEM FROM PULL-ING OUT OR UNRAVELING. I USUALLY GIVE THE DECORATIVE KNOTS TOPSIDE A FEW COATS OF WHITE PAINT TO HELP KEEP THEM CLEAN AND NEW LOOKING.

HERE ARE SOME IDEAS FOR APPLICA-TIONS OF TURK'S HEADS. I'M SURE YOU CAN THINK OF MORE:

- ON THE KING SPOKE OF THE SHIP'S STEERING WHEEL
- ON THE END OF THE TILLER
- AROUND THE OARS
- ALONG THE BOWSPRIT
- AROUND THE TOPS OF LIFELINE STANCHIONS
- AS A SLIDING RING AROUND DITTY-BAG LANYARDS
- AT THE TOP AND BOTTOM OF COACH WHIPPING AROUND THE MAST BELOW DECKS (OR THE COMPRESSION TUBE OF A DECK-STEPPED MAST)
- AROUND THE THERMOS JUG
- AROUND TURNBUCKLE BOOTS
- ON THE BELL ROPE
- AT THE ENDS OF DOCK-LINE SPLICES
- AROUND THE TOILET PUMP HANDLE
- AT THE ENDS OF TOWEL RACKS
- AROUND THE WINDLASS HANDLE
- ON THE BILGE-PUMP HANDLE
- ON A WATCH LANYARD
- AT THE ENDS OF EYE SPLICES THROUGH FENDERS
- AT THE TOP AND BOTTOM OF A FLAG STAFF
- ON A BOAT-HOOK HANDLE
- FLATTEN OUT A TURK'S HEAD TO MAKE A SMALL THUMP MAT FOR UNDER A DECK BLOCK, OR TO SERVE AS A DRINK COASTER.

Captain Dolph's Finishing Bench

B.P. Bingham

I FIRST SAW CAPTAIN DOLPH'S SHINING FACE PEERING FROM OVER A MOUND OF GIGANTIC SAIL BAGS PILED IN THE CENTER OF THE LOFT FLOOR. AS I ROUNDED THE BILLOWY WHITE MOUNTAIN, I MET HIS PLUMP LITTLE FIGURE STRADDLING A BEAUTIFUL PINE "FINISHING" BENCH WHOSE SATIN FINISH HAD BEEN WORN TO A FLAWLESS SHEEN BY ITS YEARS OF USE.

"JUST A FEW MORE!", HE MUSED, PULLING THE WAXED TWINE SNUGLY AROUND A LARGE BRONZE THIMBLE, TUGGING IT IN A FASHION BETELLING HIS YEARS AT CANVAS. I WAITED AND WATCHED HIS CALLOUSED HAND AT WORK.

"WHATCHA NEED, MY BOY?", HE QUERIED AS HIS TWINKLING EYES TURNED UP FOR THE FIRST TIME.

I EXPLAINED THAT I NEEDED A PIECE OF DACRON TO ADD TO THE BOAT'S REPAIR CHEST. "EIGHT OUNCE WILL DO NICELY. ABOUT THREE YARDS OF IT."

"OH, WHATCHA GOT?"

"A LITTLE BANKS SCHOONER ANCHORED IN THE HARBOR. SHE'S GREEN. YOU CAN'T MISS HER", I REPLIED. HE LOOKED OUT THE WINDOW TOWARD WHERE SHE LAY.

WELL, THAT'S ALL IT TOOK FOR THE CAPTAIN. HE NEEDED LITTLE EXCUSE FOR AN AFTERNOON OF SEA STORIES. HE TOLD ME ABOUT HIS FISHIN' DAYS, THE HURRICANE OF '38, HIS YEARS UNDER SAIL, THE GREAT SCHOONERS HE'D SEEN COME AND GO, ABOUT THE WHALERS THAT USED TO PLY THESE WATERS WHEN HE WAS A LAD HIMSELF. ALL THE WHILE, WE SAT TOGETHER ON THE BENCH, LAUGHIN' AND SLAPPING OUR KNEES. HE EVEN TOLD ME THE HISTORY OF EACH OF HIS SEWING MACHINES, WHICH ALL HAD ILLUSTRIOUS, SALTY NAMES LIKE *SALLY B. FARNUM (SAL)* AND *REBECCA PEASE (BECKIE).*

WHEN I ASKED HIM WHERE HE'D GOTTEN THE FINISHING BENCH (A SHORT RIGGER'S BENCH USED FOR DOING THE HANDWORK ON SAILS SUCH AS LEATHERING, SEWING BOLT ROPES, MAKING GROMMETS AND "HANKIN'"), HE TOLD ME HE'D MADE IT FIFTEEN YEARS BEFORE. AT THAT

TIME HE'D GIVEN IT FIVE COATS OF COLD VARNISH AND HADN'T TOUCHED IT SINCE. THE BENCH WAS A BUFF-TONED PINE, SIMPLE (ALMOST MODERN) IN ITS FUNCTIONAL DESIGN AND JUST AS SUGGESTIVELY NAUTICAL AS ANYTHING COULD BE (EXCEPT FOR A SHIP'S WHEEL OR SOMETHING LIKE THAT). AT ONE END HUNG AN ARRAY OF LETHAL LOOKING HOOKS (BENCH HOOKS, STRANGELY ENOUGH) FOR HOLDING CANVAS AND LINE WHILST BEING "DONE UP". AT THE OTHER END DANGLED A WELL-WORN COTTON DITTY BAG BULGING WITH THE MAKER'S GADGETS. A ROW OF FIDS AND SPIKES STOOD AT ATTENTION IN THEIR APPOINTED HOLES WITHIN THE CUTTING BOARD.

"I'VE MADE A BUNCH OF 'EM," DOLPH BOASTED. "GAVE ONE TO MY DAUGHTER. NOW SHE USES IT FOR A COFFEE TABLE, FIDS AND ALL. I'VE GOT ONE IN MY HOUSE WHAT'S USED FOR SETTIN' PLANTS AND MAGAZINES AND THINGS ON...MOSTLY THINGS. BUT IT SORTA FITS INTO THE DEN NICE. A LOTTA PEOPLE LIKE 'EM SO I MADE UP A FEW ONE WINTER OUTA SUGAR PINE BUT IT DOESN'T REALLY MATTER WHAT WOOD'S USED. WELL, NEXT THING I KNOW, I'M GETTIN' LETTERS FROM FOLKS I'D NEVER MET WANTIN' TO KNOW HOW TO MAKE THESE BENCHES. I DON'T KNOW WHY; THEY'RE JUST BENCHES."

WELL, I CAN'T AGREE WITH HIM ON THAT. THEY WEREN'T "JUST BENCHES". THEY HAD A SPECIAL CHARM FAR BEYOND THEIR UTILITY AND WERE MOST FITTING IN THE OLD SAILOR'S ABODE. WHETHER USED FOR "HANKIN'" OR SIMPLY FOR "PUTTIN'" THINGS ON," CAPTAIN DOLPH'S FINISHING BENCH WOULD MAKE FOR A DELIGHTFUL DAY'S WORK AMONG THE FRAGRANCES OF NEWLY CUT LUMBER, WITH THE REWARD OF HANDSOME CREATION. SO, I PRESENT IT TO YOU HERE.

BY THE DAY'S END, MY HEAD SWAM WITH DOLPH'S HARROWING TALES OF THE DEEP, THE WARM WELCOME INTO HIS SHOP WITH ITS SCENTS OF MARLIN AND HEMP. THEN, AS I ROWED BACK TOWARD THE COMFORT OF MY LITTLE SHIP, I SAW THE JOLLY CAPTAIN TRUDGING UP THE ROAD WITH A BAG OVER HIS SHOULDER AND A COIL OF LINE IN HIS HAND. THE LIGHTS OF THE LOFT WERE OFF AND THE DOOR DRAWN CLOSED FOR THE NIGHT. I PAUSED AT THE OARS FOR A BRIEF MOMENT OF THOUGHT. SURE ENOUGH...I'D FORGOTTEN MY DACRON!

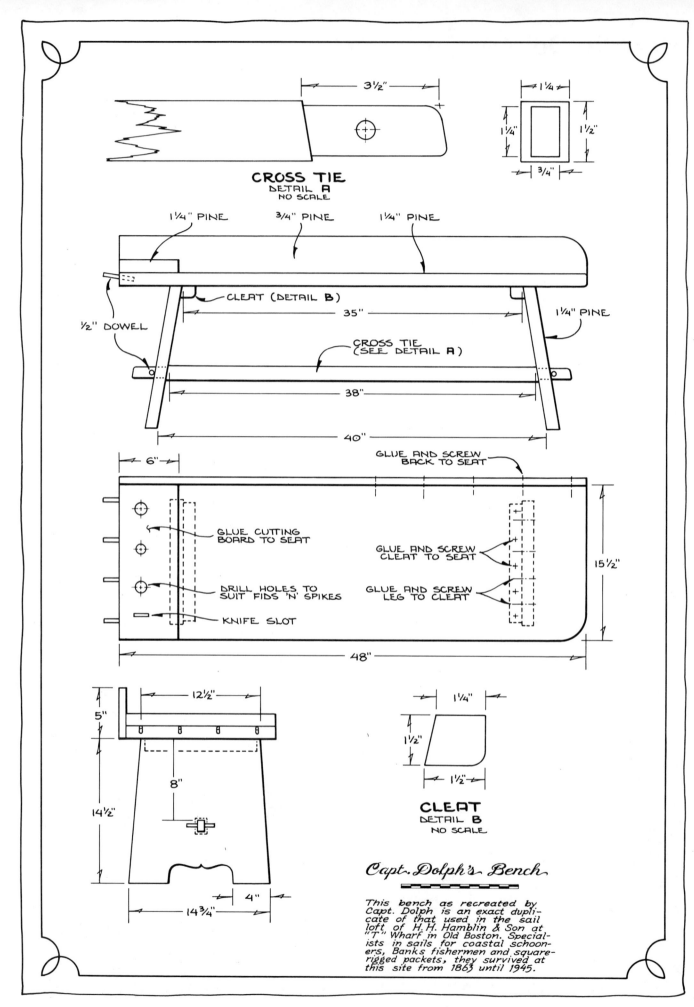

CROSS TIE
DETAIL **A**
NO SCALE

3½"

1¼"
1¼"
1½"
¾"

1¼" PINE
¾" PINE
1¼" PINE

CLEAT (DETAIL **B**)

35"

½" DOWEL

CROSS TIE
(SEE DETAIL **A**)

1¼" PINE

38"

40"

GLUE AND SCREW
BACK TO SEAT

6"

GLUE CUTTING
BOARD TO SEAT

GLUE AND SCREW
CLEAT TO SEAT

DRILL HOLES TO
SUIT FIDS 'N' SPIKES

GLUE AND SCREW
LEG TO CLEAT

KNIFE SLOT

15½"

48"

12½"

5"

8"

14½"

4"

14¾"

1¼"

1½"

1½"

CLEAT
DETAIL **B**
NO SCALE

Capt. Dolph's Bench

This bench as recreated by
Capt. Dolph is an exact dupli-
cate of that used in the sail
loft of H.H. Hamblin & Son at
"T" Wharf in Old Boston. Special-
ists in sails for coastal schooners, Banks fishermen and square-
rigged packets, they survived at
this site from 1863 until 1945.

CHAPTER 7 Fitting Solutions

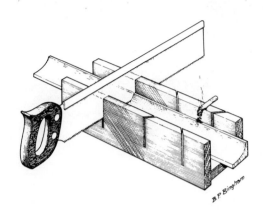

B.P. Bingham

The "Tick-Stick" Pattern Trick

I HAVE SEEN SO MANY ASPIRING BOAT BUILDERS AND FIXERS SLAVING AWAY WITH A PAIR OF DIVIDERS IN ORDER TO TRANSFER THE HULL SHAPE TO A PIECE OF PLYWOOD THAT I HAVE IMPULSIVELY JUMPED IN TO LEND THEM A HAND.

OH, THE OLD "DIVIDER-TRANSFER" PATTERN METHOD DOES WORK WELL ON SPECIAL OCCASIONS, SUCH AS WHEN SPILING A PLANK. BUT IT RARELY PROVES SUCCESSFULL WHEN BUILDING UNITS INSIDE A HULL.

THE SYSTEM I HAVE TAUGHT MOST OFTEN IS A MODIFICATION OF THE MOCK-UP PATTERN. IT LOOKS AND SOUNDS COMPLICATED, YET IT IS SO FAST AND ACCURATE THAT YOU WILL HARDLY BELIEVE THE SIMPLICITY OF IT (AFTER YOU'VE TRIED IT).

IT'S CALLED "TICK-STICKING" FOR THE LACK OF A BETTER TERM.

① CUT A SHARP POINT AT ONE END OF A PIECE OF PINE OR FIR. THIS CAN BE MADE OUT OF ANY SCRAP WOOD YOU MIGHT HAVE LYING AROUND. THIS WILL SERVE AS THE TICK-STICK. ITS LENGTH MAY RANGE FROM ONE FOOT TO THREE, DEPENDING ON THE SIZE OF THE PATTERN TO BE DRAWN.

② CUT OUT A PIECE OF PLYWOOD SOMEWHAT SMALLER, BUT FITTING CONVENIENTLY INTO THE SPACE FROM WHICH YOU ARE TAKING THE PATTERN. THIS WOOD MAY ALSO COME FROM THE SCRAP PILE AND MAY BE OF ALMOST ANY SHAPE. THIS WILL BE THE TICK-BOARD.

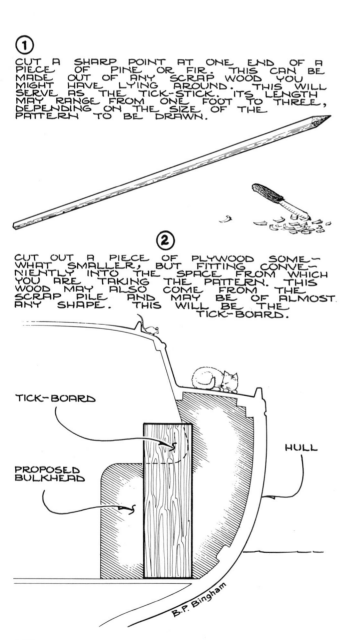

TICK-BOARD

PROPOSED BULKHEAD

HULL

B.P. Bingham

③ TEMPORARILY ERECT THE TICK-BOARD IN THE SAME POSITION TO BE OCCUPIED BY THE PROPOSED BULKHEAD (OR ON THE SAME PLANE AS THE COUNTER TOP, LOCKER PARTITION, SHELF, ETC.). LIGHT WOODEN BRACES MAY BE USED TO HOLD IT STEADY. A WOBBLY TICK-BOARD WILL SACRIFICE PATTERN ACCURACY.

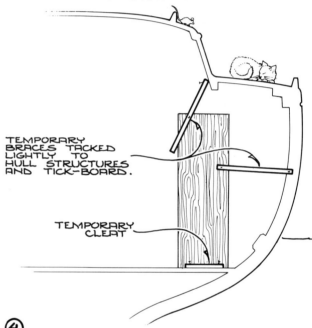

TEMPORARY BRACES TACKED LIGHTLY TO HULL STRUCTURES AND TICK-BOARD.

TEMPORARY CLEAT

④ HOLD THE TICK-STICK AGAINST THE TICK-BOARD AT ANY CONVENIENT ANGLE SO THAT THE TICK-POINT TOUCHES THE HULL OR SOME CRITICAL CUTTING OR FITTING POINT (CORNERS OF STRUCTURAL TIMBERS).

⑤ DRAW A SHARP LINE ONTO THE TICK-BOARD (USING THE TICK-STICK AS A STRAIGHT EDGE).

⑥ BEFORE MOVING THE TICK-STICK TO A NEW STRATEGIC POSITION, PLACE A REFERENCE "TICK" ON BOTH THE STICK AND THE BOARD. PLACE A NUMBER ALONGSIDE EACH TICK SO THAT THE TICKING SEQUENCE WILL NOT BE LOST.

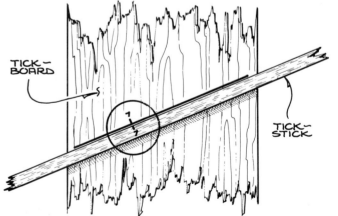

TICK-BOARD

TICK-STICK

(7) MOVE THE POINT OF THE STICK TO THE NEXT CRITICAL CUTTING POINT. DRAW A NEW LINE ON THE TICK-BOARD AND NUMBER THE STICK AND BOARD AGAIN.

(8) CONTINUE MOVING THE STICK TO NEW POSITIONS, LINING AND TICKING AS YOU GO, UNTIL YOU HAVE TICKED OFF THE ENTIRE PERIMETER OF THE SHAPE TO BE TRANSFERRED.

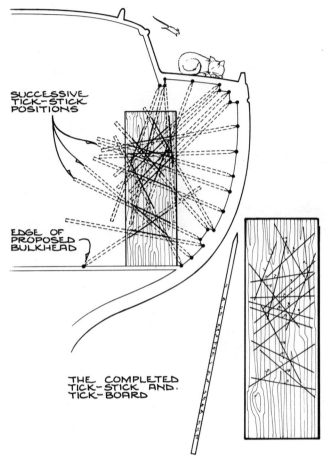

SUCCESSIVE TICK-STICK POSITIONS

EDGE OF PROPOSED BULKHEAD

THE COMPLETED TICK-STICK AND TICK-BOARD

THE TICK-BOARD WILL BECOME CRISS-CROSSED WITH STRAIGHT LINES BEARING THE MEMORY OF THE ORIGINAL TICK-STICK POSITIONS. THE MORE TICKS YOU'VE MARKED, THE MORE ACCURATE THE PATTERN WILL BE.

DRAWING THE PATTERN

(9) IT'S BEST TO LAY OFF THE PATTERN ON MEAT WRAPPING PAPER SO THAT YOU CAN ADJUST ITS POSITION ATOP THE LUMBER LATER TO MINIMIZE WASTE.

LAY THE TICK-BOARD, FACE UP, ON TOP OF THE PAPER.

(10) PLACE THE TICK-STICK ONTO THE TICK-BOARD SO THAT THE STICK ALIGNS WITH ITS ORIGINAL #1 POSITION (AS DICTATED BY THE LINE AND TICK DRAWN ON THE BOARD).

(11) PLACE A DOT ONTO THE PAPER DIRECTLY BELOW THE POINT OF THE TICK-STICK.

(12) MOVE THE TICK-STICK TO SUCCESSIVE POSITIONS ON THE BOARD, MAKING DOTS ON THE PAPER AT THE POINT OF THE STICK AS YOU GO, UNTIL ALL OF THE TICK REFERENCES HAVE BEEN USED.

(9) (10) (11) (12) CONT.

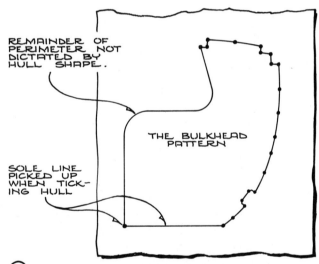

THE TICK-STICK PLACED IN ITS ORIGINAL POSITIONS ON THE TICK-BOARD.

WRAPPING PAPER FOR PATTERN

DOTS AT THE TICK-STICK POINT

TICK-BOARD

(13) REMOVE THE BOARD FROM THE PAPER. NOW CONNECT THE DOTS USING A FLEXIBLE WOODEN OR PLASTIC BATTEN (OR STRAIGHT EDGE AS CIRCUMSTANCES DICTATE).

(14) REFERRING TO YOUR CONSTRUCTION DRAWING OR SKETCHES, DRAW ALL REMAINING DETAILS REQUIRED FOR CUTTING THE FINISHED PIECE ACCURATELY.

REMAINDER OF PERIMETER NOT DICTATED BY HULL SHAPE.

THE BULKHEAD PATTERN

SOLE LINE PICKED UP WHEN TICKING HULL

(15) POSITION AND TRANSFER THE COMPLETED PATTERN ONTO YOUR LUMBER USING A TAILOR'S WHEEL. MEASURE AND NOTE ALL NECESSARY BEVELS, THEN START CUTTING.

THE TICK-STICK SYSTEM MAY BE USED FOR DRAWING ANY KIND OF PATTERN TO THE HULL OR CABIN SHAPE, WHETHER THE UNIT IS LARGE OR SMALL, VERTICAL OR HORIZONTAL, COMPLICATED OR SIMPLE. THE DEGREE OF ACCURACY WILL ASTOUND YOU AS THE TOLERANCE SHOULD FALL WITHIN A PENCIL LINE AND SAW BLADE THICKNESS.

USE TICK POINTS TO PICK UP ALL HULL IRREGULARITIES, NOTCHES, PROTRUSIONS AND STRUCTURAL MEMBERS. DON'T MISS A THING.

ONCE PRACTICED, TICKING PATTERNS WILL GO VERY QUICKLY. YOU'LL SET ASIDE YOUR OLD GUESSWORK SYSTEMS FOR GOOD; YOU'LL EVEN WONDER WHERE THIS BUILDER'S TRICK HAS BEEN ALL THESE DECADES. WELL...IT'S BEEN NEATLY TUCKED AWAY IN THE NOTEBOOKS OF THE OLD SHIPWRIGHTS, THAT'S WHERE!

Mock-Up Patterns

WHETHER BUILDING A BOAT FROM SCRATCH, RESTORING AN OLD VESSEL OR SIMPLY MAKING SMALL ADDITIONS TO YOUR MODERN STOCK YACHT, MAKING THINGS FIT CAN BE AN EXPENSIVE AND FRUSTRATING EXERCISE...UNLESS YOU KNOW A FEW PROFESSIONAL TRICKS.

I HAVE SEEN TOO MANY AMATEURS WASTE VALUABLE PLYWOOD, PLANK AND MOLDING LUMBER BY STRUGGLING WITH THE "CUT AND FIT AND WHOOPS" METHOD. BY CONTINUING TO HACK AWAY AT THE FINISHED PART IT MAY POP INTO PLACE EVENTUALLY. BUT, THEN ACCURACY MAY BE LESS THAN PERFECT.

INASMUCH AS MANY OF THE SKETCHBOOKS DEAL WITH CONSTRUCTION AND INSTALLATION OF WOODEN PARTS TO BOAT HULLS, THE NEXT THREE CHAPTERS WILL DEAL DIRECTLY WITH THE FITTING SOLUTIONS.

THE MOCK-UP

NOT THE QUICKEST SYSTEM BUT SURELY THE MOST ACCURATE AND FOOLPROOF IS THE "MOCK-UP" PATTERN. THE TIME INVOLVED IN SETTING UP THE PATTERN, THOUGH, IS PROBABLY NO MORE THAN REQUIRED FOR THE CUT, FIT, WHOOPS METHOD. SO DO GIVE IT YOUR CONSIDERATION AND PATIENCE, PARTICULARLY IF A PIECE OF TEAK, PLY, MAHOGANY OR FORMICA IS AT STAKE.

THE MOCK-UP IS VIRTUALLY A TEMPORARY BULKHEAD, PARTITION, SHELF, PLANK OR COUNTER FABRICATED IN POSITION USING SMALL PIECES OF SCRAP LUMBER. THE MORE INS AND OUTS CURVES AND CORNERS INVOLVED, THE MORE PIECES REQUIRED FOR COMPLETING THE PATTERN. THE PATTERN WILL NEED A LOT OF DIAGONAL BRACING TO "FREEZE" THE SHAPE WHILE BEING REMOVED AND TRANSPORTED.

THE ASSORTED PATTERN PIECES MAY BE NAILED, TACKED, GLUED, STAPLED OR EVEN TAPED TOGETHER DEPENDING ON THE SIZE OF THE MOCK-UP. WHEN DRIVING NAILS, HOWEVER, BE SURE TO "BUCK UP" THE BACK SIDE OF THE PATTERN WITH A LEAD OR IRON WEIGHT.

ONCE THE MOCK-UP HAS BEEN COMPLETED, REMOVE IT AND LAY IT ONTO YOUR GOOD LUMBER FOR MARKING. IF THE MOCK-UP WON'T ALLOW ITSELF TO BE REMOVED IT MEANS THAT AN IDENTICAL FINISHED PART WON'T TAKE ITS PLACE WITHOUT MODIFICATION. CHANGE THE PATTERN HOWEVER NECESSARY TO FACILITATE ITS WITHDRAWAL. THIS MAY EVEN REQUIRE TWO SEPARATE PATTERN SECTIONS WHICH FIT TOGETHER LIKE A PUZZLE.

"PENCIL THICKNESS" TOLERANCES CAN BE ACHIEVED IN PATTERN DEVELOPMENT. IT'S WORTH THE EFFORT.

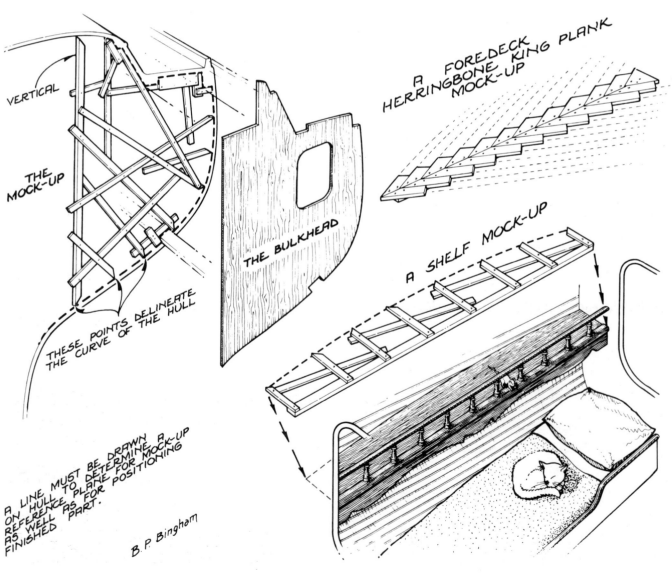

VERTICAL

THE MOCK-UP

THESE POINTS DELINEATE THE CURVE OF THE HULL

THE BULKHEAD

A FOREDECK HERRINGBONE KING PLANK MOCK-UP

A SHELF MOCK-UP

A LINE MUST BE DRAWN ON HULL TO DETERMINE A REFERENCE PLANE FOR MOCK-UP AS WELL AS FOR POSITIONING FINISHED PART.

B. P. Bingham

Making Things Fit

WHEN YOU'RE FITTING A PLANK OR TIMBER INTO A SPACE WHICH IS "DEAD ENDED" AT BOTH EX-TREMES, *i.e.* BETWEEN TWO BULKHEADS, BETWEEN THE CABIN ENDS, ETC. IT MAY BE DIFFI-CULT TO TAKE ACCURATE MEASUREMENTS WITH A TAPE RULE. SUCH WOULD BE THE CASE WHEN FITTING A CARLIN FACING OR HATCH FACING. SUCH FITTING MAY ALSO IN-VOLVE A CURVED TIMBER WITH ANGLED ENDS, THUS MULTIPLYING THE FITTING PROB-LEM. TRY THE APPROACH BELOW:

ALWAYS, ALWAYS USE A BEVEL GAUGE FOR "PULLING" ANGLES TO BE CUT (IF NOT ACCOUNTED FOR WITHIN A PAT-TERN). ALWAYS USE THE GAUGE FOR SETTING UP THE SAW FOR BEVELED EDGE CUTS. DON'T GUESS AT ANGLES.

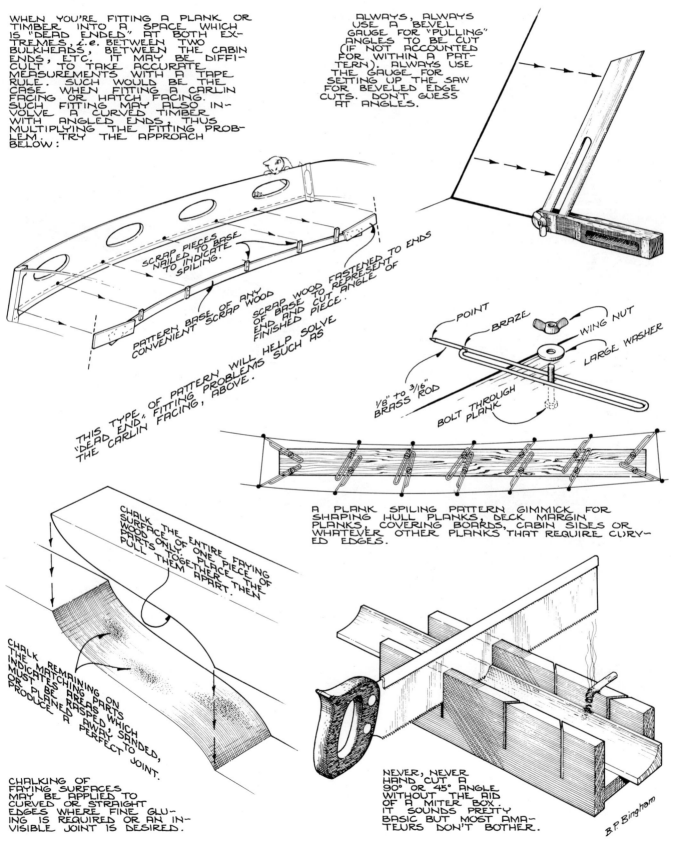

SCRAP PIECES NAILED TO BASE TO INDICATE SPILING.

PATTERN BASE OF ANY CONVENIENT SCRAP WOOD

SCRAP WOOD FASTENED TO ENDS OF BASE TO REPRESENT END AND CUT ANGLE OF FINISHED PIECE.

THIS TYPE OF PATTERN WILL HELP SOLVE "DEAD END" FITTING PROBLEMS SUCH AS THE CARLIN FACING, ABOVE.

POINT

BRAZE

WING NUT

LARGE WASHER

1/8" TO 3/16" BRASS ROD

BOLT THROUGH PLANK

A PLANK SPILING PATTERN GIMMICK FOR SHAPING HULL PLANKS, DECK MARGIN PLANKS, COVERING BOARDS, CABIN SIDES OR WHATEVER OTHER PLANKS THAT REQUIRE CURV-ED EDGES.

CHALK THE ENTIRE FAYING SURFACE OF ONE PIECE OF WOOD ONLY. PLACE THE PARTS TOGETHER THEN PULL THEM APART.

CHALK REMAINING ON THE MATCHING PARTS INDICATES AREAS WHICH MUST BE PLANED, RASPED, OR SANDED AWAY TO PRODUCE A PERFECT JOINT.

CHALKING OF FAYING SURFACES MAY BE APPLIED TO CURVED OR STRAIGHT EDGES WHERE FINE GLU-ING IS REQUIRED OR AN IN-VISIBLE JOINT IS DESIRED.

NEVER, NEVER HAND CUT A 90° OR 45° ANGLE WITHOUT THE AID OF A MITER BOX. IT SOUNDS PRETTY BASIC BUT MOST AMA-TEURS DON'T BOTHER.

B.P.Bingham

Laminating

LLOYD'S RULES FOR THE CONSTRUCTION OF WOODEN YACHTS ALLOWS A CONSIDERABLE REDUCTION IN DECK BEAM SCANTLINGS IF LAMINATED BEAMS ARE USED INSTEAD OF SOLID ONES. THE REASON IS SIMPLY THAT THEY'RE STRONGER. ALL THINGS BEING EQUAL, IT'S DUE IN PART TO THE FACT THAT THE WOOD GRAIN FOLLOWS THAT OF THE FINISHED SHAPE. A LAMINATED MEMBER IS ALSO STIFFER THAN A SOLID WHICH HAS BEEN STEAMED.

A BOAT WHICH HAS BEEN BUILT WITH ITS STEM TIMBER AND KEELSON LAMINATED AS A CONTINUOUS STRUCTURE IS, BY FAR, MUCH STRONGER THAN ONE BUILT WITH MANY PIECES AND JOINTS BOLTED TOGETHER, WITH STOPWATERS TO PREVENT MISALIGNMENT AND LEAKAGE.

LAMINATED KNEES AND FLOORS ARE SURPASSED ONLY BY "NATURAL" KNEES WHICH ARE VERY RARE AND EXPENSIVE.

A CABIN CARLIN, SHEER CLAMP OR CHINE LOG WHICH HAS BEEN LAMINATED IN THE MOST SEVERE OF ITS TWO CURVED DIMENSIONS WILL HAVE NO TENDENCY TO SPRING OUT WHEN THE VESSEL IS UNDER ABNORMAL STRESS. BUILT IN SUCH A MANNER, THE SAME BOAT WILL HAVE LESS DESIRE TO HOG.

THE STRONGEST, LIGHTEST WOODEN TILLERS ARE LAMINATED.

MOST CURVED WOODEN TRANSOMS AND CABIN ENDS ARE LAMINATED TODAY.

ALMOST ALL CABIN TOPS AND DECKS ON WOODEN BOATS ARE LAMINATED WITH AT LEAST TWO-PLY LAYERS, ALLOWING A REDUCTION IN BEAM SPACING.

STRIP-PLANKED AND COLD-MOLDED HULLS ARE TRUE LAMINATES, THUS REDUCING MUCH UNNECESSARY, HEAVY SUBSTRUCTURE.

YES, EVEN YOUR FIBERGLASS BOAT IS ALMOST COMPLETELY LAMINATED. IF IT WERE NOT SO, SHE'D BE 30% HEAVIER.

THERE'S A LOT TO BE SAID FOR WOOD LAMINATES, FOR SURE. BUT, THE PRIMARY PURPOSE FOR ADDRESSING THESE FEW PAGES...THERE IS ABSOLUTELY NOTHING AS STRIKING AS A LAMINATED TIMBER. SO STRIKING, IN FACT, THAT YOU RARELY SEE ONE THAT HASN'T BEEN OILED OR VARNISHED. AND TO ACCENTUATE THEIR INHERENT BEAUTY, MOST LAMINATES ARE SEEN IN ALTERNATING TONES OR TYPES OF WOOD.

WHAT'S MORE, LAMINATING IS EXTREMELY EASY. ANYONE CAN DO IT WITH A MINIMUM OF EQUIPMENT. ONCE SANDED TO FINISHED SHAPE, EVEN A BAD JOB LOOKS GOOD!

HERE'S HOW

LAY OUT THE DESIRED CURVE ONTO A SHEET OF PLYWOOD (FOR LARGE PIECES) OR A SCRAP PLANK (FOR SMALL WORK).

COVER THE BOARD WITH WAXED PAPER.

NAIL 1½" SCRAPWOOD BLOCKS (MIN.) TO THE BOARD AT CLOSE INTERVALS ALONG THE CURVE LINE ON ONE SIDE ONLY. JUST TOUCH THE LINE. DON'T COVER ANY PART OF IT.

ONLY IF YOU HAVE NO "C" CLAMPS: NAIL A SECOND ROW OF BLOCKS ALONG THE OPPOSITE SIDE OF THE LINE. THE SPACE BETWEEN THE TWO ROWS MUST BE ENOUGH TO ACCOMMODATE THE FINISHED PART PLUS, SAY, 1" FOR WOODEN WEDGES.

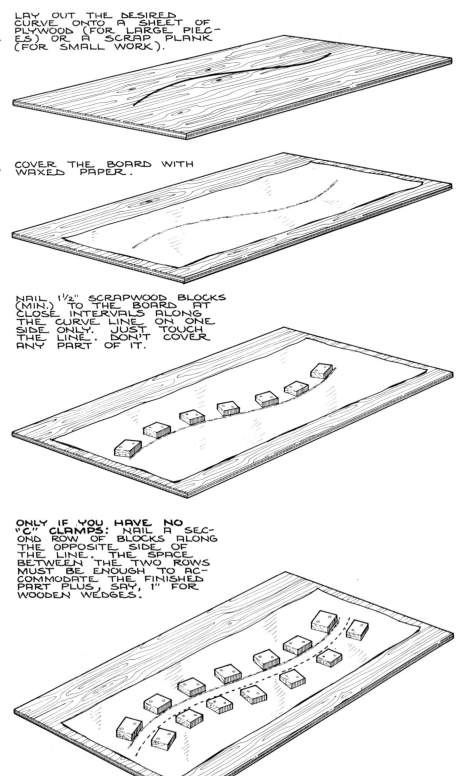

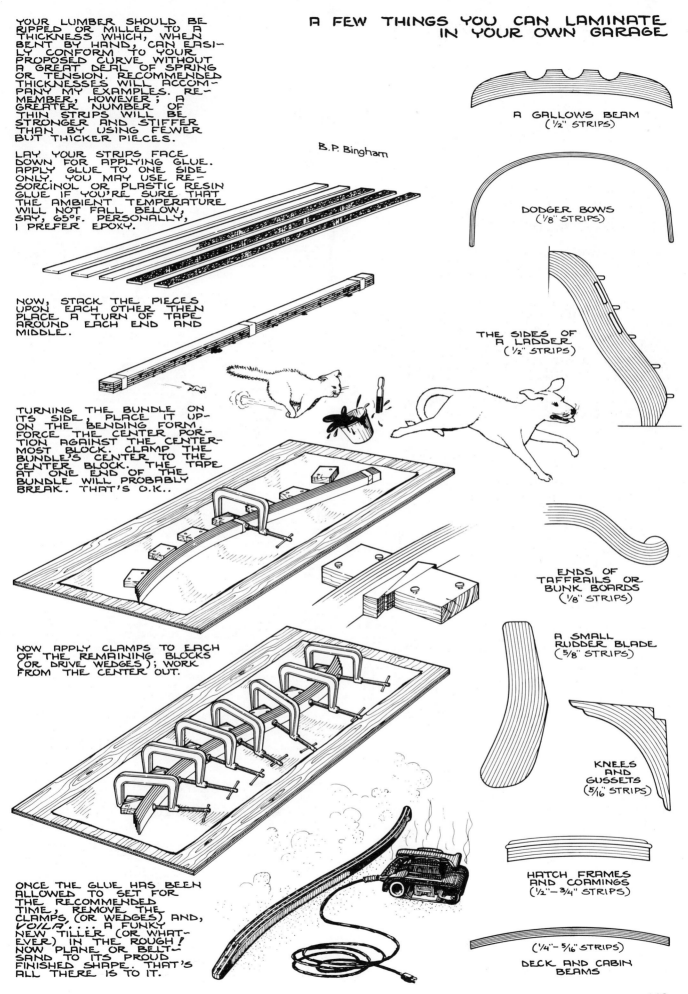

YOUR LUMBER SHOULD BE RIPPED OR MILLED TO A THICKNESS WHICH, WHEN BENT BY HAND, CAN EASILY CONFORM TO YOUR PROPOSED CURVE WITHOUT A GREAT DEAL OF SPRING OR TENSION. RECOMMENDED THICKNESSES WILL ACCOMPANY MY EXAMPLES. REMEMBER, HOWEVER; A GREATER NUMBER OF THIN STRIPS WILL BE STRONGER AND STIFFER THAN BY USING FEWER BUT THICKER PIECES.

LAY YOUR STRIPS FACE DOWN FOR APPLYING GLUE. APPLY GLUE TO ONE SIDE ONLY. YOU MAY USE RESORCINOL OR PLASTIC RESIN GLUE IF YOU'RE SURE THAT THE AMBIENT TEMPERATURE WILL NOT FALL BELOW, SAY, 65°F. PERSONALLY, I PREFER EPOXY.

B.P. Bingham

NOW, STACK THE PIECES UPON EACH OTHER THEN PLACE A TURN OF TAPE AROUND EACH END AND MIDDLE.

TURNING THE BUNDLE ON ITS SIDE, PLACE IT UP-ON THE BENDING FORM. FORCE THE CENTER PORTION AGAINST THE CENTER-MOST BLOCK. CLAMP THE BUNDLE'S CENTER TO THE CENTER BLOCK. THE TAPE AT ONE END OF THE BUNDLE WILL PROBABLY BREAK. THAT'S O.K..

NOW APPLY CLAMPS TO EACH OF THE REMAINING BLOCKS (OR DRIVE WEDGES); WORK FROM THE CENTER OUT.

ONCE THE GLUE HAS BEEN ALLOWED TO SET FOR THE RECOMMENDED TIME, REMOVE THE CLAMPS, (OR WEDGES) AND, VOILA'.... A FUNKY NEW TILLER (OR WHAT-EVER) IN THE ROUGH! NOW PLANE OR BELT-SAND TO ITS PROUD FINISHED SHAPE. THAT'S ALL THERE IS TO IT.

A FEW THINGS YOU CAN LAMINATE IN YOUR OWN GARAGE

A GALLOWS BEAM
(½" STRIPS)

DODGER BOWS
(⅛" STRIPS)

THE SIDES OF A LADDER
(½" STRIPS)

ENDS OF TAFFRAILS OR BUNK BOARDS
(⅛" STRIPS)

A SMALL RUDDER BLADE
(⅝" STRIPS)

KNEES AND GUSSETS
(5/16" STRIPS)

HATCH FRAMES AND COAMINGS
(½" – ¾" STRIPS)

(¼" – 5/16" STRIPS)
DECK AND CABIN BEAMS

A Simple Scarfing Jig

IF YOU WERE BUILDING A STRIP-PLANKED HULL, YOU'D HAVE TO MAKE SEVERAL HUNDRED WATER-TIGHT AND STRUCTURALLY SOUND SCARF JOINTS. IF YOU WERE CONSTRUCTING A HOLLOW MAST, EIGHT PERFECT SCARFS MIGHT BE REQUIRED. IF YOU WERE TO REPLACE A TOERAIL OR CAP, SIX FINE SCARF JOINTS WOULD PROBABLY BE NECESSARY AND OF AN INVISIBLE QUALITY WHICH WOULD WARRANT VARNISH.

WHETHER YOU'RE BUILDING A BOAT, FINISHING A KIT OR JUST TINKERING AROUND, EVEN-TUALLY SCARFING IS GOING TO CATCH UP TO YOU. YOU CAN'T AVOID IT FOREVER.

BUT, SOMETHING ABOUT SCARF JOINTS: EITHER THEY'RE **ALL** RIGHT OR...THEY'RE **ALL** WRONG! THERE'S JUST NO IN BETWEEN ABOUT IT. THE ANGLES OF THE JOINING PIECES MUST MATCH EXACTLY. THEIR SURFACES MUST BE ABSO-LUTELY FLAT SO VOIDS WILL NOT DEVELOP WITHIN THE GLUE LAYER. THE FAYING SUR-FACES MUST NOT BE TEXTURED BY SAWING SCORES OR RAISED GRAIN. FOR A SCARF TO BE OTHERWISE DESTROYS BONDING STRENGTH, ENCOURAGES ROT AND EVENTUAL FAILURE.

PRODUCING A PERFECT "COMMON" SCARF (EASIEST TO MAKE) ISN'T TERRIBLY DIFFICULT IF YOU KNOW HOW. BASICALLY, IT REQUIRES THE USE OF AN EASILY-CONSTRUCTED JIG. HERE'S HOW:

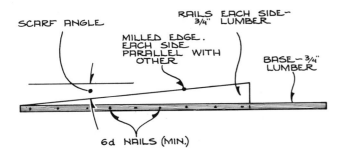

SCARF ANGLE

RAILS EACH SIDE- 3/4" LUMBER

MILLED EDGE. EACH SIDE PARALLEL WITH OTHER

BASE— 3/4" LUMBER

6d NAILS (MIN.)

SIGHT ACROSS THE TOPS OF RAILS TO ASSURE PARALLEL

RAILS

BASE

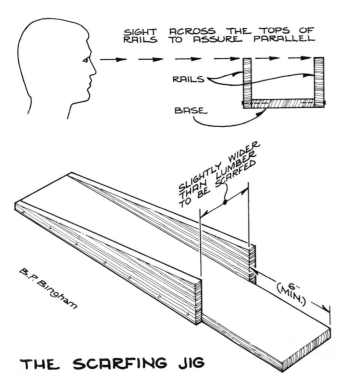

SLIGHTLY WIDER THAN LUMBER TO BE SCARFED

6" (MIN.)

B.P. Bingham

THE SCARFING JIG

USING THE JIG

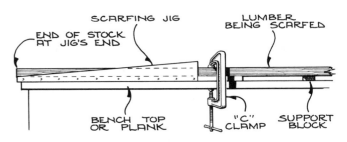

SCARFING JIG

END OF STOCK AT JIG'S END

LUMBER BEING SCARFED

BENCH TOP OR PLANK

"C" CLAMP

SUPPORT BLOCK

PLACE THE LUMBER INTO THE JIG AS SHOWN THEN CLAMP IT FIRMLY IN PLACE.

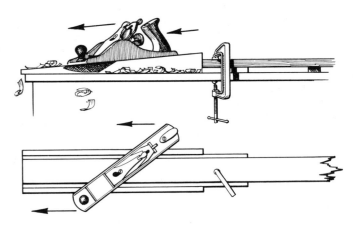

HOLDING A PLANE AT AN ANGLE TO THE LUMBER, PLACE THE EXTREME ENDS OF THE SOLE (THE BOTTOM OF THE PLANE) ONTO THE OPPOSING JIG RAILS. AS YOU PUSH THE PLANE FORWARD, MAINTAIN THE ANGLE. DO NOT ALLOW THE BLADE TO NICK THE JIG RAILS.

BEGIN PLANING WITH DEEP CUTS. AS THE LUMBER NEARS ITS FINAL SHAPE, REDUCE THE DEPTH OF THE CUT.

WHEN FINISHED PLANING, SAND THE SURFACE WITH MEDIUM PAPER WRAPPED AROUND A WOODEN BLOCK. THE ENDS OF THE BLOCK MUST EXTEND BEYOND THE PAPER. WHEN SANDING, PLACE ONLY THE BLOCK ENDS UPON THE JIG RAILS.

EACH FINISHED PIECE REMOVED FROM THE JIG WILL BE IDENTICAL TO ALL OTHERS SO, WHEN GLUED AND CLAMPED, YOU'RE BEST ASSURED OF A PERFECT JOINT. A ROUTER MAY BE USED IN LIEU OF A PLANE IF YOU WISH.

SCARF PROPORTIONS (ANGLES) VARY WITH THEIR USES BUT THE LONGER THE BETTER. 12 to 1 IS IDEAL FOR MASTS; 10 to 1 FOR TOERAILS; 7 to 1 FOR SUPERFICIAL JOINTS. 7 to 1 SHOULD BE CONSIDERED MINIMUM.

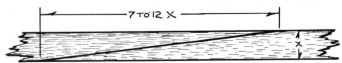

7 TO 12 X

X

CHAPTER  **Practical Potpourri**

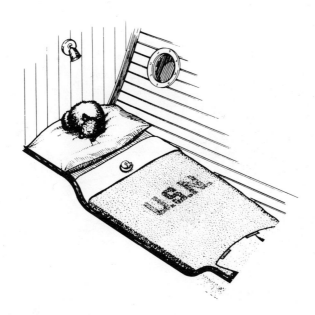

An Entertaining And Useful Flytrap

ONE EVENING IN NEWPORT, STEVE McNALLY ARRIVED FOR DINNER BEARING GIFTS OF WINE AND CHEESE AS A CONTRIBUTION TOWARD THE NIGHT'S MEAL. AS IF THIS WAS NOT ENOUGH, HE ALSO PROVIDED ANOTHER SURPRISE THAT HAS REMAINED WITH US SINCE. IT WAS A LITTLE TRICK THAT WE HAVE SHARED WITH OUR MANY CRUISING FRIENDS TO THEIR UTTER AMAZEMENT AND DELIGHT. IT HAS PRODUCED A THOUSAND LAUGHS AND ENTERTAINMENT WHILE FULFILLING A VALUABLE ON-BOARD SERVICE...FLY CONTROL!

IT'S SO SIMPLE AND FOOLPROOF THAT YOU JUST WON'T BELIEVE IT UNTIL YOU'VE TRIED IT FOR YOURSELF.

① FILL A GLASS TO WITHIN 1½" OF THE RIM WITH WATER. ANY GLASS (OR PAPER CUP) WILL DO BUT I'VE FOUND THAT ONE OF CLEAR PLASTIC WORKS BEST.

② TO THE WATER, ADD A SQUIRT OF LIQUID DISHWASHING SOAP.

③ NOW, COVER THE TOP OF THE GLASS WITH THE PALM OF YOUR HAND THEN SHAKE IT VIGOROUSLY UNTIL THE WATER HAS PRODUCED A NICE HEAD OF SUDS. YOUR FLY CATCHER IS READY FOR ACTION.

④ HAVE YOU SPOTTED A FLY? IT MUST BE ON THE OVERHEAD OR UPSIDE DOWN UNDER A HATCH OR SHELF. DO YOU SEE HIM? SLOWLY RAISE THE GLASS UNDER HIM. HE WON'T TAKE OFF IF YOU KEEP YOUR MOVEMENTS FLUID. WHEN THE GLASS IS ABOUT AN INCH FROM HIM... **BLOOP**... HE'LL DIVE RIGHT INTO THE SUDS!

THE PRINCIPLE IS THAT AN UPSIDE DOWN FLY MUST FIRST DROP VERTICALLY IN ORDER TO GAIN ENOUGH AIR SPACE TO ACHIEVE ADEQUATE FLIGHT VELOCITY. WHATEVER THE THEORY... IT WORKS. ONCE A FLY HITS THE SUDS, IT'S TRAPPED. I'VE BEEN ABLE TO COMPLETELY CLEAR A BOAT OF AS MANY AS THIRTY FLIES IN AS LITTLE AS FIVE MINUTES. WHAT'S MORE, IT'S MUCH NEATER THAN THE OLD SWATTER.

"Velcroisms"

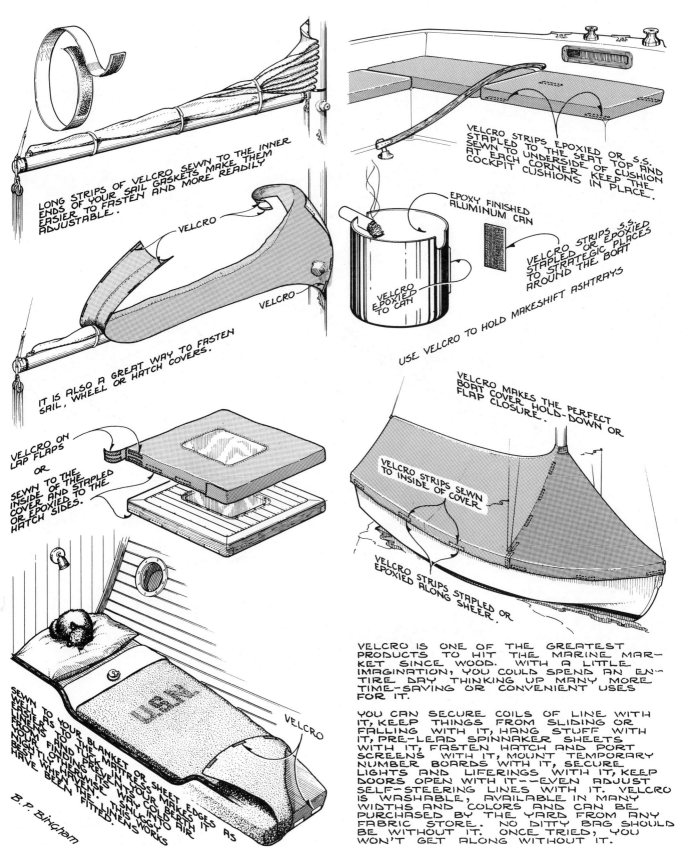

LONG STRIPS OF VELCRO SEWN TO THE INNER ENDS OF YOUR SAIL GASKETS MAKE THEM EASIER TO FASTEN AND MORE READILY ADJUSTABLE.

VELCRO STRIPS EPOXIED OR S.S. STAPLED OR SEWN TO THE SEAT TOP AND TO UNDERSIDE OF CUSHION AT EACH CORNER KEEP THE COCKPIT CUSHIONS IN PLACE.

VELCRO

VELCRO

IT IS ALSO A GREAT WAY TO FASTEN SAIL, WHEEL OR HATCH COVERS.

EPOXY FINISHED ALUMINUM CAN

VELCRO EPOXIED TO CAN

VELCRO STRIPS S.S. STAPLED OR EPOXIED TO STRATEGIC PLACES AROUND THE BOAT

USE VELCRO TO HOLD MAKESHIFT ASHTRAYS

VELCRO ON LAP FLAPS

or

SEWN TO THE INSIDE OF THE COVER AND STAPLED OR EPOXIED TO THE HATCH SIDES.

VELCRO MAKES THE PERFECT BOAT COVER HOLD-DOWN OR FLAP CLOSURE.

VELCRO STRIPS SEWN TO INSIDE OF COVER

VELCRO STRIPS STAPLED OR EPOXIED ALONG SHEER.

SEWN TO YOUR BLANKET OR SHEET EDGES AS WELL AS TO THE MATTRESS, COLD BERTH LINERS TO THE TUCK IN AND TO PREVENT FROM NIGHT FINDING YOUR MAKES IT EASIER AROUND THE OTHERWISE WAY. SNUG INTO HAVE BEST WHATEVER. THIS UGLY AIR HAVE BEEN THE LINENS WORKS.

B.P. Bingham

VELCRO

VELCRO IS ONE OF THE GREATEST PRODUCTS TO HIT THE MARINE MAR-KET SINCE WOOD. WITH A LITTLE IMAGINATION, YOU COULD SPEND AN EN-TIRE DAY THINKING UP MANY MORE TIME-SAVING OR CONVENIENT USES FOR IT.

YOU CAN SECURE COILS OF LINE WITH IT, KEEP THINGS FROM SLIDING OR FALLING WITH IT, HANG STUFF WITH IT, PRE-LEAD SPINNAKER SHEETS WITH IT, FASTEN HATCH AND PORT SCREENS WITH IT, MOUNT TEMPORARY NUMBER BOARDS WITH IT, SECURE LIGHTS AND LIFERINGS WITH IT, KEEP DOORS OPEN WITH IT—EVEN ADJUST SELF-STEERING LINES WITH IT. VELCRO IS WASHABLE, AVAILABLE IN MANY WIDTHS AND COLORS AND CAN BE PURCHASED BY THE YARD FROM ANY FABRIC STORE. NO DITTY BAG SHOULD BE WITHOUT IT. ONCE TRIED, YOU WON'T GET ALONG WITHOUT IT.

Bug Screens

SOONER OR LATER, YOU'RE BOUND TO HAVE A BOUT WITH BUGS. THEN YOU'LL WISH YOU HAD BUG SCREENS. UNFORTUNATELY, I DON'T KNOW OF A SINGLE YACHT MANUFACTURER WHO PRODUCES THEM FOR OWNERS. FOR YEARS, I'VE USED SCREENS WITH RIGID WOODEN FRAMES. THEY EITHER RESTED UPON THE NARROW LEDGES FASTENED TO THE INNER FACES OF THE HATCH COAMINGS OR SLID INTO THE VERTICAL CRIBBOARD CHANNELS, THUS REPLACING THE COMPANIONWAY CRIBBOARDS.

THE RIGID SCREENS POSED A STOWAGE PROBLEM, HOWEVER. SO I CAME UP WITH A FANTASTIC ALTERNATIVE.

I MADE SCREENS AFFIXED WITH VELCRO PERIMETERS THAT CAN BE ROLLED UP AND STOWED ALMOST ANYWHERE. THE HATCHES AND VERTICAL COMPANIONWAY ARE RIMMED WITH MATING VELCRO STRIPS WHICH MAKES INSTALLATION QUICK AND EASY. THE SEAL IS ALSO VERY POSITIVE.

NOW, THE VELCRO CORPORATION DOES PRODUCE A SCREEN KIT, BUT IT SUPPLIES ONLY NARROW, WHITE VELCRO (AS WELL AS THE SCREEN, OF COURSE) AND THE VELCRO GLUE IS OFTEN DRY IN THE TUBE IF THE KIT ISN'T FRESH.

BY MAKING YOUR OWN SCREEN SET FROM SCRATCH, YOU HAVE THE ADVANTAGE OF BEING ABLE TO PURCHASE FRESH GLUE AS WELL AS 3/4" VELCRO IN A VARIETY OF COLORS (BROWN VELCRO REALLY LOOKS GOOD ON WOODEN HATCH COAMINGS).

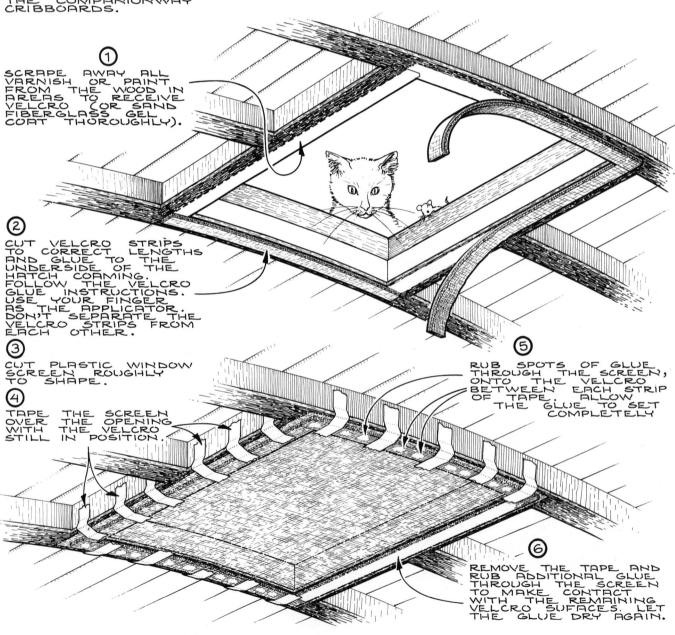

① SCRAPE AWAY ALL VARNISH OR PAINT FROM THE WOOD IN AREAS TO RECEIVE VELCRO (OR SAND FIBERGLASS GEL COAT THOROUGHLY).

② CUT VELCRO STRIPS TO CORRECT LENGTHS AND GLUE TO THE UNDERSIDE OF THE HATCH COAMING. FOLLOW THE VELCRO GLUE INSTRUCTIONS. USE YOUR FINGER AS THE APPLICATOR. DON'T SEPARATE THE VELCRO STRIPS FROM EACH OTHER.

③ CUT PLASTIC WINDOW SCREEN ROUGHLY TO SHAPE.

④ TAPE THE SCREEN OVER THE OPENING WITH THE VELCRO STILL IN POSITION.

⑤ RUB SPOTS OF GLUE THROUGH THE SCREEN, ONTO THE VELCRO BETWEEN EACH STRIP OF TAPE. ALLOW THE GLUE TO SET COMPLETELY

⑥ REMOVE THE TAPE AND RUB ADDITIONAL GLUE THROUGH THE SCREEN TO MAKE CONTACT WITH THE REMAINING VELCRO SUFACES. LET THE GLUE DRY AGAIN.

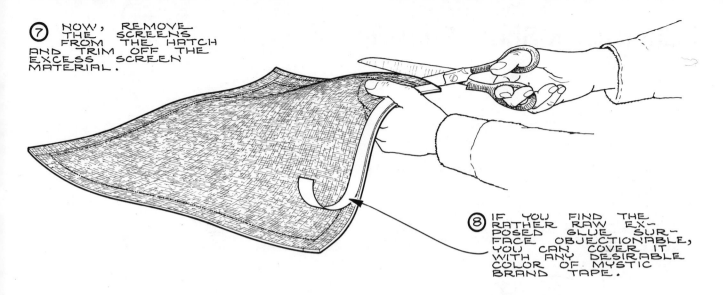

(7) NOW, REMOVE THE SCREENS FROM THE HATCH AND TRIM OFF THE EXCESS SCREEN MATERIAL.

(8) IF YOU FIND THE RATHER RAW EXPOSED GLUE SURFACE OBJECTIONABLE, YOU CAN COVER IT WITH ANY DESIRABLE COLOR OF MYSTIC BRAND TAPE.

THE SCREEN FOR THE COMPANIONWAY IS A VARIATION OF THE FOREGOING ASSEMBLY IN THAT IT MUST BE MADE WITH TWO DISTINCT SECTIONS, ALTHOUGH CONSTRUCTED WITH ONE CONTINUOUS PIECE OF SCREEN. THE VERTICAL SECTION COVERS THE CRIBBOARD PORTION OF THE COMPANIONWAY WHILE THE HORIZONTAL SECTION

COVERS THE SLIDE HATCH PORTION OF THE COMPANIONWAY. THE TWO SCREEN SECTIONS ARE DIVIDED BY A 3/8" WOODEN DOWEL THAT SERVES AS A RIDGE ROD, THUS PREVENTING THE SCREEN FROM DROOPING AND ALLOWING EITHER SECTION TO BE OPENED INDEPENDENTLY OF THE OTHER. THE DOWEL

ALSO HELPS IN THE ROLLING OF THE SCREEN FOR STOWAGE. THE COMPANIONWAY SCREEN USES THE SAME VELCRO PERIMETER AND IS FITTED IN THE SAME MANNER AS PREVIOUSLY DESCRIBED... BUT ONLY AFTER THE DOWEL HAS BEEN ATTACHED TO THE SCREEN. THIS IS HOW IT'S DONE:

(A) CUT THE SCREEN TO ROUGH SHAPE.

(B) LOCATE THE POSITION OF THE RIDGE ROD ON THE SCREEN.

(C) HAND SEW THE SCREEN TO THE RIDGE ROD.

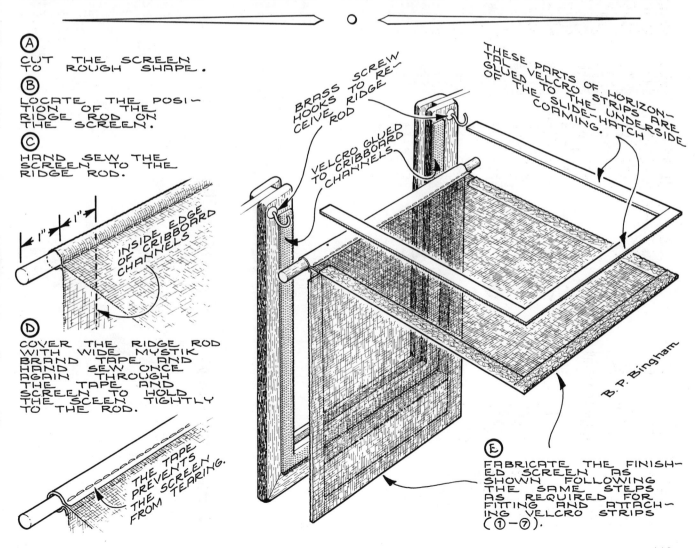

INSIDE EDGE OF CRIBBOARD CHANNELS

1" 1"

(D) COVER THE RIDGE ROD WITH WIDE MYSTIK BRAND TAPE AND HAND SEW ONCE AGAIN THROUGH THE TAPE AND SCREEN TO HOLD THE SCEEN TIGHTLY TO THE ROD.

THE TAPE PREVENTS THE SCREEN FROM TEARING.

BRASS SCREW HOOKS TO RECEIVE RIDGE ROD

VELCRO GLUED TO CRIBBOARD CHANNELS

THESE PARTS OF HORIZONTAL VELCRO STRIPS ARE GLUED TO THE UNDERSIDE OF THE SLIDE-HATCH COAMING.

B.P. Bingham

(E) FABRICATE THE FINISHED SCREEN AS SHOWN FOLLOWING THE SAME STEPS AS REQUIRED FOR FITTING AND ATTACHING VELCRO STRIPS (1 - 7).

Sherman's Short Ship Tips

EVERY NOW AND THEN, POUR A SHOT OF COOKING OIL OR BRAKE FLUID (HYDRAULIC OIL) INTO YOUR MARINE TOILET, ESPECIALLY IF IT'S DIFFICULT TO PUMP. THIS WILL LUBRICATE THE SEALS, "O" RINGS AND MOVING PARTS. THIS WILL IMPROVE THE TOILET'S OPERATION DRAMATICALLY AND REDUCE REPAIRS. **DO NOT USE LUBE OIL.**

TO PROTECT YOURSELF FROM "NO SEE'UMS", THOSE PESKY, INVISIBLE WATERFRONT GNATS, USE MINERAL OIL AS A REPELLENT. AVON COSMETIC'S *SKIN SO SOFT*® IS ALSO GOOD.

IF YOU MUST BATHE IN SALT WATER, USE SHAMPOO OR *JOY*® INSTEAD OF BATH SOAP. A RICH, CLEANSING LATHER WILL RESULT.

IF YOUR STAINLESS-STEEL CLEATS, STANCHIONS AND OTHER TOPSIDE HARDWARE ARE RUSTING AND DIFFICULT TO MAINTAIN, USE *AJAX*®, *BON AMI*®, *COMET*®, OR OTHER SUCH ABRASIVE-BASED CLEANSER AS A POLISH. RINSE WELL AFTER USE; THEN COAT WITH AUTO PASTE WAX.

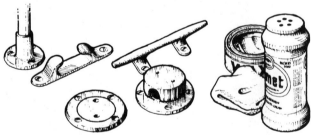

ADD A LITTLE RICE TO YOUR SALT SHAKER TO HELP KEEP THE CONTENTS FLOWING EASILY.

BEFORE STEPPING INTO YOUR DINGHY FROM A SANDY BEACH, JUST TOUCH THE SOLES OF YOUR SHOES ON THE WATER, ONE AT A TIME. ALL THE GRIT WILL FALL OFF.

CLEANING YOUR LEATHER MOCCASINS WITH SADDLE SOAP (OR ANY SOAP OR DETERGENT, FOR THAT MATTER) FOLLOWED BY A RUBDOWN WITH *VASELINE*® WILL BRING THEM BACK TO ALMOST-NEW CONDITION AND LENGTHEN THEIR LIVES.

TO KEEP SUGAR, FLOUR, COCOA, ETC. FRESH AND MOISTURE-FREE, FILL A BABY STOCKING WITH VERMICULITE (FROM A GARDENING STORE) OR NON-SCENTED KITTY LITTER; THEN PLACE THE STOCKING INTO ITS RESPECTIVE CONTAINER. YOU CAN ALSO USE SILICA-GEL BAGS. FROM TIME TO TIME, DRY OUT THE STOCKINGS OR SILICA BAGS IN A LOW OVEN.

IN CASE YOU'VE WONDERED WHAT SOME OLD SAILORS OF THE CLIPPER ERA USED AS A FINE-WOOD OIL, HERE'S A FORMULA YOU CAN MIX YOURSELF:

1/3 TURPENTINE, 1/3 LINSEED OIL, 1/3 CARNUBA WAX.

STIR THEN SHAKE THIS MIXTURE JUST BEFORE USE. APPLY WITH A RAG AND ALLOW TO SET FOR, SAY, ONE HOUR. WIPE AWAY THE EXCESS WITH A CLEAN, DRY RAG.

THE BEST BOTTOM SCRUBBERS ARE 3M COMPANY'S *SCOTCH-BRITE*® SCOURING PADS. THEY'RE AVAILABLE IN THREE GRITS: USE FINE GRIT TO REMOVE LIGHT SCUM, MEDIUM GRIT FOR GRASS AND HEAVY SCUM, COARSE GRIT FOR BARNACLES. THESE PADS ARE MANUFACTURED WITH AND WITHOUT HANDLES AND CAN BE BOUGHT AT ALMOST ANY FOOD STORE. THEY'RE ALSO GOOD FOR CLEANING OTHER PARTS OF THE BOAT WHERE STUBBORN DIRT PERSISTS.

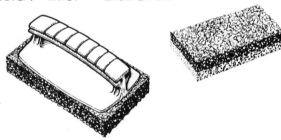

TO RESEAL A GUN-TYPE TUBE OF CAULKING COMPOUND TO PRESERVE THE REMAINING CONTENTS AND TO PREVENT THE NOZZLE FROM JAMMING WITH HARDENED COMPOUND, TURN A MACHINE SCREW INTO THE NOZZLE HOLE. THE SCREW SHOULD BE SLIGHTLY LARGER THAN THE HOLE.

B.P.Bingham

NOW AND THEN, TAKE ALL OF YOUR FIBER SHEETS, GUYS, HALYARDS AND DOCK LINES TO A LAUNDROMAT. GIVE THEM A GOOD WASHING AND THOROUGH RINSE. THEY'LL NOT ONLY COME OUT BRIGHT AND CLEAN BUT SUPPLE AND LONGER LASTING. BE SURE TO REMOVE ALL SHACKLES, THOUGH, OR THEY'LL BEAT THE HELL OUT OF THE WASHER! DRY THE LINES IN FRESH AIR, NOT IN A DRYER.

REMOVE MASKING TAPE BY PULLING AT A 90° ANGLE AWAY FROM THE FRESHLY PAINTED SURFACE. MASKING TAPE SHOULD BE REMOVED AS SOON AS THE PAINT HAS TACKED. THESE MEASURES WILL PREVENT THE LIFTING OF THE EDGE OF THE NEW PAINT.

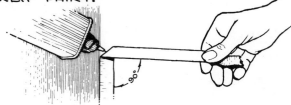

IF MASKING TAPE IS ALLOWED TO REMAIN IN THE SUN FOR A LONG TIME, IT WILL BE DIFFICULT TO REMOVE. IT WILL HELP TO RUN A LITTLE LIGHTER FLUID UNDER THE TAPE AS YOU PULL.

ADHESIVE THAT REMAINS ON ANY SURFACE AFTER REMOVING TAPE CAN BE EASILY DISSOLVED WITH A SMALL RAG OR PAPER TOWEL SATURATED WITH LIGHTER FLUID.

TO PREVENT THE LOSS OF YOUR ENSIGN STAFF ON BREEZY DAYS, DRILL A HOLE SIMULTANEOUSLY THROUGH THE SOCKET AND THE STAFF; THEN INSERT A ⅛" BRASS-ROD "KEEPER PIN." AN ALTERNATIVE IS TO ATTACH A CLIP PENDANT TO THE STAFF.

GOVERNMENT REGULATIONS PROHIBIT THE ADDITION OF MILDECIDES (MILDEW INHIBITORS) TO PAINTS. YOUR PAINT DEALER, HOWEVER, WILL SELL YOU THE MILDECIDE IN SMALL POWDER PACKETS. WHEN MIXED INTO INTERIOR PAINTS, THEY BECOME MILDEW RETARDANT.

AFTER WASHING THE INTERIOR OF YOUR BOAT, ADD MILDECIDE POWDER TO THE RINSE WATER.

TO HELP KEEP CLOTHING, CHARTS AND INTERIOR WOODWORK FRESH AND MILDEW FREE, PLACE A WAX-MILDECIDE DISC INTO EVERY DRAWER, LOCKER AND BIN. REPLACE THE DISCS EVERY FOUR MONTHS. YOU'LL FIND THEM AT YOUR LOCAL HARDWARE STORE.

FOR SCRUBBING IN HARD-TO-GET-AT PLACES, SUCH AS AROUND ENGINE PARTS, UNDER HANDRAILS, ETC., TRY USING A TOOTHBRUSH. THEY'RE EASY ON FINISHES AND WON'T GOUGE AWAY TEAK GRAIN.

TOOTHBRUSHES ARE ALSO GOOD FOR DISLODGING IMPACTED DIRT IN TIGHT PLACES PRIOR TO VARNISHING OR PAINTING. THEY'RE ESPECIALLY USEFUL FOR CLEANING NEWLY REEFED DECK AND HULL SEAMS PRIOR TO REPAYING FRESH COMPOUND.

IF YOU'RE HAVING TROUBLE KEEPING YOUR TURNBUCKLES, ANCHOR SHACKLES, RUDDER PINTLES AND HATCH HINGES LUBRICATED...NO MATTER HOW OFTEN YOU SPRAY THEM WITH "MAGIC SLICK"...TRY USING WATER PUMP GREASE. IT SEEMS TO HOLD UP FOREVER.

SPEAKING OF GREASE, DURING YOUR NEXT HAULOUT POLISH YOUR PROPELLER; THEN GIVE IT A COATING OF TEFLON GREASE. NO LIVING CRITTER CAN HOLD ONTO THIS STUFF, SO ONCE THE SCREW BEGINS TO TURN, EVEN BARNACLES LET GO.

BRASS SUEDE BRUSHES, PURCHASED AT ANY SHOE STORE OR SHOE REPAIR SHOP, ARE PERFECT ON BOARD FOR ANY SMALL SCRUB-BRUSH JOB. FINGERNAIL BRUSHES ARE ALSO GOOD.

IF YOU'RE CLEANING TEAK WITH A POWDER-TYPE BRIGHTENER BUT THE WIND BLOWS IT AWAY AS FAST AS YOU SPRINKLE, POUR A LITTLE INTO A BOWL, ADD SOME WATER, THEN STIR IT INTO A SYRUP. IT WILL THEN STAY WHERE YOU PUT IT.

IF YOU'RE USING L.P. GAS (PROPANE) FOR GALLEY FUEL, A 50-POUND FISHERMAN'S SCALE IS INDISPENSABLE FOR KEEPING TRACK OF YOUR GAS LEVEL. IF A FULL 20-POUND TANK WEIGHS 38.5 POUNDS...YOU'LL KNOW YOU'RE ALMOST OUT WHEN IT SCALES-IN AT 22 POUNDS.

TO HELP YOU GET THROUGH THOSE CHILLY SPRING EVENINGS, TRY PLACING A CLAY FLOWER POT ON ONE OF YOUR STOVE BURNERS. THIS WILL RETARD THE CONVECTION HEAT FROM SIMPLY RISING TO THE OVERHEAD AND, HENCE, PROMOTE MORE EFFICIENT RADIATION.

B.P.Bingham

IF YOU HAVE A PERSISTENT DECK OR PORT LEAK THAT REPEATEDLY SOAKS YOUR BOOKS, PILLOWS OR CLOTHING, TRY TAPING A SUPER SANITARY NAPKIN UNDER IT. IT MIGHT BE A LITTLE EMBARRASSING BUT IT BEATS GETTING THINGS WET. THEIR ABSORBENT QUALITIES ARE REMARKABLE AND THEY CAN BE USED OVER AND OVER.

DRYING OUT IS THE WORST THING THAT CAN HAPPEN TO ANY BRUSH. IF IT'S GOING TO BE STORED FOR MORE THAN A WEEK OR SO, SQUEEZE A LITTLE CLEAN LUBE OIL INTO THE BRISTLES THEN WRAP IT IN FOIL. RECLEAN THE BRUSH BEFORE ITS NEXT USE.

Secret Super Solvent

THE STUFF HAS BEEN ON THE MARKET FOR OVER TEN YEARS AND IS PRODUCED BY MANY COMPANIES. IT'S AVAILABLE AT ANY HARDWARE OR PAINT STORE. IT'S CHEAP. IT WILL CLEAN ALMOST ANYTHING FAR BETTER THAN THE HEAVY-DUTY SPRAY SOLUTIONS, YET MOST SAILORS DON'T KNOW IT EXISTS.

- IT WILL REVITALIZE PAINT BRUSHES THAT HAVE BEEN LEFT TO HARDEN FOR YEARS. IT WILL EVEN CLEAN BRUSHES THAT HAVE BEEN USED FOR VINYL BOTTOM PAINT. IT WILL ALSO CLEAN THE HANDLES TO LIKE-NEW CONDITION.

  I'VE SAVED HUNDREDS OF DOLLARS BY SIMPLY CLEANING BRUSHES THAT HAD BEEN THROWN AWAY IN BOATYARDS.

- IT WILL CLEAN UP UNCURED POLYESTER RESIN, NOT ONLY FROM BRUSHES, BUT FROM HANDS AND FIBERGLASS WORKING TOOLS. THE STUFF DOESN'T EVAPORATE AS QUICKLY AS ACETONE (NORMALLY USED FOR THESE JOBS) SO YOU DON'T USE AS MUCH. IT NEVER LEAVES A STICKY RESIDUE (AS ACETONE ALWAYS DOES) AND IT WON'T BURN YOUR HAND IF YOU HAVE A SMALL CUT (ACETONE NEVER MISSES).

  THE STUFF IS SO GOOD THAT IT CAN EVEN SAVE A RESIN BRUSH LONG AFTER ACETONE WOULD HAVE FAILED.

  I DO A LOT OF FIBERGLASS WORK AND I RARELY USE MORE THAN TWO BRUSHES FOR EVEN THE LARGEST JOBS. I ALWAYS KEEP A RAG SATURATED WITH THE STUFF NEARBY SO I CAN PERIODICALLY WIPE MY HANDS AND TOOLS, THUS MAKING THE WORK FAR MORE PLEASANT AND NEAT. I HAVEN'T BOUGHT A DROP OF ACETONE IN SEVEN YEARS.

- IT REMOVES CREOSOTE FROM HULLS, SHOES, DINGHY GUNWALES AND FENDERS.

- IT CLEANS TO LIKE-NEW CONDITION VINYL LIFELINES, FENDERS, COWL VENTS AND WINCH-HANDLE HOLDERS.

- IT CLEANS UP AFTER EPOXY WORK IN THE SAME WAY AS FOR POLYESTER RESIN.

- IT REMOVES ENGINE-EXHAUST STAIN FROM THE HULL.

- IT REMOVES ROAD TAR AND EXHAUST GRIME FROM TRAILERABLE BOATS AND NEW YACHTS THAT HAVE BEEN TRANSPORTED LONG DISTANCES.

- IT REMOVES CIGARETTE AND COOKING-SMOKE STAINS FROM THE CABIN OVERHEAD.

- IT REMOVES ALMOST ALL KINDS OF UNCURED GLUE DRIPPINGS FROM FIBERGLASS AND WOOD WHEN DOING REPAIR WORK.

- IT CLEANS HANDS, TOOLS AND SMEARS WHEN WORKING WITH POLYSULPHIDE AND SILICONE CAULKING COMPOUNDS.

- IT DISSOLVES ENGINE OIL AND GREASE SO IT'S GREAT FOR CLEANING YOUR ENGINE, ENGINE PARTS AND YOURSELF AFTER A TUNEUP. WIPE UP THE TOOLS AND WORK AREA, TOO.

- IT REMOVES WATERLINE SCUM FROM FIBERGLASS BOATS. DON'T USE IT ON A PAINTED WATERLINE (BOOT TOP).

- IT REMOVES SPILLED OIL OR GASOLINE FROM DECK SURFACES.

- IT'S AN EXCELLENT GENERAL WIPE-DOWN BEFORE PAINTING OR VARNISHING, REMOVING ALL TRACES OF OIL AND FINGER PRINTS.

- IT CLEANS THE GALLEY AND STOVE OF COOKING SPATTERS.

- YOU CAN CLEAN VINYL UPHOLSTERY WITH IT IF YOU RINSE THOROUGHLY WITH WATER WHEN YOU'RE FINISHED.

- IT REMOVES PENCIL AND CRAYON FROM ANYTHING.

- IT REVITALIZES FORMICA® TABLE AND COUNTER TOPS.

- IT REMOVES SMUDGES FROM ALL STAINLESS STEEL AND CHROME.

- IT REMOVES THE BUILDUP OF GRIME ON MASTS AND RIGGING THAT MIGHT OTHERWISE END UP ON YOUR SAILS.

I COULD GO ON, BUT YOU GET THE IDEA. IT DOES A LOT OF CLEANING JOBS THAT WOULD BE DIFFICULT OR IMPOSSIBLE WITH HEAVY-DUTY, GENERAL-MAINTENANCE DETERGENTS OR SOLUTIONS.

BUT... DON'T CLEAN A.B.S. PLASTICS SUCH AS PORTHOLE RIMS AND HAND PUMPS. DON'T USE IT ON LEXAN®, BUT IT'S O.K. ON PLEXIGLAS®. IF YOU'RE NOT SURE, DON'T USE IT. KEEP IT AWAY FROM VARNISH AND PAINT EXCEPT AS A PREFINISH WIPEDOWN.

IT'S COMBUSTIBLE, SO USE IT IN VENTILATED SPACES. BE SURE TO OPEN YOUR PORTS AND HATCHES WHEN USING IT BELOW.

SO... WHAT IS THIS SECRET SOLUTION? IT'S **BRUSH CLEANER!** DON'T CONFUSE IT WITH PAINT THINNERS, MINERAL SPIRITS, TURPENTINE OR ACETONE. **BRUSH CLEANER** IS USUALLY FORMULATED OF TOLUAL (OR TOLUENE), PETROLEUM DISTILLATE, METHYLENE CHLORIDE, SOMETIMES ACETONE, M.E.K., EVEN LANOLIN. THE KEY IS THAT IT IS SOLUBLE IN FRESH OR SALT WATER. WHEN LOOKING FOR IT, BE SURE IT INSTRUCTS YOU TO RINSE YOUR BRUSHES IN WATER AFTER CLEANING. THEN YOU'LL KNOW YOU'VE GOT THE RIGHT STUFF.

ONCE YOU'VE TRIED IT, YOU'LL WONDER WHY IT'S BEEN SUCH A SECRET. YOU'LL SOON DEVELOP YOUR OWN LIST OF "IMPOSSIBLE" CLEANING JOBS THAT HAVE SUCCEEDED WITH THE SUPER SOLVENT.

CHAPTER **A Seagoing Gallery**

. . . for Moments Like These

A pencil sketch of Vince Lazarra's Mercer 44 sloop, *Avanti*, for the author's 1965 Christmas card.

Atlantic Gale

A sketch made during the author's naval service on a bleak February afternoon in 1961 in the North Atlantic, while standing by the disabled German freighter *Nordmeer*. Within a year of the drawing, the *Nordmeer* rolled over and sank directly under the Ambassador Bridge in the Detroit River as the result of a collision. The site of the incident was less than five miles from the author's Michigan home.

Wing 'N' Wing

A little conceptual sketch of a gaff-rigged, Flicka-class sloop drawn at the bottom of a letter during the development of her design. The sketch was actually drawn with coffee rather than ink in the wee hours of the morning.

What Dreams Are Made Of

An imaginary schooner reaches out of a fantasy harbor on a Utopian morning. This drawing was done for the cover of the author's first book, *Ferro Cement Techniques,* published by Cornell Maritime Press.

Frostbiting

A sketch of Commodore David O. Kennedy in his dinghy, *Jinks.* The drawing was etched for a trophy in gratitude to the Seawanhaka Corinthian Yacht Club for its kindness during the author's frozen-in winter aboard *At Last* in the record-breaking year of 1977.

Winter's Rewards

A sketch for a 1974 Christmas card of the author and his Labrador, Sabrina, enjoying the warmth of a cozy cabin.

Tender Towing

The 8-foot Trinka dinghy was towed over more than 18,000 miles of protected water and open ocean behind the author's schooner, *At Last,* and his little sloop, *Sabrina.*

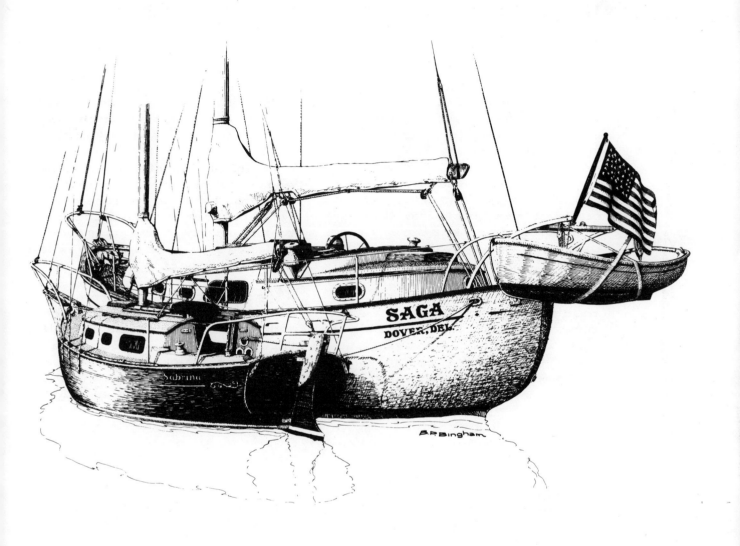

Rafting Relatives

Sabrina and *Saga,* both of the author's design, served as homes as well as drawing platforms for most of these *Sketchbook* pages.

A YACHT

A yacht is, indeed, a boat but a boat is not necessarily a yacht. I do not fully agree with the dictionary's definition: "a yacht is a boat used exclusively for pleasure." While this is true, it is much more than that: a boat is only a yacht when she has dignity, polish and class. Size or cost has little to do with achieving the stature of a yacht. I have known many yachts no larger than eighteen feet capable of far outshining boats of much greater sizes. I have been dazzled by examples set by yachts costing less than that of the sail covers on "gold platers" nearby.

A yacht may be a racer or a cruiser, constructed of any material and built in any year. She needn't be profuse of brightwork nor fancy gear. In fact, she may not have any brightwork at all if it is the nature of her character. She doesn't have to belong to a yacht club—a club cannot create a yacht; nor can any builder, try as he may.

It is the owner who makes a yacht from a boat or, conversely, who makes a boat out of a yacht.

What a boat and yacht have in common, besides being able to float, is the unique ability to reflect their owner's attitudes and degrees of fortitude, patience, attention to detail and the desire for beauty and respect for things produced through human effort. A yacht is the mirror of the owner's self esteem.

A yacht announces to those who view her that her owner is proud of her, caters to her appearance and attends to her health. She is never neglected, abused or treated with disrespect.

A yacht stands out among boats wherever she may be and sets an example for all those around her. But she does not stick up her nose nor is she ever pretentious in her ways. She is a lady.

A yacht, however large or small...old or new, tells who and what we are: caring owners and loving friends. She is the profound expression and extension of ourselves. You'll know her when you see her.

B.P.Bingham

A Yacht Owner's Checklist

Do not use ease of maintenance as a reason for a lack of maintenance.

Wash (and wax) topsides to remove salt, grime and stains whenever they begin to accumulate. And don't let your boot top get slimy.

Polish your metal hardware from time to time then give it a coat of wax.

Have your sails and sail covers cleaned when they become deeply soiled.

Don't hang dirty fenders.

Keep your ports and windows clean. Don't just let the salt build up on them.

Varnish or oil all natural wood trim to bring out its real personality. Don't let it turn dingy gray.

Keep the ends of all lines neatly whipped.

Enter port without fuss. Go about your business quietly, with confidence and dignity.

Clear the foredeck of headsails as soon as practical. Enter port ship-shape and squared away.

Keep your boomed sails furled and covered when not in use.

Flemish the tails of your dock lines on deck and ashore.

Coil and stow all lines when you're finished with them.

Never admonish or embarrass your crew in the presence of others.

Fly the correct flags in the right places at the proper times. Don't fly a dirty or frayed ensign or burgee.

Don't try to be a big shot with the size of your boat, your mouth or your purse. Maintain a low profile and leave your captain's hat below.

Address unknown skippers of other yachts and dockmasters as "Captain".

Be courteous to all dockside personnel and launch tenders.

Keep the deck clear of clutter such as bicycles, fuel cans, laundry, tools, garbage, surfboards and inflated rubber boats when possible.

Don't take advantage of a marina's facilities unless you are a paying guest. Always offer to pay for water.

Don't be loud or boisterous in an otherwise quiet marina or anchorage. Keep your language clean. Don't impose your verbal abuses upon the harbor's wives or children.

Don't run a loud generator or noisy machinery when it would intrude upon the peace or privacy of others.

Keep your personal duties private. Don't relieve yourself over the side to the embarrassment of those nearby.

Maintain your tender to the same standard as your yacht.

Great Names Sail On

ALMOST AS LONG AS I'VE BEEN WRITING AND ILLUSTRATING FOR BOATING PUBLICATIONS, THE MOST-ASKED QUESTION OF ME IS, "DO YOU REALLY HAVE A CAT AND MOUSE ABOARD?" HUNDREDS OF PEOPLE HAVE COME ABOARD AT BOAT SHOWS AND ALONGSIDE IN HARBORS JUST TO FIND OUT. HARDLY AN ANCHORAGE IS ESCAPED WITHOUT AT LEAST ONE QUERY.

THE ANSWER USUALLY SEEMS TO BE THE OPPOSITE OF THE ONE EXPECTED, SO I THINK IT'S TIME TO MAKE SOME INTRODUCTIONS.

YES, THERE IS INDEED A HANDSOME LITTLE MOUSE WHO HAS LOGGED MANY THOUSANDS OF MILES WITH ME. HE'S THREE YEARS OLD AT THIS WRITING, SILKY BROWN WITH A SOFT WHITE TUMMY AND ABOUT THE SIZE OF THE MAIN TOP'N'LIFT BLOCK. HIS HOME IS AN ELABORATE, FOUR-ROOM, CLEAR ACRYLIC TRI-LEVEL, FURNISHED WITH TOYS, GAMES, TUNNELS, LADDERS, PLACES TO HIDE AND SNUGGLE, AND A LARGE WHEEL IN WHICH TO JOG.

HE HAS FREE ACCESS TO A COUNTER TOP, NAVIGATOR'S BOOKSHELF AND OFTEN RUNS FREELY IN THE COCKPIT, BUT BEING VERY TERRITORIAL, HE PREFERS HIS OWN COZY DEN AND CAN USUALLY BE FOUND AT HOME.

HE'S NEVER BEEN AFFECTED BY THE MOTION OR HEELING OF THE SHIP, REGARDLESS OF THE SEA CONDITION. HE GOES ABOUT HIS DAILY AFFAIRS WITH THE BEST OF SEA LEGS. MICE ARE VERY BUSY PEOPLE, YOU KNOW. THEY'RE ALWAYS BUILDING, CLIMBING, DIGGING, RUNNING AND GENERALLY MOVING THINGS AROUND.

HE'S HAD MANY PREDECESSORS OVER THE YEARS. THE FIRST MOUSE JOINED ME IN MY SLEEPING BAG IN FORT LAUDERDALE WHILE I WAS LAYING OVER BETWEEN YACHT DELIVERIES AT FRITZ SKOGLUND'S SAIL LOFT. THE MOUSE SEEMED TOTALLY UNAFRAID AND SHORTLY JOINED ME IN A SPOT OF COCOA. I'VE BEEN SAILING WITH THESE LITTLE CREW MEMBERS EVER SINCE: *CAPTAIN CHARLIE BARR*, *SIR THOMAS*; *CORNELIUS SHIELDS*; *BRIGGS CUNNINGHAM* AND OTHERS NAMED AFTER GREAT YACHTSMEN OF THE WORLD.

HE CARRIES HIS OWN PASSPORT (A CERTIFICATE OF ORIGIN, COMPLETE WITH PHOTO, CUSTOMS STAMPS, BILL OF HEALTH AND THE ASSOCIATED ARRAY OF PAPERWORK) TO ALLEVIATE PROBLEMS OF ENTRY INTO FOREIGN PORTS. HE'S BEEN MORE A SOURCE OF FASCINATION TO BOARDING OFFICIALS THAN A HINDRANCE, MORE THAN ONCE DIVERTING THE ATTENTIONS OF INSPECTORS FROM A QUESTIONABLE CARGO OF GRAPEFRUIT.

THE MOUSE GETS ALONG FAMOUSLY WITH *NATASHA*, MY GOLDEN LABRADOR. BETWEEN THEM, THERE IS NO SIGN OF AGGRESSION; BUT ONLY A MILD CURIOSITY. AFTER A SNIFF OR TWO, THEY USUALLY GO THEIR SEPARATE WAYS.

MY AFFECTION FOR MICE HAS NOW EXPANDED TO A LONG SHELF IN THE SALON, WHERE THERE RESIDES A LARGE FAMILY OF CERAMIC, FELT, STRAW, PLASTIC, SHELL, BRASS AND PEWTER MICE, EVEN MICE OF CRYSTAL AND SILVER. MANY HAVE BEEN SENT OR GIVEN BY *SKETCHBOOK* AFICIONADOS FROM AROUND THE WORLD.

SO NOW, *SKETCHBOOK* FRIENDS, THE ORIGIN OF THE MOUSE IS KNOWN. HE IS REAL, ALIVE AND CRUISING THE EAST COAST. WHEN PASSING CLOSE ABOARD, YOU MIGHT SEE HIM DUCKING INTO A VENTILATOR, PEEKING THROUGH A SCUPPER OR JUST ENJOYING THE BREEZE ON THE TAFFRAIL. GIVE HIM A LITTLE SALUTE... HIS NAME IS *SHERMAN HOYT!*

WHAT ABOUT THE CAT? THERE IS NONE ABOARD, BUT MANY HAVE BEEN KIND ENOUGH TO MODEL FOR ME ALONG THE WAY: *FINGERS, JASMINE, GOTCHA, GERALDINE* AND OTHERS. ALL WISHED TO HAVE MADE *SHERMAN'S* ACQUAINTANCE, I'M SURE. UNFORTUNATELY, CLOSE MEETINGS JUST DIDN'T SEEM VERY PRACTICAL!